HOLLYШOOD
DOЦBLE AGEИT

HOLLYWOOD DOUBLE AGENT

THE TRUE TALE OF BORIS MORROS,
FILM PRODUCER TURNED COLD WAR SPY

JONATHAN GILL

ABRAMS PRESS, NEW YORK

CONTENTS

PART II

PROLOGUE
ENDGAME, JANUARY 20, 1957

It had been a bad night, as usual. But the old man's hotel room in Munich was comfortable enough. What was troubling him was a secret rendezvous with a KGB agent scheduled for later that winter day in 1957 in Vienna. Operating under the code name "Frost," the man had for more than a decade been considered by the intelligence services of the Soviet Union to be key to their American operations, though they suspected but were never able to confirm that at some point he became a double agent for the United States. As the morning sun filtered through the curtains and lit up the room, the man, Hollywood movie producer Boris Morros, tried to push fears of exposure out of his mind and focus on something simple: whether to catch the early train to Vienna or sleep in and take the plane. The latter won out. After all, the FBI was paying. But Boris couldn't get back to sleep. He hadn't slept well in years, always waking up in a different hotel room in a different city, always afraid of being unmasked. It wasn't paranoia. Most of the Soviet agents he had worked with had met a gruesome end: exiled, shot, strangled, poisoned, or simply disappeared.

Every little noise kept him awake: the clanking of the heat pipes, the noise of water running in the next room, a door closing. Then, at five minutes to seven, footsteps came down the hall and stopped before his door. Someone knocked three times, paused, attempted to turn the doorknob, then slipped something under the door. Boris crept out of bed, picked up the blue envelope, and tiptoed to the bathroom, where he opened it and saw one word—CINERAMA—that told him it was all over.

Cinerama was Hollywood's latest gimmick, a curved panoramic screen that covered the entire front wall of the cinema. But for Boris, "CINERAMA" was also the code word he had arranged with the FBI in case he was unmasked. It meant: "They're coming for you."

He dressed quickly and crammed his belongings into a valise. If he made it back to America in one piece, would he be celebrated as a national hero, reviled as the dupe of J. Edgar Hoover's anti-communist hysteria, or perhaps viewed as a villain who had sold his soul to the highest bidder? The scene seemed to resemble something out of a movie, and he ought to know. Boris had been a Jewish musical prodigy in imperial Russia who escaped revolution and civil war before coming to America and becoming one of the top executives at Paramount Pictures in the 1930s, even as he was drawn into the shadowy world of international espionage. In the 1940s he became an unlikely central figure in the Cold War intelligence arsenals of both the Soviet Union and the United States. An apolitical figure by nature, he had survived and flourished by telling people what they wanted to hear, and if his story took on Shakespearean proportions, it was still unclear in that Munich hotel room whether it would be history, comedy, or tragedy.

Boris Morros has been long forgotten by everyone, it seems, except Cold War historians and fans of Hollywood's Golden Age, and many of the people who do remember him today wish they didn't. Even his surviving family members, including his widow, his daughter-in-law, his grandchildren, and his great-grandchildren, don't quite seem to know what to think about their interesting family member, who took such dramatic advantage of the intersection of "real life and reel life," as *Time* magazine once put it. If it's not clear to them whether he was Nathan Hale or Benedict Arnold, they can blame Boris's constantly changing sense of his own history, as well as the culture of secrecy that still determines what we know about the "wilderness of mirrors," as the CIA's James Jesus Angleton put it, that was the Cold War.

But with the release of a treasure trove of previously classified documents from both the FBI and the KGB, Boris's thrilling and disturbing story, which the *New York Times* called "one of the most fantastic and astounding spy careers of them all," can finally begin to be told. The man who made his life into what one writer called "the most fascinating myth of a generation" may be largely forgotten, but his story is as relevant as ever, shining new light on issues that are still with us, and not just when it comes to accepting the truth about the threats that communism posed to American national security in the 1950s or to restoring credit to blacklisted filmmakers. It is the story of Russian attempts to infiltrate and influence the integrity of the American political system, a story that is not only relevant but not even over. Raising perennially important questions about privacy, loyalty, and the relation between the two, it is the tale of a self-made immigrant turned Hollywood hustler who became the FBI's "special special agent," whose restless ambition helped him exemplify a generation of Jews in the entertainment world who remade themselves even as they remade America. It is also the story of tragic contradictions and missed opportunities, the inspiring successes and breathtaking accomplishments of one man's American Century, a story that would have ended right there, in that hotel room in Munich in 1957, if the old man hadn't been able to get away.

Boris dashed down the stairs, found a taxi to the airport, and managed to get on board the first flight home. After a lifetime of suiting his past to fit his present, all Boris now had to do was to tell his story, for the very first time, the whole story, perhaps even, finally, the real story.

PART I

CHAPTER ONE
ENTER BORIS, 1891–1914

Boris Morros was born on January 1, 1891, though the papers couldn't agree on the date when he died seven decades later in a New York City hospital bed. Determining the date of his debut, not to mention understanding what happened between then and the rolling of the credits, is no simple matter, because nothing about Boris Morros was simple.

Well into the twentieth century, Russians paid little attention to birth dates. Stalin himself died without ever knowing for sure when he was born, and like Stalin, who would claim different birth dates to serve different political goals, Boris took advantage of the confusion. As he later put it: "A little embellishment never ruined a good story," which is why at one point or another he claimed no fewer than four different birth dates, though the overwhelming documentary evidence, including his Social Security records and his World War II draft registration card, as well as investigations by Soviet intelligence, points to New Year's Day of 1891.

It is just as difficult to discover where Boris was born. Over the years he claimed St. Petersburg as his birthplace, but the most reliable evidence, including his Ellis Island arrival documents and background checks by the FBI, points to Bobruisk, then a town of forty thousand in what is now southern Belarus. Smaller than Minsk, but bigger than Pinsk, as the old joke went, Bobruisk was a lively port town, and most of its inhabitants made their living in lumber, bricks, turpentine, tar, grain, shoes, textiles, and beaver hats.

Bobruisk is often remembered as the birthplace of Vintsent Dunin-Martsinkyevich, the founder of modern Belarusian literature, but the town was mostly famous for its mud. Between April thaw and November freeze, its unpaved streets turned into rivers of knee-deep muck. Simply walking the streets required strength and ingenuity, and indeed, throughout Belarus, Bobruiskers were renowned improvisers, smart and inventive, always in motion, always in search of a way over and across any obstacle. This description certainly fits Boris, who was the first of nine children born to Mendel and Malka Morros, a Jewish couple who gave their son a traditional Jewish education consisting of Torah and Talmud. But Boris, like so many of his friends, was interested in more worldly pursuits. For many of the town's Jews in the late nineteenth century, the future wasn't in the Yiddish used at home and in the schools, markets, and streets, but in the Russian used by anti-tsarist revolutionaries in St. Petersburg, the Hebrew used by Zionists in Palestine, or the English used by those who ended up in America.

Bobruisk's Jewish residents had long bemoaned the town's poverty and overcrowding, the illness and hunger. They lived in constant fear of conscription: Involuntary military service in the Russian army, which might last decades, was an ever-present threat. Worst of all were the waves of both informal anti-Semitic persecution and government-orchestrated mass violence against Jews that followed the 1881 assassination of Tsar Alexander II. Alexander had freed the serfs and made important gestures toward ending the anti-Semitic policies of his predecessors, who had given many Jews a strong incentive to escape the "walled-in dungeon," as Boris later described the towns and villages of the Pale of Settlement, where Russian Jews were required to live. But Tsar Alexander III, unlike his more progressive father, was determined to solve Russia's "Jewish problem" by converting a third of them to Christianity, using work restrictions to encourage another third to leave the country altogether, and exterminating those who remained. Bobruisk's Jewish community dwindled accordingly. Terrible fires in 1899 and 1902 destroyed most of the town. If that wasn't enough, there were mass arrests of students and government-directed pogroms against Jews following the assassination of the Russian minister of education in 1902.

It was clearly time for the Morros family to leave. But how? The answer was literally in Boris's hands. A contemporary of Boris's from Bobruisk remembered: "A Jew in Bobruisk has actually two businesses—forestry and 'arranging' for his son to get into a gymnasia," or secular secondary education that would lead to admission to a university in Moscow or St. Petersburg. That was the plan of Boris's father, a humble locksmith whom Boris later preposterously claimed was the scion of seven generations of teachers, philosophers, and musicians who had performed at the court of the tsars and who supposedly served as the conductor of the Imperial Symphony Orchestra. It was actually Boris's mother, an amateur singer, who engineered the family's escape from Bobruisk. She gave Boris a quarter-size cello and found him a teacher who soon recognized that he was dealing with a child prodigy that might indeed change the fortunes of the whole Morros family.

Around the turn of the twentieth century, the theaters and concert halls that dotted the towns of the Pale of Settlement offered both vaudeville and classical music, with frequent outdoor summertime concerts. But Bobruisk was no place for a musical prodigy. The writer Isaac Babel recalled in his 1931 autobiographical story "Awakening" that virtually every Jewish family in every Eastern European backwater was willing to stake its future on one of its sons making his way to the St. Petersburg Conservatory of Music, which was among the few institutions of higher education in tsarist Russia that enrolled Jews and provided their families with the residence permits that allowed them to live legally in the city. So in 1903, Mendel and Malka Morros packed up Boris and his eight younger siblings and moved them to the capital of the Russian Empire. Whether the family would be able to remain and start a new life would be up to the twelve-year-old prodigy.

Located on a swamp on the Gulf of Finland, St. Petersburg was founded by Peter the Great in 1703 as Russia's "Window to the West." It replaced Moscow as the official capital of the tsar's empire long before it became the country's primary center of culture and business. When Boris and his family arrived in 1903, it was a heady time in the city's history, and the Morros family got an unsettling welcome. The city was under martial law, yet striking factory workers and revolutionary students bravely covered the city with their red flags, marching as they sang "Hymn to Liberty" in place of "God Save the Tsar!" Boris's parents heard with horror that the tsar's security forces were breaking up the demonstrations and arresting hundreds of young men. Those who weren't immediately executed were sent to the tsar's brutal prison colonies in Siberia, never to be heard from again. The crackdown offered a lesson in the consequences of political commitment that Boris never forgot.

Boris was hardly the only child prodigy studying at the St. Petersburg Conservatory at this time. Opening in 1862 as the first Russian music school of its kind, the conservatory offered a ten-year course of study that included six years at the high school level followed by four years at the college level, as well as lessons for young talents who were not formally matriculated full-time. Boris's time there coincided with the waning of what is often called Russian music's Silver Age, but the faculty still included such legends as Anatoly Liadov, Alexander Glazunov, and Nikolai Rimsky-Korsakov. The student body, which had once included Piotr Ilyich Tchaikovsky and Sergei Rachmaninoff, was in Boris's time no less distinguished. Boris studied alongside numerous prodigies who later dominated the world of classical music, among them Jascha Heifetz, Serge Koussevitzky, and Sergei Prokofiev. They all practiced obsessively, learning to play every instrument in the orchestra, sometimes less out of musical passion than a desperate effort to stay warm during St. Petersburg's long winters.

A degree from the St. Petersburg Conservatory all but guaranteed Jewish graduates a future that would have been otherwise impossible in tsarist Russia. The conservatory had been founded by a converted Jew, Anton Rubinstein, who made sure that Jews were welcome. In the early years of the twentieth century, half of the conservatory's twelve hundred students were Jewish, at a time when Jews comprised 4 percent of the Russian population and most institutions of higher education capped their Jewish enrollment at 3 percent. A joke from the period calls the St. Petersburg Conservatory the only school in Russia that had a quota to keep out the goyim.

The Jewish atmosphere of the conservatory dominated not only head counts but musical content, which could be awkward for students like Boris who were interested in art, not religion. While Russian and German classics still predominated in the concert halls, St. Petersburg's Jewish musicians were carrying out a revolution of their own, with the city becoming the center of efforts to document and promote the traditional Jewish religious and folk music of Eastern Europe as an art in its own right. Under the auspices of the Society for Jewish Folk Music, the movement attracted many of the conservatory's most talented musicians, but Boris never joined in the events they sponsored. Indeed, he refused to identify himself with any religion or political party, fearful that a reckoning was coming, when Jews—who were already considered insufficiently Russian and who were seen as foreigners and strangers, prone to violence, criminality, and revolution—could no longer depend on the meager protections offered by the tsar. Early on, Boris was an outsider among outsiders.

But it was impossible to escape history. In early 1905, midway through Boris's second year at the conservatory, the tsar's failure to approve a constitution guaranteeing basic civil rights, combined with widespread discontent with his war against Japan, in which more than a hundred thousand Russian soldiers had lost their lives, resulted in an enormous strike that shut down St. Petersburg. A peaceful crowd of more than a thousand men, women, and children gathered on Sunday, January 22, at the Winter Palace, the imperial family's official residence, to demand economic and political reform. They were savagely attacked by the tsar's troops, and more than two hundred civilians were killed.

Boris read about the incident in the newspapers and went back to practicing. But in the wake of what became known as Bloody Sunday, the country descended into chaos, with disruptive waves of protests, marches, and strikes. Eventually the tsar backed down and proposed the creation of an elected assembly called the Duma, with limited legislative and administrative powers. The gesture was inadequate: Only ten thousand of Russia's 130 million inhabitants would be eligible to vote, legislative sessions were to be closed to the public, the Duma would have no oversight over the tsar's ministers, and the tsar could dissolve the Duma at any time for any reason. Not surprisingly, public unrest, stoked by communist revolutionaries, intensified, and in December 1905 protesters shut the city down once again. Residents were left without power, transportation, mail, telegraph service, or newspapers. All of the city's shops, as well as the conservatory, closed their doors as communists fought the tsar's troops for ten days before surrendering, having seen hundreds of their comrades shot in the streets or arrested and sent into exile.

The tsar finally relented in May 1906, consenting to the establishment of a Duma that would be more broadly representative, even as he shut down dozens of newspapers and jailed their editors. Still, only a third of the Duma membership came from anti-tsarist parties, so it was unsurprising when their demands for land reform, a new education policy, and wider suffrage were all refused by the tsar, who dissolved the Duma in July. Then a wave of political assassinations convinced the tsar to crack down even more brutally on the press and opposition parties: He restricted voting rights, executed or exiled radicals, and orchestrated more pogroms in the provinces. By the time yet another Duma was seated in February 1907, it was clear that the tsar would continue to reign supreme, no matter how many of his ministers were assassinated, no matter how many young people marched, no matter how many workers went on strike. The dissolution of the newest version of the Duma in June 1907 and the seating of a much more conservative legislative later that month that backed anti-Semitic riots throughout the empire sent shock waves through Russia's provincial Jewish communities, which lost more than two thousand of their own in the massacres. St. Petersburg's Jews were relatively safe, for the moment, but more than one million Jews living in the provinces, about 40 percent of Russia's Jewish population, left the country during the period between the Revolution of 1905 and the outbreak of the Great War.

Students at the St. Petersburg Conservatory were at the forefront of these events, which Lenin later called a dress rehearsal for 1917. They paid the price. The government expelled and arrested dozens of students and closed down the conservatory indefinitely. When Boris's teacher, Rimsky-Korsakov, took the side of the students, he was dismissed. It was only after three hundred students quit school and threatened further unrest that Rimsky-Korsakov was reinstated and the school reopened.

Far from manning the barricades, Boris locked himself in his practice room, working on his counterpoint and perfecting his vibrato. It was a survival mechanism, and it worked. His reluctance to identify as a Jew and his lack of political commitment paid off when things returned to normal. Boris was a seasoned performer by the time he graduated in 1914, his father having taken him on concert tours of the provinces every summer since 1904. That was no doubt one of the reasons he was selected, while still a student, to serve as assistant musical director for the Imperial Opera Orchestra's conductor, Eduard Nápravník, who appreciated Boris's combination of artistic gifts and organizational talents. Upon Boris's graduation, Nápravník recommended him for a position organizing and directing musical activities at the Imperial Court. At a time when the tsar's popularity was at its lowest, Boris would be responsible for recruiting, rehearsing, and conducting the ensembles performed for the tsar and his government, and he would write and arrange much of the music as well. Mendel and Malka were overjoyed by their son's success, but they worried about whether Boris would end up on the right side of the revolution that everyone knew was coming.

CHAPTER TWO
BROKEN CHORDS, 1914–22

St. Petersburg's Winter Palace was the most luxurious of the tsar's seven residences, a vast eighteenth-century baroque structure with more than fifteen hundred rooms on the banks of the Neva. It was a fitting monument to the world's oldest and biggest empire, and it would be Boris's new home, a world away from the cramped apartment that he had shared with his family. The entire ground floor of the Winter Palace was dominated by a state room that could accommodate ten thousand visitors and a dining room that could host a thousand guests at its central table. The third floor was reserved for living quarters for court officials like Boris, while the piano nobile in between served as the imperial family's official home. The tsar and his family spent little time there, however, because the tsarina despised St. Petersburg, with its freezing winters and stifling summers. Moreover, because of the political turmoil that started in 1905, she felt safer in one of the tsar's several palaces outside the city. She also had a strong distaste for the corruption and decadence of court life and tried to convince the tsar to scale back his official public duties. That wasn't difficult, given the tsar's preference for quiet evenings at home with his family. But there were still grand receptions for which Boris had to select the music and the musicians, rehearsing and conducting the ensembles in programs that ranged from military marches to the latest in social dancing imported from Western Europe. In 1913, Boris recalled, he organized the entertainment for a massive celebration of the three hundredth anniversary of the Romanov dynasty's ascension to power. The next year, when Russia entered the Great War, Boris conducted the military orchestra that played as the tsar and tsarina bid farewell to troops leaving for the front. If the music didn't satisfy Boris's artistic appetites, the prestige of the position more than compensated. The tsar's guests must have been surprised to learn that the portly, already balding conductor providing the music was only in his early twenties, and they were often disturbed to hear the rumors that he was Jewish, but the tsar was happy to have found someone who could play anything and who never talked politics. Years of concertizing had given Boris a reputation in St. Petersburg as a crowd-pleaser, but Boris's most frequent and appreciative listener was the "Emperor and Autocrat of All the Russias," as the tsar was formerly known, a dignified, delicate, and well-bred man who insisted that Boris lead an ensemble to entertain the royal family at mealtimes. Boris also provided the keyboard accompaniment to the silent films the royal family loved to watch together on Saturdays, and he even performed for them aboard the imperial yacht. Much of this history comes from Boris's own later accounts and is impossible to verify, given the chaos and destruction that the historical record was subject to during the Russian Revolution and the Soviet era. By the same token, there is nothing in the surviving archives to contradict most of Boris's account. If nothing else, it leaves us with a very good idea of how Boris wanted this part of his life story to be written.

In 1915, when part of the Winter Palace was converted into a military hospital, a gesture aimed at appeasing the public's outrage at the number of dead and wounded soldiers, Boris and his musicians were relocated to the nearby village of Tsarskoe Selo. There the Romanovs, insulated from the public unrest of St. Petersburg—the tsar read special newspapers printed just for him that didn't include bad news—occupied the sumptuous neoclassical Alexander Palace, located in a sprawling complex of imperial palaces, churches, and gardens.

Despite the hardships that the war caused the average Russian, the tsar kept up appearances. A typical state dinner at Tsarskoe Selo included up to five hundred aristocrats, diplomats, and politicians who would be escorted into the palace's semicircular gilt-and-marble Portrait Hall to the sounds of Boris's orchestra. Seated under massive palm trees grown in the imperial greenhouses, guests enjoyed a French-style seven-course meal, starting with a traditional buffet of caviar, cheeses, cured meats, and smoked fish, and accompanied by copious amounts of champagne and vodka, which were poured by the two liveried servants assigned to each guest. Next came the dancing, again with music provided by Boris: The traditional polonaise was first, followed by waltzes and quadrilles, and then the tsar's favorite opera arias and chamber works, church and military music, and Russian folk songs.

Boris tried to stay out of politics, but his role in the court put him square in the middle of the turmoil. In addition to providing entertainment at balls and receptions, he was charged with providing music at sessions of the Duma, which meant performing both the Russian national anthem, "God Save the Tsar!," after major speeches by politicians who were partial to the tsar, and "The Marseillaise," after addresses by members of the opposition parties.

Despite the enormous authority of the tsar and the considerable power of the Duma, the future of the empire, it was widely believed, was actually controlled by a filthy, smelly, rail-thin priest whom Boris encountered shortly after he came to the court. The notorious Grigori Yefimovich Rasputin's supposed powers of prophecy and healing—he claimed to be able to treat the hemophilia that afflicted the young heir apparent, Alexei—captivated the superstitious tsarina and gave him entry to the most refined of St. Petersburg's social and political circles. Boris came to know Rasputin, treasuring a set of amber beads that the "Mad Monk" gave him, but he knew to keep his distance, especially after Rasputin tried to convince the tsar to stay out of the Great War. That made Rasputin some very powerful enemies. Boris had heard the rumors that Rasputin was even secretly advocating for a separate peace with Germany, which was a very unpopular position in the tsar's inner circle of advisors. Boris was shocked but perhaps not surprised to learn that on December 30, 1916, the tsar's closest advisors tried unsuccessfully to poison Rasputin with a chocolate pastry. Hours later, they finished the job by shooting him in the back, beating and castrating him, drowning him, and then dumping his body into a St. Petersburg canal. Objects associated with Rasputin were soon in demand as collectors' items and talismans, including his penis, which one of his paramours apparently preserved for decades. Boris already had his own relic, the amber beads, but he also learned a lesson about the wages of being close to power.

Boris witnessed the decline of Russian Empire firsthand. The tsar had declared war on the country's age-old Teutonic foe with a poorly prepared army and an outraged populace that remembered 1905 all too well. Despite early successes on the battlefield, the tsar's forces were soon in retreat. Public support for the war declined even further as millions of Russians were injured, killed, or captured and sent to German prisoner-of-war camps. The tsar knew he couldn't fight a civil war at home and a world war abroad, so in March 1917 he abdicated and was replaced by a provisional government operating out of the Winter Palace. Boris had a new employer, but he remained with the tsar's inner circle in the relative safety of the Alexander Palace, where he continued to perform for the family most evenings. Amid widespread strikes and army deserters, in the summer of 1917, Bolshevik revolutionaries overran the Alexander Palace, arrested the tsar and his family, and sent them all into internal exile, where they were soon executed.

Boris feared that same fate awaited him, but when Red soldiers knocked on his door in the middle of the night, it wasn't to throw him into jail but to demand that he organize a hundred-piece military brass band for the next evening. The revolution needed music and Boris delivered, even if it meant calling in every favor he was owed by his comrades from the St. Petersburg Conservatory. But Boris's concerns about having been a member of the tsar's court were well grounded. He later recalled that he was "the first of the court personnel tried by the Bolsheviks," who could not forgive him for the fact that while performing for the Duma, he had once mixed up his tunes, playing "God Save the Tsar!" after a speech by a member of one of the anti-tsar parties. He was able to survive formal accusations of anti-revolutionary leanings by reminding his accusers of his middle-of-the-night musical services just a few days earlier. Boris's position still wasn't as secure as he would have liked, but once again, he was protected by his status as a musician. When Red Army units randomly stopped him after Vladimir Lenin's November 1917 election as chairman of the Council of People's Commissars, Boris was glad to take off his hat to prove his identity: "Everyone in Petrograd knew that Conductor Morros has a bald head," he remembered.

Boris survived the Russian Revolution by switching sides, but enduring the civil war was a different matter. Boris later remembered: "During and after the Revolution I had many bizarre and thrilling experiences." But he rarely spoke about the destructive conflict between the communist Reds and the monarchist Whites. Boris did not trust Lenin's promise upon his assumption of power that "Doers in the Arts and Sciences" would be protected and accepted in the new nation, no matter their past political affiliations. At the same time, the Whites who still controlled much of the country considered all Jews to be communists and organized numerous pogroms and assassinations accordingly. It confirmed in Boris the lesson that every Jew in tsarist Russia had learned: No matter how influential or successful you might become, no matter which side you are on, even if you're on no side at all, you remain vulnerable.

Boris hoped that the civil war would be short-lived and that things could get back to normal, whatever that might be. In the meantime, self-preservation demanded that he choose the side that was winning, and he was rewarded by the Bolsheviks with a position running what until recently been the Imperial Music School in Poltava, in northeast Ukraine. It didn't offer Boris much artistically, but for the time being, he preferred the boredom of a civil servant's job in a provincial town to a Bolshevik firing squad in St. Petersburg. Eventually, he appealed to Lenin's government for a better position and was transferred to Moscow, where he worked at the Commissariat of Education, a position that first led to a job organizing local music education departments in the Ukrainian city of Ekaterinoslav (now known as Dnipro), and then to the post of head inspector of military orchestras on the southwest front.

In late 1919, with the end of the civil war nowhere in sight, Boris was captured by the Whites and briefly held in a prisoner-of-war camp, before being released in a prisoner exchange. He was determined to make his way back to St. Petersburg, but he stopped first in Alexandrovsk (later known as Zaporozhye), a Bolshevik-held town in Ukraine, where his parents had fled to escape the dangers of St. Petersburg. Because the Whites, who in addition to targeting former Bolsheviks were viciously anti-Semitic, still held territory to the north, Boris had initially decided to wait out the end of the civil war with his family; however, when he heard rumors that the Whites were approaching Alexandrovsk, he remembered he might also be considered a deserter by the Bolsheviks, and he decided to flee Russia altogether. One of Boris's cousins remembers being told by family members that Boris implored them to join him, but in the end he was unsuccessful, so he made his way alone to Rostov-on-Don and booked passage aboard a British boat making its way to Baku, the capital of Azerbaijan. The city was at the time controlled by the Bolsheviks, but many monarchist Russians had also ended up there, some waiting for the Whites to prevail so they could return home, others determined to put Russia behind them entirely. Boris hadn't yet decided which group he belonged to.

With its numerous oil wells providing almost half of the world's petroleum, Baku was crucial to the Bolshevik effort in the civil war and was one of the first provincial capitals they seized after the revolution. When Boris arrived in early 1920, he went straight to the Bolsheviks, told them that he had escaped from a White prisoner-of-war camp, and volunteered to rejoin the cause. He was appointed chairman of the local branch of the Soviet Union of Art Workers. Ever the opportunist, Boris made sure that when the city hosted the weeklong First Congress of Eastern Peoples in September 1920, he was put in charge of the teams of translators who were rendering speeches by hundreds of orators, among them the legendary American radical John Reed, into Russian. At one point, Boris found another focus for his attention: a wealthy singer and actress named Yekaterina Yefimova Modina, a native of Rostov-on-Don who lost most of her family when they sided with the Whites.

From the start, the love affair had a practical side. The two met when Catherine, as Boris always called her, registered as a singer and actress at Boris's offices. They quickly became intimate, but remained pragmatic: Boris promised to get them out of Baku, with the help of a velvet sack of diamonds around Catherine's neck that would pay for a new life somewhere else. The fact that she was married with two children, sixteen-year-old Constantin and thirteen-year-old Liouba, was barely an impediment: Her husband was old and sickly, virtually on his deathbed. He realized that Boris was Catherine's best hope and that their teenaged children were almost old enough to take care of themselves. Sometime in late 1920, Boris arranged for Catherine and her family to travel with him to Constantinople, where they hoped to find a way to Europe or America.

Constantinople wasn't much better than Baku. The Turks had backed the losing side in World War I, after which England and France divided up the Ottoman Empire, while Greece invaded mainland Turkey. Before he abdicated, the tsar had agreed to a deal in which Constantinople would end up in Russian hands, but the Bolsheviks refused to abide by that agreement, so the city remained under control of the Allies. It was a situation intolerable to Turkish nationalists who were suffering under postwar terms even harsher than those famously imposed on Germany. Agitation for an independent Turkey coalesced under the leadership of Mustafa Kemal Ataturk, who unilaterally rejected the terms imposed by the Allies and convinced Lenin to supply him with arms to be used against the Greeks. Lenin was not oblivious to the fact that these weapons would be used on Russian exiles, who were the targets of Ataturk's campaign of ethnic cleansing. Until the Turks finally vanquished the Greeks in the summer of 1922, the French, British, and Italian troops patrolling the city could do little to protect non-Muslims from mob violence.

Boris had taken Catherine and her family to Constantinople in search of a safe haven, but they found themselves living between two war zones. As many as 160,000 Russians had taken shelter in Constantinople, a city of under one million, according to the Turkish Red Crescent at the time. It was a hopeless, desperate situation. Work was difficult for Russians to find, and there were severe shortages of food. Overcrowding reached crisis proportions, with an astonishing seven thousand people living on the grounds surrounding the Russian embassy. Typhus and tuberculosis coursed through Constantinople's shantytowns where other refugees took shelter, though the ever-resourceful Boris found an apartment for all of them together. When Catherine's husband's heart finally gave out, Boris saw an opportunity and married her, though it would never be clear whether it was for the companionship or for the diamonds. Most of his fellow countrymen weren't so lucky. A European journalist observed in *National Geographic*:

> Russian refugees are everywhere, selling flowers, kewpie dolls, oil paintings of Constantinople, cakes and trinkets, books and newspapers printed in Russia. They sleep in the open streets and on the steps of mosques. They loaf, beg, work when they can find a job, and sometimes sob with hunger. A few Russians have been lucky enough to find positions in restaurants as waitresses or coat boys. A princess may bring the patron's coffee and a general may hand him his stick. Professors, ex-millionaires, women of high birth beseech one to buy cigarettes or paper flowers.

In such an atmosphere, diversion was welcome. For those refugees who were "more interested in Mozart than Marx," as Boris later put it—among them Vladimir Nabokov, who was also looking for a way out—a comedy revue called *The Bat*, which had been a huge hit in Moscow before World War I, supplied entertainment. Boris fell in with the troupe, earning some extra cash by providing musical backing for the show, which included what were then known as gypsy tunes, as well as ballads, folk melodies, opera arias, marches, polkas, and comic routines that comprised the show. But when *The Bat* moved on to Paris in late 1920, Boris began dipping into Catherine's little velvet bag of diamonds again.

The situation in Constantinople was deteriorating fast. News of massacres of non-Muslims and other atrocities committed by Ataturk's forces convinced a group of Russians to try to return home in 1921, but they were shot on arrival in Odessa. Boris knew it was time to leave, especially since he was now fully responsible for Catherine and for her children, whom he had adopted. Going back to Russia was not an option, and not simply because of the events in Odessa. The civil war continued to rage, and word had reached Boris that famine was killing millions, even as Lenin orchestrated thousands of extrajudicial executions and show trials. Most European countries refused to take in Russian refugees, so Boris turned his eyes to America, which had recently opened its borders after halting immigration completely during the Great War. But he still needed departure papers, which were notoriously difficult to procure amid all of the chaos. Remembering that the Allies' main representative in Constantinople, the French high commissioner Maurice Pellé, had been to see *The Bat* more than once when Boris was part of the crew, Boris decided to request an audience with Pellé in early November 1922. It was granted, and he walked away with departure papers for the whole family.

Days later, Ataturk's forces took control of the Sultan's army in Ankara, and Ataturk's nationalist followers in Constantinople stepped up attacks on foreigners. European troops were to leave the city immediately as part of the Allies' full recognition of Turkish independence, and that any Europeans who remained in the city did so at their own risk. Boris managed to book passage for the family on the SS *Constantinople*, a steamship leaving for America the next day, November 10, 1922. They escaped just in time.

The family travelled with a small group of Russian refugees who had also been stranded in Constantinople, in addition to passengers from Greece, Syria, Armenia, and even America. Third-class tickets were $120 each, almost $7,000 for the family in today's figures, an amount that almost depleted their funds, but they were grateful to gather their few belongings, board the massive vessel, a veritable Noah's ark of the displaced and the desperate, and head for Greece, through the Strait of Gibraltar, and then out into the stormy Atlantic.

Boris never spoke publicly about the voyage, which could not have been an easy one. He and his new family shared a third-class cabin with two other families. It wasn't steerage, but it wasn't much better. There were long lines to use the bathrooms, especially in the mornings, and the food left much to be desired, but all of the Russians onboard had seen worse. The crossing was scheduled to take ten days, but engine trouble added more than a week to the trip. They also encountered severe weather along the way. When the SS *Constantinople* finally steamed into New York Harbor on December 8, 1922, the passengers crowded onto the deck for the boat's ceremonial loop around the Statue of Liberty. Then Boris and his family, along with the rest of the third-class and steerage passengers, climbed into rowboats that took them through the cold and fog to Ellis Island.

Boris wasn't like the majority of these immigrants—he never had been and never would be. While most Russian immigrants were illiterate, uncultured, unskilled, and destitute, Boris had—even as an adolescent—entertained the world's most powerful man with his musical talents and dazzled the aristocracy who gathered at his court. His restless, haunted sense of destiny had allowed him to outrun regicide and revolution. The $130 he had in his pocket was almost enough to start a new life.

CHAPTER THREE
THE GOLDEN LAND, 1922–25

For most of the Russian Jewish immigrants who landed at Ellis Island on December 8, 1922, the past was something to be as forgotten as soon as possible. The more naive among them knew that the tsar and the Russian Empire were gone forever, but they thought that the Bolshevik Revolution was temporary and that a new, more moderate government would soon take Russia from the Reds and welcome back those who fled. The wiser among them knew better: With European nations reluctant to take in refugees, America was their best chance, perhaps their only chance. They questioned this wisdom, however, when they arrived at Ellis Island, the notorious "Gateway to America."

Today, Ellis Island is a museum celebrating America's embrace of the castoffs of European society, warmly remembered by the 40 percent of Americans whose ancestors landed there. But every new arrival soon learned why the primary entry point for the newest Americans was also known in the years after World War I as the "Isle of Hope and Tears." Corruption was rife, with doctors demanding payment for signing off on medical exams, and security personnel accepting bribes to smuggle rejects into Manhattan. Sanitation was substandard: The bathrooms were filthy, and the mattresses, sheets, and towels were infested with vermin. After advocates for immigrants publicly condemned the situation at Ellis Island, a *New York Times* article from May 1922 warned of a "Health Peril" on Ellis Island and detailed how new arrivals detained overnight were crammed thirty-five to a 24-by-14-foot cell. Later that year, a *Times* editorial called the twenty-seven-acre island in Upper New York Bay "a New Inferno," where immigrants were met with "the first and worst sample of America." The US secretary of labor, whose portfolio included immigration services, denied the charges, but when President Warren G. Harding addressed Congress on immigration policy later that year, he deplored what he called the "pathos at our ports," in which arrivals were treated like anything but future citizens.

The problem, and the solution, dated back to the years after the Civil War, two decades before the construction of Ellis Island, when it became clear that the arriving passengers didn't resemble the makeup of the nation's ruling class. In an effort to promote a vision of a nation populated by healthy, self-sufficient, law-abiding, well-educated Protestants, federal law barred entry to prostitutes, ex-convicts, the mentally ill or intellectually challenged—"lunatics" and "idiots" in the parlance of the day—and anyone "likely to become a public charge." Shortly before the turn of the century, the restrictions were expanded to deny entry to beggars, vagrants, paupers, alcoholics, felons, homosexuals, epileptics, consumptives, the "physically defective," and anyone who was judged to be "feebleminded." Officials also began to pay attention to the racial and ethnic origin of arrivals, favoring Anglo-Saxons and Scandinavians, who were overwhelmingly Protestant, over the largely Jewish and Catholic masses from eastern and southern Europe. Still, almost 1.5 million Jews from Russia and Poland, fleeing anti-Semitic pogroms, a crushing lack of economic opportunity, or both, were offered entry in the first decade and a half of the twentieth century, and more than twice that number arrived from Italy.

The doors to Ellis Island that had been closed during World War I opened when the conflict ended. Nonetheless, fears that the newest wave of arrivals threatened to undermine American values and bloodlines led Congress to begin imposing draconian restrictions not only on the total number of immigrants but on their national origin and religion as well. In 1922, fewer than 38,000 steerage passengers were allowed in, compared to more than 210,000 the year before, according to official figures. New legislation limited the number of arrivals from any individual country to 3 percent of the number who had arrived from that country in 1910. The date was chosen strategically in order to limit immigration from eastern Europe: The number of Jews arriving from Russia and Poland had peaked years earlier.

On Ellis Island itself, the legislation translated into an experience that was confusing at best and harrowing at worst. After the passengers finally reached dry land, carrying all of their worldly possessions on their backs, they lined up before immigration officers who hung identity tags around their necks. Next came the medical inspection, a terrifying moment for the new arrivals, who were well aware that anyone with an infectious disease, a physical or mental disability, or a moral failing like an association with communists or anarchists might be quarantined or even sent back to Europe. After that came a hot meal, which was often inedible, and never kosher. Finally there was the interview to determine whether they had what it took to become proper Americans.

Boris didn't look all that different from his fellow passengers. But unlike his mostly unskilled, uneducated, and destitute shipmates—a popular joke from the period told that of every three Jewish immigrants, one was a tailor and three were luftmenschen, which was Yiddish for someone who lived in the clouds and subsisted on air—he used to be somebody back in the old country. He was an educated and talented professional, someone who had been an insider, even something of a celebrity. Unlike them, he even had a bit of money in his pocket. So despite his heavy accent in the few English words he knew, and despite the burden of having to support a wife and two teenagers, he believed it wouldn't be that difficult for him to make it to the top again.

Still, as Boris waited in line with Catherine, Liouba, and Constantin, he tried to overcome a deep fear that they would be turned back. It took all of his skills as an entertainer to maintain an optimistic attitude for the sake of his wife and children, knowing that they had nowhere else to go. When they fled Russia, they forfeited their citizenship, and even if they had Russian passports, even if they wanted to return, the borders had been closed. Even so, as a member of a small cohort of political exiles from Bolshevism—artists, intellectuals, professionals, nobility, clergymen, and demobilized soldiers—he had good reason to hope that his family would be offered entry and a chance at citizenship. As he waited to approach the counter and face the notoriously fearsome immigration officer, Boris silently rehearsed his story. It was to be one of the most important performances he had ever given, and it was filled with lies.

The document that Boris filled out that day, or rather dictated to the clerk in broken English, appears to be the earliest piece of surviving physical evidence attesting to his life. It is also a record of the kind of man he wanted America to think he was, a testament to his mastery at reshaping his past in order to build his future. Boris claimed he was thirty-two years old but then corrected himself, instructing the clerk to cross out the typewritten figure and make him a year younger. He described himself as five feet four inches tall, which was optimistic, to say the least. He announced he was in good health and watched the clerk type that his eyes were blue, his skin fair, and his hair black, though again, that wasn't quite accurate, because Boris had been almost completely bald since his teens. He claimed to have paid for his own ticket, arriving from Constantinople with $130 in cash. As a native of "Bobroyski," as the town was known in Russian, Boris confirmed that he read and wrote the language. His "Race or People" was "Hebrew," and since the Soviet Union had yet to be formally established, much less internationally recognized, he claimed Russian nationality, though he had no plans to return, instead declaring that he hoped to become an American citizen as soon as possible. In the column asking for the "name and complete address of nearest relative or friend in country from whence alien came," most of his fellow passengers had listed "Nobody." Boris listed "General Pelle, High Commissioner of France," a gesture that was almost pitiful in its effort to impress. Strangest of all, he described himself not only as unmarried but as Catherine's cousin.

The performance was a success, and Boris and his family were admitted. They lugged their belongings onto the ferry that took them to the southern tip of Manhattan. Most of their shipmates intended to settle in New York City, but Boris had other plans. His arrival documents indicate that his next destination was to be Philadelphia and then Reading, Pennsylvania, where a man Catherine listed as her brother-in-law, a Russian immigrant named Charles Solov, owned a mattress shop. Solov met them at the ferry terminal, but instead of heading to Pennsylvania Station, where they could take the train to Philadelphia, he brought them to Grand Central Station. There the eighteen-year-old Constantin apparently went his own way and disappeared from Boris's life, while the rest of the little family got on a train to Boston, where Solov had friends who could find the family a place to live and set up Boris with a job.

Boris's first day in America was a bittersweet one. He had escaped from hell, a point brought home to him when he saw in the papers that Russia was pushing its weight around in a disarmament treaty with its neighbors. There were also articles about the US State Department's efforts to beseech Turkish officials to do more to prevent the massacre of its non-Christian minorities. But it wasn't clear that he had made it to heaven either. Although the arrival of *The Bat*, which had made it to America before Boris, had capitalized on a craze for all things Russian in fashion, music, dance, and the theater world, public opinion was different when it came to actual Russians. The Bolsheviks had for a time taken America's side against the Germans in the Great War, but eventually Lenin withdrew from the Allies and declared neutrality. By the end of the war, a full-blown Red Scare began sweeping across the United States, targeting both home-grown communists and the Russians who, in the public mind, were all Bolsheviks bringing with them a socialist revolution. The movement resulted not only in immigration restrictions but the infamous Palmer Raids, which were named after the attorney general who didn't hesitate to put public safety before civil liberties after a series of terrorist bombings masterminded by Italian radicals. (Palmer also didn't bother to distinguish between Italian anarchists and Russian socialists.)

Palmer's efforts to deport suspected radicals coincided with a disturbing rise in anti-Semitism in the United States in the 1920s. The Ku Klux Klan was nationally resurgent at that time, endorsed indirectly by the pseudoscientific anti-Semitism of figures like Henry Ford and Harvard University president A. Lawrence Lowell. Tensions were particularly high in Boston, where the Jewish population doubled in the years before World War I. New immigrants competed with members of the long-established Irish community for jobs in factories or on construction sites. Nat Hentoff, who became one of the country's most celebrated jazz critics and civil libertarians, grew up in Boston in the twenties and remembered it as America's most anti-Semitic city. Irish gangs, egged on by Sunday church sermons calling Jews "Christ-killers," regularly attacked Jewish boys who strayed into gentile territory with rocks, chains, baseball bats, and anti-Semitic taunts. Boris, who had seen worse in Russia and Turkey, wasn't too worried.

Within a few days Boris had settled his family into an apartment at 24 Creston Street, a three-unit, three-story clapboard house just off Blue Hill Avenue, commonly known as "Jew Hill Avenue," in Roxbury, which was then Boston's main Jewish neighborhood. Unlike the grim tenements of New York's Jewish ghetto, where most Russian Jewish immigrants in the early 1920s ended up, the Morros's new home was a spacious fifteen-hundred square feet apartment. Once the weather warmed, they could relax on their front porch and watch the local boys play stickball; among those boys was Theodore H. White, born in 1915 into a Russian Jewish family that lived on nearby Erie Street. White, who grew up to become the premier historian of the American presidency, remembered Roxbury as a friendly neighborhood of kosher butchers, grocers with pickles and crackers in oak barrels, horse-and-wagon peddlers, and lamplighters criss-crossing the neighborhood at dusk.

Boris wouldn't be able to get proper work anywhere while his legal status was in doubt, so as soon as he had settled Catherine and Liouba into their new home, Boris and Catherine paid a visit to the federal courthouse in downtown Boston. There, they renounced their allegiance to Russia and declared their intention to become American citizens. The Department of Labor form that Boris used on December 13, 1922, to start the naturalization process was brief, but his responses were predictably inconsistent. The blue-eyed, fair-complexioned Hebrew "artist" from Bobroyski was now a brown-eyed, medium-complexioned white "composer and professor of piano" from Minsk.

Next, Boris turned his attention toward finding a job, which would prove more difficult than finding an apartment. Boris arrived in Boston during the economic crisis that had followed the end of World War I and lingered well into 1923. Good job opportunities were uncommon, especially for those whose English was poor. Most newly arrived Russian Jews were happy to find work in Boston's garment factories, sweatshops, or slaughterhouses. Those who could speak English often found work as waiters or doormen. Those were the sorts of jobs that the friends of Catherine's brother-in-law were offering. But the former director of music at the court of the last tsar thought he could do better, and he started by going to the movies.

In the years after World War I, even Boston's poorest families could afford an afternoon at the theater to experience the new fad called "moving pictures," which in the days before talkies used live musical accompaniment. Boris quickly picked up work as an organist at Roxbury's half-dozen theaters, but it was in the world of Jewish music that he supported his family and began to build a career. Although he'd been given a proper Jewish education back in Russia, he was never a religious man, nor was he interested in Zionism, until now. In between providing organ accompaniment for showings of Buster Keaton's *The Paleface* and *Robin Hood* with Douglas Fairbanks, Boris began writing an opera called *Ahasverus Play* about the Jewish holiday of Purim, which began on March 1 that year, and knocking the doors of Roxbury's theaters in the hope of finding a collaborator.

With the holiday only a few weeks away, and local amateur synagogue musical ensembles looking for something less formidable than a full-scale work of musical theater, the work was never performed. Boris toned down his ambitions, and with an eye—and ear—toward the next Jewish holiday, he composed a shorter work based on the psalm traditionally heard on the Sabbath after Passover, which in 1923 fell on March 31.

This work, called the "Hymn of Palestine," which borrows from the 126th Psalm and its plea for the Lord to restore Israel's fortunes, had genuine resonance for Boris, who had indeed fallen very far from his glory days in St. Petersburg.

Boris had no more success pitching "Hymn of Palestine" in Roxbury than he did *Ahasverus Play*, but he did publish it with a local music management company as "Opus 47 Number 3," which suggests he already had a career's worth of compositions in his portfolio, or that he wanted to give that impression. His next composition, a collaboration with the well-known Yiddish singer and actor Julius Nathanson, was an operetta called *Shayne Khaleynes*, or *Beautiful Dreams*. This time, Boris found an audience, performing selections for a gathering of Young Judaea, a national Zionist organization, at the house of a local supporter.

Beautiful Dreams attracted the notice of a local weekly newspaper called the *Jewish Advocate*, which referred to him as "Professor Boris Morros," the composer of a slew of popular Jewish folk tunes, and claimed he was just back from a visit to Palestine—all out-and-out untruths. What the newspaper got right was that Boris was being hired to organize and conduct a choir composed of local Young Judaea members. But the meager salary that Young Judaea paid him wasn't enough to cover the rent on the spacious rooms on Creston Street, so that summer he moved his family into a humbler abode, a fifth-floor tenement apartment at 218 Humboldt Avenue. It was smaller and less comfortable but a step up in terms of social class, because it was located in a neighborhood that was home to fancier, single-family homes with front yards and backyards, and just two blocks from the Crawford Street Synagogue, the neighborhood's most prominent and progressive temple.

Boris had failed as a composer, and he wasn't making much progress as a performer or teacher either, having traded in a seat at the organ, where he provided the soundtrack for the vampires, tramps, and bullfighters dominating America's cinema screens, for the even less fulfilling task of rehearsing a choir of bored teenagers. It's no surprise that Boris grew restless, realizing that he couldn't afford to wait for opportunities to come to him. According to the *Boston Daily Globe*, in August 1923, "Prof. Boris Morros, composer and musical director" invited a group of "representative Jewish men" to his new home for the first of a series of meetings to plan for the upcoming visit to Boston of the famed cantor Pincus Minkowsky and to lay the groundwork for a national conservatory devoted to Jewish music and the training of cantors. Boris appointed himself and Catherine to the conservatory organizing committee, which came with a ·title and the promise of a salary.

Boris's career was back on track, but life at home wasn't particularly happy. He had officially married Catherine, who played the role of the devoted Jewish wife in public, but the desperate circumstances that threw them together in Baku and Constantinople resulted in a partnership that was less passionate than pragmatic. Now Catherine was increasingly resentful of Boris for having promised her the world and then reduced her to pinching pennies in the worst apartment on Roxbury's best block.

Catherine couldn't accuse Boris of laziness. October 1923 found "Professor Morros" conducting a vocal quartet and accompanying the violinist Gertrude R. Nissenbaum in a concert sponsored by the Roxbury Agudath Ivrith, a society dedicated to Hebrew language and literature. The event, held at Hebrew Teachers College, only attracted an audience of one hundred, but Boris was making a name for himself locally. A few weeks later he provided a "musical interlude" at a meeting at the synagogue of another local Jewish group, the Young Zionists of nearby Somerville.

Boris's self-promotion began to pay off. In November 1923, readers of the *Jewish Advocate* were drawn to an advertisement that announced A GREAT EVENT! PROVIDENCE! PROVIDENCE! A closer look revealed that "The Famous Piano Artist and Composer, Prof. Boris Morros," shown in the first known photo of him, would be at the piano bench for a Hanukkah concert on Sunday afternoon, December 2, 1923, to accompany three of the most celebrated cantors in the world, Pincus Minkowsky of Odessa, Isaac Glueckstein from Budapest, and Isidore Andelsman of Boston.

By this time it was becoming clear that the conservatory job would not materialize, so when the parent institution of the Hebrew Teachers College, the Crawford Street Synagogue, began looking for a new director of music, Boris made sure he was the first in line to apply. To bolster his application, he wrote an article for the *Jewish Advocate* on Jewish music as a universal art form, one that was essential to the development of European classical music. The "zeal and idealism characteristic of the Russian artists" like Rimsky-Korsakov, Liadov, and Glazunov, all professors at the St. Petersburg Conservatory in the years before the revolution, Boris wrote, could be traced to the Hebraic passions that reverberated through the practice rooms and hallways. Naturally Boris put himself at the forefront of such developments, preposterously claiming that he had been one of the primary exponents of the Jewish folk music movement at the conservatory before World War I. The strategy worked. The Crawford Street Synagogue hired him.

It wasn't an ideal job. Most of his time was spent either in the synagogue, accompanying services or rehearsing choirs of bored children and out-of-tune housewives, or in its Hebrew College, teaching music in the afternoons to 150 future teachers headed for positions in Boston's Jewish schools.

Boris began to look beyond the narrow confines of Roxbury's Jewish enclave. He took a leadership position in the Jewish Culture Club of Boston, which was part of the Jewish National Workers Alliance. The fact that the club was officially socialist didn't seem to bother Boris, who had learned back in Russia how to be politically flexible. The point for Boris was to find a way out of the literal and musical ghetto in which he'd found himself. The all-male club, which met at the tony Parker House Hotel in downtown Boston and the elegant American House Hotel in the North End, conducted its meetings in Yiddish and was nominally devoted to sponsoring cultural and educational programs, including initiatives to assist Jews in need in Europe and Palestine. The best part for Boris was that it provided him with an excuse to get out from under the disapproving stare of Catherine, who was now pregnant and housebound.

On October 12, 1924, Catherine and Boris welcomed into their family Richard Hyman Morros, whom they called Dick. Boris was ecstatic, determined to make his son proud, and he redoubled his efforts to escape Roxbury's orbit. Later that month he managed to convince WBZ, a radio station owned by the *Boston Herald-Traveler* and Westinghouse, to feature him performing his own "Prelude in D Major," "Fantasy," and "Prelude in G-Major," as well as selections from his 1923 operetta, *Beautiful Dreams*. But Boris's meal ticket was still kosher. In between his increasingly dreary and demeaning duties on Crawford Street, he composed the soundtrack for the Zionist documentary film *Land of Promise*, accompanied the great cantor Yossele Rosenblatt when he came to Boston, and was commissioned by the prominent Zionist Elihu Stone to collaborate on a song in Yiddish called "My Homeland." The sheet music holds no revelations in terms of musical artistry, but it does feature the second known photograph of Boris, balder and chubbier, with a broad smile hiding his increasing professional frustration.

Then came a cable from Jerusalem offering Boris the conductorship of the Hebrew Opera Company in Palestine and the musical directorship of the Palestine Conservatory of Music beginning in early 1926. Boris's connections—some of America's most prominent Zionists—were behind the offer, so he wasn't surprised, but he was uncertain about what to do. On the one hand, he was getting nowhere in Boston, locked into an endless round of synagogue services and lessons for amateurs that left little room for him to make his own music. The work barely paid the bills, especially now that Boris and Catherine were overwhelmed by the expenses of a new baby. An occasional appearance at a memorial or benefit concert or political gathering was exciting, but someone else was always in the spotlight. On the other hand, while becoming the face of classical music in Palestine was tempting, it seemed like Roxbury writ large. Though the Hebrew Opera Company's 1924 season had featured operas by Gounod, Verdi, Wagner, Saint-Saëns, Meyerbeer, Rimsky-Korsakov, and Puccini, the company was only able to offer such a wide selection of performances in minimalist versions, without full sets, costumes, or a full orchestra.

Moreover, the fact that the works were staged in Hebrew ensured that they would be as artistically estranged from the rest of the opera world as they were geographically distant.

Boris wanted something more, something better, somewhere else, and he got it. On July 26, the *Boston Daily Globe* reported that Boris, "one of the foremost composers of Yiddish and Hebrew operas in America," had turned down the position of conductor of the Hebrew Opera and managed to negotiate the terms of the Palestine Conservatory offer so that he could go to New York and become the director of the administrative council of the Association for the Erection of a Conservatory of Music in Memory of Jewish Soldiers Killed in the World War. Boris had finally made it back to New York City.

CHAPTER FOUR
THE ENTERTAINER, 1925–33

Boris moved to "the monster known as New York," as another Russian exile, Leon Trotsky, called it, in the fall of 1925 and was soon using the offices of the Palestine Conservatory to look for another job. It didn't take long. By the end of the year Boris was working at Times Square's Rivoli Theatre as the assistant conductor under Hugo Riesenfeld, the famed Viennese-born violinist, composer, and conductor who had given up the concert hall for the cinema. Until 1918, when Riesenfeld replaced Samuel "Roxy" Rothafel at the Rivoli, the organ music that accompanied most silent films was considered incidental. It was Riesenfeld's innovation to write original scores for a full pit orchestra that would not simply keep the ears of the audience busy but intensify their experience of the film. More important to Boris was the fact that Riesenfeld's orchestras had a reputation as breeding grounds for new musical talent. More than one of Riesenfeld's assistant conductors had gone on to significant careers of their own on Broadway and even in Hollywood.

After his years of exile in Boston's Jewish ghetto, the tsar's musical director felt at home at the Rivoli, at West 49th Forty-Ninth Street and Broadway. It was the grandest of all the Broadway cinemas. The theater boasted the biggest screen in the world and had the capacity to seat 2,270 people in air-conditioned comfort. The exterior boasted Doric columns in the Greek Revival style, while the inside was, according to architect Thomas Lamb's vision of Italian Renaissance Revival style, entirely gold, marble, and ivory. Male ticket holders were required to wear jackets, and there were separate lounges for the ladies. The Rivoli was a place to see and be seen, but as a venue it had been expressly designed to foreground its musical offerings. It housed the largest organ of any cinema in the world, had room for a fifty-piece orchestra, and was ready for the sound revolution that Riesenfeld knew was coming.

Boris was now working seven days a week, from the matinee until after the midnight showing. That meant he didn't have much time to spend with Catherine or Dick—Liouba, who no longer appears on official records as a member of the household, seems to have remained in Boston—whom he had installed in an apartment at 345 West Fifty-Fifth Street, a relatively new nine-story building that was popular in New York's music and theater world. But Catherine didn't complain that Boris wasn't around much, now that Boris was finally making enough money to maintain her in the style to which she'd once been accustomed back in the old country.

Boris reported to Riesenfeld, but he was officially an employee of the Paramount organization. At the time, Paramount was not only one of the most successful entertainment companies in the country but one of the most powerful corporations in the world. Founded in 1912 by Adolph Zukor, a furrier from Hungary who went into the movie business after making a fortune in penny arcades that showed two-minute films known as "peep shows," Paramount was focused almost solely on movies by the time Boris came onboard. Nonetheless, live entertainment was still being used to draw audiences to the two-thousand cinemas that the company controlled from coast to coast through its Publix Theatres subsidiary.

One of Boris's colleagues recalled that Boris was a friendly second-in-command, perhaps too friendly, since he gained something of a reputation for pinching cheeks and swatting behinds. But in the few months he worked under Riesenfeld, Boris made quite an impression on Zukor. When Riesenfeld resigned in late 1925, Zukor promoted Boris, making him music advisor to the well-known Broadway showman John Murray Anderson, who was in charge of putting together the vaudeville revues that ran between films at the Rivoli. Since Anderson was charged with coming up with a new show every month, Boris was not simply composing and conducting music to accompany films but also scouting musical acts, dancers, acrobats, jugglers, comics, and anything else that might keep audiences entertained. If this wasn't the job that Boris had been waiting for, it did offer him the money, authority, and renown that he had been dreaming of since he was a child.

Boris's ascent in the world of American entertainment was still just starting. He turned out to be so good in this new position that Zukor made him a travelling "fixer" for Publix theaters nationwide that were not drawing the expected crowds. Boris was now responsible for everything from hiring and firing musicians, to adjusting the programs to suit local tastes, to conducting orchestras himself. It was difficult work that kept Boris on the road for weeks at a time, mostly in the South and Midwest, but he didn't mind time away from Catherine and Dick. He found plenty of temporary female companionship among the showgirls and starlets, but it was the attention he attracted in his capacity as a Publix executive that he found most satisfying.

For much of 1926 and 1927, when he wasn't on the road, Boris was based in Memphis, Tennessee, where he was officially the musical director at Paramount's Loew's Palace. Boris had never imagined himself in a small Southern city, but he realized that Memphis could be a stepping stone to a better position at Paramount. The Palace, a twenty-two-hundred-seat cinema that had been built in 1920 by Thomas Lamb, was located on Union Avenue, Memphis's main commercial thoroughfare. It was the latest word in garish, with an impossibly ornate interior accented by pink neon lighting, and it had a twenty-five-cent ticket price that bought entry not only to a feature-length film but to a full-length variety show. Still, the crowds just weren't showing up. When Boris arrived, he dedicated himself to improving the tastes of Tennessee filmgoers by leading the pit orchestra in everything from sentimental ballads to Wagnerian lieder to jazzy dance tunes. There was even room for his own compositions. But Boris did what he had to do to bring in audiences. In March 1927 he introduced Memphis audiences to a series of decidedly lowbrow features, including segments called "Around the World in Rhythm," "Milady's Love Songs" (complete with a trumpeter playing at the back of the balcony), and "The Road to Romany." The new programming worked, and Boris became something of a celebrity. Back East, the industry newspaper *Film Daily* began noticing the unusual goings-on in Memphis and announced that Boris was "putting them over in great style."

When a disastrous flood inundated the Mississippi delta region in 1927, Boris staged several concerts to benefit the victims. He was able to convince an engineer-turned-politician named Herbert Hoover, who chaired the Mississippi Flood Relief Commission, to lend his voice to the effort. The two became close friends, and in Hoover's successful campaign for president the next year, Hoover used his experience in the Memphis floods as evidence of his compassion and competence. Hoover even invited Boris and Catherine to the White House for his inauguration, Boris later claimed, and Catherine danced the first waltz with the new president at the festivities that evening. At least, that is the way Boris told the story, and though it seems improbable, like so many of his stories, a close inspection of a photograph of Hoover's swearing-in ceremony reveals a prematurely balding man who looks very much like the young Boris. As with much of Boris's early history, the facts are ultimately unknowable, and one suspects that Boris preferred them that way.

Eventually Zukor, who had placed that admiring item in *Film Daily*, realized that Boris's instincts for what audiences wanted made him too valuable to keep down in Memphis. Zukor called Boris back to New York to become associate director of music at Publix, working with a team of booking agents that filled stages from coast to coast. The pay raise that came with the job allowed Boris to move his family into a new apartment at 320 West Eight-Ninth Street, a nine-story luxury building just off Riverside Drive, in the more family-friendly neighborhood of the Upper West Side.

It took only a few months for Zukor to promote Boris to general musical director, with responsibility for the music at more than a thousand theaters across the United States. More responsibility meant even more money, and Boris began to get a taste for spending it. This wasn't difficult in Jazz Age Manhattan, especially because Boris was expected to make appearances at all the right restaurants and nightclubs. At first, Catherine came along, showing off an updated version of the kind of luxurious evening wear she had worn back in tsarist Russia, clothes that Boris was for the first time able to afford. Although she liked to keep an eye on Boris as he hobnobbed with Broadway's most powerful men, beautiful women, and brightest new talents—among them the young Milton Berle, Bob Hope, George Burns and Gracie Allen, and Jack Benny—she just couldn't keep up with him as he hopped from theater to nightclub night after night. In the beginning, he had no problem affording the lifestyle, but eventually he starting taking advances on his salary. Then he began borrowing from friends. Three months after Black Tuesday ushered in the Great Depression, Boris declared bankruptcy. Coming soon after he had become an American citizen, it was a move that shamed him so deeply he never mentioned it again, not even to his intimates; but anyone who could read the public announcements in the newspapers on January 29, 1930, learned that after almost a decade in America, Boris Morros had liabilities of $13,666, the equivalent of almost $60,000 today, and no assets.

Declaring bankruptcy in those early dark days of the Great Depression was by no means uncommon, and Boris soon bounced back, in part because he gave journalists what they wanted: a good story. Boris, who had managed to charm Southerners that might not have otherwise warmed to a Jew with a thick Russian accent, was becoming nationally known as someone who attracted attention wherever he went. An article in the *Atlanta Constitution* in July 1930 announced his arrival in the city to prepare music for the grand reopening of the Paramount Theatre and called him "one of the most picturesque characters in the theater business today."

It wasn't just the accent and the brash wardrobe that made him a magnet for publicity; it was also his biography, much of which he compulsively embellished or outright invented. The story was irresistible to the newspapers: Russian prodigy wins highest honors at the St. Petersburg Conservatory and becomes the musical director of the tsar's Imperial Court, where he meets Rasputin. Then he serves in the Russian

Revolution and the ensuing civil war and lands in Constantinople. That much seems to be mostly true, though unverifiable. Much of the rest, from directing *The Bat*, to writing its most popular song, "March of the Wooden Soldiers," to getting hired by Paramount right off the boat and helping Zukor turn the company into a nationwide entertainment powerhouse, is contradicted by the historical record or dismissed by the people who were there. In addition to the invented facts, there was also much missing from this narrative: his Judaism, his demoralizing flight from both the Bolsheviks and the Whites, the desperation of his time in Constantinople, the years leading synagogue choirs in Boston, and his recent bankruptcy. That might have made for a truer story, but Boris was in search of a better story.

Boris's tall tales were excellent publicity for Paramount, but the fact is that he was very good at his job. Despite his strict classical training, he had been studying what American audiences wanted: a real show. In this sense, Paramount was the perfect place for him. After Paramount won the very first Academy Award for Best Picture in 1929 with *Wings*, Zukor took as the company motto "If it's a Paramount Picture, it's the best show in town." Zukor may have sold the public on the quality of his films, but the thirty-nine-story corporate headquarters that rose above the theater at West Forty-Third Street and Broadway was a symbol of the studio's devotion to unadulterated commerce. In addition to putting together orchestras, Boris hired organists, negotiated with sheet music publishers, and even became a radio personality, promoting Paramount acts via the weekly show he hosted on the nationwide Mutual Broadcasting System. Boris's favorite part of the job was holding daily auditions, judging everything "from fire eaters, dog acts, and acrobats to comics and coloratura sopranos," as he later remembered. This was how Boris claimed to have discovered Bing Crosby, Ginger Rogers, and Artie Shaw, among many other marquee-quality names.

Boris also took credit for having discovered one of the most popular child stars of the Great Depression, the boy singer Bobby Breen. The six-year-old Canadian prodigy showed up at Boris's office in the Paramount

Building every day for two weeks, waiting for Boris to spare a few minutes to hear his act. In fact, once Boris looked at the boy's last name, he became convinced that he was the grandchild of a famed Ukrainian cellist who was one of the earliest Bolshevik martyrs, and he decided to give the child a tryout. Boris was unimpressed by the boy's voice, but when he saw that his secretary was moved to tears when Breen sang "Boulevard of Broken Dreams," he assumed Paramount audiences would have the same response, and he offered Breen a contract. The boy was soon wowing audiences in New York and later become one of the greatest Hollywood child stars of the era.

Boris had accomplished almost everything he had set out to do in America, but thoughts of his family back in Russia haunted him. He had always tried to keep in contact. Even if the Morros family hadn't been scattered by war and revolution, postal and telephone contact was unreliable, in part because the United States still hadn't recognized the Soviet Union diplomatically. Most of the letters he sent were returned as undeliverable, and he received very little mail from back home. Travelling there wasn't a good option either, at first because Boris couldn't afford it in terms of time or money and later because he wasn't even sure if he would be allowed back in the country, given his service to the tsar and ensuing flight into exile. Nonetheless, when Boris learned via telegraph cable that his father, Mendel, was ailing, he booked a trip with Catherine and Dick to France, where he hoped to travel by plane or train to Russia. *Film Daily*, which by this point was almost his personal publicity machine, reported on a farewell party that Publix executives threw for Boris at the Waldorf-Astoria Hotel on September 29, 1932, before his ship sailed the next day. Boris never gave any details about what happened on this trip, beyond telling a reporter from the *Baltimore Sun* that they had made it to Moscow, where, Boris claimed, the Soviet authorities, who were well aware of Boris's membership in the tsar's inner circle, would only approve a brief meeting with his father at the airport. That was when Boris began to wonder what it would take to bring some or all of his family to the United States. Little did Boris know that the Soviet secret police was wondering the same thing.

CHAPTER FIVE
COVER STORIES, 1933–34

In his line of work, Boris met many people only once, but he rarely forgot a face, so he was intrigued when in February 1933 the agent who had convinced Bobby Breen to camp out in Boris's lobby showed up at his office with a most unusual offer. Boris was expecting another child prodigy. He didn't foresee getting the chance to put Leon Trotsky on the Paramount stage. The incendiary hero of the Russian Revolution had been ejected from the Communist Party in 1927 because of his insistence on global social revolution, whereas Stalin was determined to focus his efforts on the Soviet Union alone. Trotsky was sent into exile and infuriated Stalin by organizing anti-Soviet socialist groups across the globe. By 1933, the world's most committed communist was having money problems. A contract for an American lecture tour, with a gig at the Paramount as its centerpiece, would mean financial stability for Trotsky's family and funding for the international conference he was organizing that would challenge Stalin's stranglehold over socialism.

Boris demurred, in part because of politics. His experience during the Russian Revolution and the civil war that followed convinced him that he wanted nothing to do with communism. Moreover, with the rise of Hitler, it was Stalin and not Trotsky who was America's best bet to fight the Nazis. Boris also doubted signing Trotsky on less lofty grounds: Boris rarely erred when it came to understanding what his audiences wanted, and he was convinced the Trotsky show wouldn't sell tickets. Trotsky had spent time in New York City in 1917, but whatever English he had picked up was gone after almost two decades, so his speech would have to be in Russian. Still, Boris didn't reject the offer outright. Instead, he said he would think it over.

Thinking it over meant thinking about his family back in Russia. Ever since he had left, Boris had struggled to keep up with the news from the old country. American newspapers had celebrated the Russian Revolution as a victory over feudalism, and despite the Red Scare of the postwar period, the Bolsheviks were widely praised in the United States. But the news that Boris was able to glean from letters from his family or from fellow émigrés who had visited Russia was troubling. The Morros family, like so many Russians, struggled to feed and clothe themselves. Boris also heard that his brothers had been running into difficulties with the authorities because of their outspoken criticism of Stalin, whose disastrous collectivization of fourteen million Soviet farms beginning in 1930, was causing mass starvation. A few weeks after Bobby Breen's agent made the Trotsky offer, Boris learned that a friend, the well-known promoter Sol Hurok, who specialized in importing Russian musicians and dancers for American stages, would be travelling to the Soviet Union. Boris asked if Hurok would look up his family and deliver gifts and clothes on his behalf. Hurok was glad to help, but on his return, he had disturbing news. Hurok had managed to meet with two of Boris's brothers, Serge and Savely, but they hadn't accepted the packages Boris had sent, because they refused to accept charity from any capitalist, not even their own brother. Both were now working as engineers and were delighted to hear that their older brother was doing so well in America, Hurok reported. Though their clothing was threadbare, they seemed physically healthy, and as true believers in the communist revolution, they had no complaints about life in the Soviet Union; but they refused to offer Hurok any information about how the rest of the family was doing, or even how to find them. Nor did they offer any criticism of Stalin. "They are either shy or very proud men," Hurok explained to Boris. "Perhaps like everyone else in that terror-filled world they are too frightened to say anything—or even to think."

Hurok encouraged Boris to keep sending packages but advised him to use Union Tours, a travel agency that specialized in sending American tourists to the Soviet Union under the letterhead of Amtorg, the Soviet agency responsible for promoting economic relations between the Soviet Union and the United States. Boris contacted the head of Union Tours in New York, M. B. Horton, who was happy to help.

Within days, Boris began receiving telephone calls from a man who called himself Gregory Melamed and claimed to be an official from Amtorg, but who was in fact a Soviet spy named Lev Nikolaevich, operating under the code name "Ossip," though it would be years before Boris discovered his true identity. Boris agreed to lunch with Melamed in the Hotel Astor's Hunting Room, a male-only preserve of Midtown wheelers and dealers right around the corner from the Paramount. Melamed, a dour, balding figure, began by asking what family Boris still had back in Russia. Might Boris write down their names and addresses? It seemed like an innocuous gesture, but Melamed recognized the names and was sorry to tell Boris that not just Serge and Savely, but two of his other brothers, Isaak and Aleksander, had been identified by the government as potential counterrevolutionaries. Melamed, Boris began to suspect, was not what he seemed.

Boris didn't have to ponder long about why a Soviet trade representative in America had such up-to-date information about his family back in Russia. Boris had seen first-hand how the Soviet secret police, known as the Cheka, behaved in the years after the civil war, and he had heard rumors about how prison camps were filled with people like his brothers. So when Melamed offered to help get Boris's packages through, Boris correctly assumed that Melamed wanted something else in return: to keep Trotsky off the Paramount's stage. Boris, who had always been a quick learner, realized that he had some leverage, but over whom?

Boris got back to Trotsky's agent, and though he had no intention of following through, Boris told him he would consider putting the Russian revolutionary onstage. It was Boris's way of turning Melamed's quid pro quo around, and it worked. "It would make a sensation, you know," he told Melamed, who understood and answered: "We can be very useful to one another, my friend. Isn't there something else I can do for you besides this small matter of seeing that your parcels get through? Wouldn't you like me to try to get your parents sent here?"

Boris had become increasingly pessimistic about the possibility of ever seeing his family again and left lunch thinking he had come out on top. "I got a big favor in return for not doing something I had never intended to do anyway," he remembered. What Boris, in his naivete, didn't realize was that it was the wrong favor, because it left his brothers vulnerable, which gave the Soviets a very significant advantage.

It wasn't long before letters from Boris's family, which had arrived so sporadically in the past, began piling up in his mailbox, filled with joyous plans about Mendel and Malka's impending visit, not to mention thanks for the packages. But in late November some bad news came: Malka was reportedly too sick to travel, so Mendel started alone on the long, arduous journey from his home in Leningrad, as St. Petersburg was now known. He travelled to Riga to acquire his visa, then returned to Leningrad before making his way by train to Cherbourg, France, where the SS *Majestic* sailed on November 19, 1933. The elderly, bearded locksmith arrived at Manhattan's West Side cruise-ship terminal two weeks later and burst into tears upon seeing his dapper, successful son. Boris, too, couldn't keep himself from weeping at the sight of the old man, much changed after years of hardship.

Boris settled his father into his own bedroom in the family's new apartment at 586 West End Avenue, which represented yet another step up economically. Boris didn't have much time to babysit him, but he was determined to show Mendel a good time in America and even took him on a trip to Florida. Mendel wasn't happy that his son, a classical music prodigy, was now working in vaudeville, and he saw little of Boris, instead spending most of his time tracking down acquaintances from the old country. Ultimately, even though Mendel had declared upon his arrival that he intended to seek US citizenship, he was mostly occupied with thoughts of returning to his wife, and he began to plan a journey back to the Soviet Union.

In the beginning of May 1934, Boris took his father to the Soviet consulate to make sure his travel documents were in order. There was the matter not only of Mendel's exit visa but of gifts he wanted to make sure would make it through customs. The official they dealt with was Peter Davidovitch Gutzeit, the Soviet vice-consul in New York, though Boris's experience with Melamed made him suspect, again correctly, that the people working out of the consulate might be leading double lives. He would learn later that Gutzeit, a longtime veteran of Soviet intelligence, had recently been made the New York station chief of Stalin's international espionage operations, code name "Nikolai."

It was a friendly conversation, especially after Gutzeit learned that Mendel was anxious to return home, having become "disgusted with the capitalist country," as Gutzeit wrote in a secret cable sent to Moscow that has only recently been declassified and translated. Boris held back until Gutzeit, who had been well prepared by Melamed, asked what kind of work he did. Then Gutzeit allowed Boris to do what he did best: brag about his accomplishments, especially his meteoric rise in the Paramount ranks. By the time Boris stopped to take a breath, Gutzeit realized that Boris's usefulness to the Soviet Union extended far beyond keeping Trotsky off Paramount's stages. Gutzeit wrote to Moscow: "During a conversation with Morros, I got the impression that he might be used to place our operatives in Paramount offices situated in every country and city," that he "could be brilliantly put to use providing our workers with a cover."

Boris would later claim he was aggressively recruited by Melamed and Gutzeit, but the declassified Soviet archives tell a very different tale, one in which Boris himself took the lead. After Mendel and Boris left, Gutzeit wrote back to Moscow that Boris's views of the Soviet Union were sympathetic and that he "would like, in some capacity, to offer his services to Soviet organizations." Moscow responded that Gutzeit should begin recruiting Boris. The task was assigned to consular official Gaik Ovakimian, a spy with code name "Gennady," who specialized in gathering scientific and technical information, with a sideline in hunting down Trotskyites. Ovakimian was to start by taking advantage of Boris's vanity, eventually broaching the idea of Boris getting one of Ovakimian's friends or family members a job at Paramount in Germany, where they could build an anti-Nazi espionage network. Boris was flattered, listening to the proposal "with perfect composure," according to the report that Gutzeit filed. Within a few days Ovakimian reported that Morros "was ready to arrange this when there was an opportunity." It referred to Boris by the code name "Frost," which, as bizarre as it may seem, is simply the Russian translation of "Morros." In a twist of events that even an ambitious dreamer like Boris couldn't have predicted, he was now working for the communists again. Boris had become a spy.

When Mendel left for the Soviet Union at the end of May 1934, he wept at the thought that he might be seeing his son for the last time. Boris was not as emotional. Part of him was glad to see Mendel go, the two having grown so far apart, but he still felt responsible for his father. Mendel wanted to bring home the American phonograph Boris had given him as a gift, but he failed to declare it at customs in Moscow, and the apparatus was seized. If Gutzeit was trying to find new ways to put Boris in his debt, he couldn't have done a better job: "F. begged Ossip to help the old man with this," Gutzeit wrote, instructing the recipient to make sure that the phonograph made its way back to Mendel without any further complications. Boris was getting in even deeper, though he didn't realize it yet.

Anxious to please Gutzeit, Boris started planning how he might be able to put a Soviet operative on the Paramount payroll in Berlin, though he hoped to come up with lots of impediments, a sign that he had already started to think like a spy. He told Ovakimian that through discreet inquiries he discovered that Paramount would have to put up $1,000 for each employee stationed in Berlin, insurance against them remaining there beyond the time period specified in their visa. That kind of money would attract attention, Boris explained. Ovakimian began to have second thoughts about how useful Boris might be. Gutzeit's superiors in Moscow, who followed every step of this seduction, wrote that Boris was "a valuable acquisition, one worth holding on to."

CHAPTER SIX
PARADISE AND ITS DISCONTENTS,
1934–35

Boris later claimed that he clung to the hope that he would never see Melamed or Gutzeit again, but in late July 1934 they showed up together, unannounced, in his offices at the Paramount Building. This time they were accompanied by a short, burly redhead who peered through his blue-tinted glasses as he stuck out his hand and, in a heavy Russian accent, introduced himself as Edward Herbert. This newcomer, whose real name was Vasily Mikhailovich Zarubin, was not yet forty years old, but he was already a legend back in the Kremlin, a spy whose career dated to the earliest days of the revolution and one of the Cheka's first foreign agents. Now Stalin was counting on Zarubin, a former Olympic athlete whose stint in the tsar's army turned him into a Bolshevik, to enlist Boris in the fight against fascism. Boris never imagined that this barrel-chested but strangely meek fellow would become the serpent in his American paradise.

One reason that Boris was so easily lured into unwilling service of the Soviet intelligence service was that he knew little for certain about them. On that midsummer day in 1934, he raised a glass of vodka with Zarubin and made a toast to their shared future. Had Boris, never much of drinker, known more about Zarubin's place in the history of espionage in Russia, he might have emptied the bottle.

The first organized espionage agency in Russia predated not only the first tsar but the very concept of the Russian nation. It was Grand Prince Ivan of Moscow who in 1565 began depending on a brotherhood of black-clad mercenaries called *oprichniki* to provide him with political intelligence. They were so brutal in their methods that after only eight years they had completely wiped out all of their contacts, friendly and unfriendly. Ivan put them all to the sword and erased their names from the official record. But it wasn't until the white-gloved Russian police were flummoxed by the revolutionary terror that swept across Europe starting in the 1870s—they were unable to predict or prevent the assassination of Tsar Alexander II in 1881—that Russia's intelligence operations entered the modern era, one that saw both the tsar's forces and the opposition vying to capitalize on new technologies like railroads, dynamite, and rotary printing.

Until the revolution, the police, security, and intelligence groups, whose nominal job was to protect the imperial family, focused on anti-tsarist revolutionaries and terrorists. These four thousand agents, known collectively as the Okhrana and identifiable by their bowler hats, umbrellas, and green military-surplus coats, constituted a tiny force in a country of more than 150 million inhabitants, but they compiled a list of as many as three million suspected revolutionaries and beat, shot, hanged, drowned, and poisoned as many as thirty thousand of them in the years between the turn of the twentieth century and the beginning of World War I. By complementing such raw force with the development of subtler weapons, including secret recordings, wiretapping, and code-breaking, the Okhrana could keep anti-tsarist dissent under control. Members of the Okhrana were known to Russians as resourceful and oblivious, morally superior and dastardly, subtle and blunt, but always to be feared—when they could be identified. London's Jack the Ripper is thought by many historians to have been an Okhrana agent provocateur named Mikhail Ostrog, only one of many mysteries guarded by the organization's still inaccessible archives held by Moscow's Department of Police Records. The tsar's secret police infiltrated Russian trade unions and planned the strikes that threw the country into turmoil in 1903, and it's commonly thought that the Okhrana was behind two of the assassinations that sparked the Revolution of 1905 in Russia. The 1911 assassination of the Russian prime minister was carried out by an Okhrana agent posing as a revolutionary, according to some historians, although it may have been a revolutionary pretending to be a government agent. Of thirteen Bolsheviks in attendance at a 1912 conference in Prague, no fewer than ten worked for the tsar's secret police, and it's still not clear which side they were ultimately on. The wild-eyed radical who led the combat unit of the Socialist Revolutionary Party, Evno Azev, was also a member of the Okhrana, and to this day it's uncertain where his true loyalties lay. It was this kind of ambiguity that eventually led the tsar to rein in the Okhrana by limiting its powers and centralizing its activities in bureaus in St. Petersburg, Moscow, and Warsaw, but by then it was too late. In the years before the revolution, it was not food or fuel that was in the shortest supply but trust and truth.

Lenin had predicted that when the revolution came, the Workers' Paradise wouldn't even need police, but just six weeks after his Bolsheviks seized power, he founded the All-Russian Extraordinary Commission for Combating Counter-Revolution and Sabotage, known by its acronym in Russian, the Cheka. Its spies, trained at the facility that would eventually be named the International Lenin School in Moscow, studied the gray arts of secret communications, encryption, and the use of invisible ink, not to mention advanced techniques in extracting information from detainees. With their long, black leather coats, amber worry beads, and *klichkas*, or code names, Chekists also engaged with cruel impunity in more distasteful but effective activities known as "wet work," which included ethnic cleansing and genocide, as well as more personalized atrocities in which suspected enemies of the revolution were kidnapped, scalped, electrocuted, crucified, stoned, skinned alive, boiled in water, or frozen to death. More than three hundred thousand people died at the hands of the Cheka from 1917 to 1922 during the Russian Civil War, including many of the Cheka's own agents, who were "put on ice," as it was not so delicately phrased by their own colleagues. No wonder most Russians feared the Cheka, which by 1923 had been renamed the Joint Political Directorate, or the OGPU, as much as they had feared the tsar. After Lenin's death in 1924, the OGPU became the chief instrument of Stalin's obsession with his rival, Trotsky, who was increasingly marginalized, exiled to Siberia, and eventually thrown out of the country.

Stalin's secret police was extraordinarily effective at rooting out domestic dissent because its agents were above the law. But tracking down enemies of the revolution abroad posed a much greater challenge. Soviet spies needed a pretext for being in a foreign country, a legitimate source of income, a reasonable explanation for travel, a justification for making contacts with government figures in the host country, and convenient access to secure communications with each other and Moscow.

Soviet spies who settled in other countries under their own names were known as "legals," a situation most common in liberal democracies, which guaranteed privacy, due process, and freedom of speech and assembly even to suspected spies. They often worked for trade missions, which was the case with Gregory Melamed, Boris's first contact with Soviet intelligence back in 1933. The foreign service, where Gutzeit and Ovakimian could be found, was also a common setting for legals, who could take advantage of diplomatic mail services to communicate quickly and discreetly with Moscow. There were, however, disadvantages to legal status. It was easy for the host country to identify and track legals, and potential sources might not want to be seen or heard talking to officials of the foreign government.

These were not problems for the other kind of Soviet agent abroad, known as "illegals," who, like Zarubin, operated without diplomatic cover and lived a clandestine existence, complete with false names and histories. They usually posed as businessmen, tourists, or journalists. Illegals at first perfectly suited the goals of Soviet intelligence, especially since the Soviet Union had no formal diplomatic relations with the United States for the first decade of its existence and therefore no ability to plant legals in embassies and consulates. Moreover, it was difficult for the host country to keep tabs on illegals. If diplomatic relations were broken off, illegals could still continue to operate. But functioning as an illegal required considerably more preparation and training, starting with the establishment of legitimate cover, which often cost a great deal of time and money. Boris, who held an important position in one of America's biggest corporations, who could operate as a legal even as he provided cover for Soviet illegals, whose circle of acquaintances included the rich and famous, was more than just another Soviet agent; he was central to Stalin's long-range international plans to wipe out Trotskyite counterrevolutionaries once and for all. Boris's troublesome brothers, his murky history during the revolution and the civil war, and his uncertain patriotism were all problems that Moscow thought it could make go away.

Stalin's interest in Boris was also a matter of timing. After Lenin's death, Stalin was slow to devote significant intelligence resources to the United States. The postwar Red Scares led American immigration officials to refuse leftist radicals entry to the country and resulted in the mass deportation of communists already on American soil, limiting the ability of Soviet spies to operate in the United States. In addition, Stalin was worried about the recent formation of the General Intelligence Unit of the Justice Department, led by a lawyer fresh out of law school named J. Edgar Hoover, who started out fighting organized crime but soon began targeting political radicals. Finally, the almost simultaneous identification in 1927 of dozens of Soviet agents in England, Poland, Switzerland, Turkey, China, Austria, and France led Stalin to withdraw or deactivate the spies in all of the major Soviet areas of operation that remained and start from scratch.

It wasn't until 1933, with the rise of the Nazis in Germany, along with the United States' need for trading partners during the Great Depression, that the United States formally recognized the Soviet Union. The start of diplomatic relations allowed Stalin to set up a functioning and sustainable spy network of legals in America. It was a gamble, since the FBI considered spying on friends during peacetime to be conduct unbecoming of a civilized nation. But for Stalin, who had a very different idea of what civilization meant, and who was squeezed between the twin dangers of Trotsky and Hitler, the stakes were too high not to be in the game.

When Moscow sent Piotr Gutzeit to New York in 1933 as a consular official with diplomatic immunity, his task was to take charge of the OGPU's New York *rezidentura*, as the local headquarters was known, and build a network of illegals that would fight both Trotsky and Hitler on American soil. It was blind luck that he found in Boris someone who would be more broadly useful in building an anti-fascist network in Germany as well, because he could supply the superstructure. Gutzeit, himself a legal, knew that the most trustworthy spies were ideological recruits whose motivation, character, and circle of acquaintances could be observed and analyzed long before contact. "Walk-ins," or volunteers, on the other hand, were less trustworthy because they might be motivated by private or even mercenary considerations. Boris wasn't quite either, and Moscow should have known better than to try to turn him into an agent so quickly, without so much as a look into his past, much less his present. It never seems to have dawned on them that Boris would reject Trotsky's Paramount offer on commercial and not ideological grounds. Indeed, a simple glance at any of the dozens of newspaper articles or trade journals that outlined Boris's history as a supposed intimate of the tsar who fled the civil war and came to America to seek fame and fortune should have set off alarm bells in the New York *rezidentura*. Despite the requirement of the Soviet Communist Party's Central Committee that recruiters exercise "caution and purposefulness in the selection of agents," Gutzeit and his comrades were admittedly taken with the glamourous worlds of Times Square and Hollywood, which seems to have clouded their judgment when it came to Boris. If celebrities were the unacknowledged legislators of the United States, as Stalin believed, Boris was his entrée into that world. But they still needed an entrée to Boris.

This was the unspoken background to the conversation, in a mishmash of Russian, heavily accented English, broken French, and even a smattering of German, that ensued between Melamed, Gutzeit, Zarubin, and Boris on that summer day in 1934 in the Paramount Building. Boris nonetheless made it clear that he was prepared to risk his own reputation and that of Paramount to make Zarubin Stalin's man in Berlin. By the time he broke out the vodka, Boris had become a Soviet spy, and an American traitor. The Soviet archives emphasize Boris's political motivation, but it is difficult to know how much to trust that version over the story Boris later told, in which it took threats to his family back in Russia to bring him onboard, in which he resisted every step of the way. It is worth remembering that during the Russian Revolution, Boris sympathized with the Reds or the Whites opportunistically, and in the 1920s in Boston, he considered his association with a variety of Zionist, socialist, and labor causes as career moves. Even after moving to New York and rising to the top level of the Paramount organization, he lent his talents to politics only when it suited him. Even before Melamed, Gutzeit, and Zarubin recruited Boris to help to build an anti-fascist underground in Germany, Boris served as executive chairman, along with investment banker Otto Kahn, Hollywood director Ernst Lubitsch, and RCA president David Sarnoff, of a December 1933 fundraiser for the Federation for the Support of Jewish Philanthropies, held at the Waldorf-Astoria. The money went to the victims of German anti-Semitism, which had reached alarming proportions since the Nazis' rise to power and Germany's withdrawal from the League of Nations in 1933. In Boris's case, being apolitical meant picking and choosing among political commitments according to his momentary needs.

After the meeting in summer 1934 that marked Boris's formal entry into the services of Soviet intelligence, Melamed cabled back to Moscow that "there is no hesitation or fear on Frost's part," which suggests either that Boris was lying to protect himself when he later claimed to have been forced to cooperate or that he was lying to his new friends to give them the impression that he was an enthusiastic recruit. Either way, Boris was putting on an act. In the weeks that followed, Zarubin met several times with Boris at the Paramount Building to arrange exactly how Boris would be supporting the Soviets' efforts to establish an intelligence network in Germany. It was a perilous undertaking on Zarubin's part. Boris was taking risks as well. He would need to do more than write a single form letter authorizing Zarubin to scout talent for Paramount. Rather, Boris would have to fabricate a stream of business correspondence and even send a fifty-dollar-per-month salary that "Herbert" could use to prove his legitimacy.

It wasn't long after Zarubin's departure for Germany in October 1934 that "Center," as Moscow's intelligence headquarters was referred to in classified cable traffic, began noting how impressed they were by the smooth recruitment of Boris, envisioning that he might prove valuable in a variety of other ways. Gutzeit's superiors urged him to use great care in developing Boris, especially after Gutzeit told them that Boris was being promoted at Paramount. "Frost received a new appointment as director of all the company's production in Hollywood," Gutzeit wrote to Moscow in late October 1934. That promotion would have come as quite a surprise to Paramount founder and head Adolph Zukor, who valued Boris, but apparently not as much as Moscow did.

The negotiations that Boris had been conducting with Zukor in the late summer and early fall of 1934 were not about making Boris chief of the entire studio but head of the studio's music operations. In misrepresenting his position with Paramount, Boris was perhaps attempting to extricate himself from his obligations to Gutzeit, Melamed, and Zarubin. Boris might have also hoped his new friends would reason that Southern California would be inconveniently far from Soviet intelligence's American headquarters, and as the head of Paramount's Hollywood operations, Boris would be so in the public eye that it would be difficult to engage freely in dubious dealings with the shadowy and dangerous world of Soviet espionage. Gutzeit saw it differently: It would be more difficult for him to supervise Boris when he was living and working on the other side of the continent, but the promotion meant Boris would no longer have to worry about his boss finding out about the phony letters to Zarubin and the secret envelopes of cash being sent to Germany every month. In fact, Gutzeit reported, the transfer meant that they didn't have to limit Boris's involvement to Zarubin: "We asked Morros about taking one or two people for training in his studios." Boris's lie about what exactly he would be doing in Hollywood had made him even more attractive to Moscow.

After accompanying Zarubin to the West Side piers to bid him farewell in October, Boris settled back into his normal routine. With Zarubin far away in Berlin, all Boris had to do for the Soviets was keep writing and sending cash. For the first few months, Boris followed his instructions diligently, which allowed Zarubin to establish his Paramount cover identity in Berlin and set up a network of Soviet agents that eventually included a Gestapo officer and an employee of the Nazi Foreign Office, both of whom became crucial to Stalin's efforts to discern Hitler's future plans.

Back in New York, Boris was left with plenty of time to pursue not only an active social life in the golden age of Manhattan entertainment but a dizzying array of extracurricular activities. In addition to his duties at Paramount, Boris was becoming the go-to man in New York for an endless string of benefits, charities, clubs, balls, and galas. Sometimes he served as master of ceremonies or led the orchestra. Other times he simply showed up, checkbook in one hand and Catherine's hand in the other, and smiled for the cameras. Either way, Boris was becoming a bona fide celebrity.

At many of these events, which were covered breathlessly in the press from coast to coast, celebrities raised money for Jews fleeing Germany. For another charity event at the Waldorf-Astoria, Boris shared the stage with Mayor Fiorello La Guardia, film director Ernst Lubitsch, comedian Eddie Cantor, and Wall Street titan Felix Warburg. The scale was even grander when Boris produced and staged a revue called "Night of the Stars" at Yankee Stadium to benefit the United Jewish Appeal's efforts on behalf of Jewish refugees. The talent roster was a virtual Who's Who of Depression-era celebrities, including Bill "Bojangles" Robinson, Leopold Stokowski, Jack Benny, and Walter Winchell, with no fewer than a thousand musicians on three stages. It was so successful that the Jewish National Fund brought in Boris to organize a massive charity ball to support the organization's efforts to buy land for an eventual state in Palestine. By then, the press was presenting Boris not only as a formidable fundraiser but as a "sophisticated taste-maker" and "probably the most cultivated of New York's movie palace impresarios," according to one journalist.

But "the man of a thousand smiles," as a radio industry annual called him, came across as a slightly ridiculous figure: a bald, rotund glad-hander who was always in search of a card game and whose "vivid haberdashery" on the golf course made him visible no matter how thick the rough, though he cheated by using a rubber ball. At an October 30, 1934, charity baseball game in Nyack, New York, an all-star cast including William

Randolph Hearst Jr., Ben Hecht, Billy Rose, and James Thurber all took to the field, but only after Boris had paraded three elephants across it. The acid-tongued reporter for the *Brooklyn Daily Eagle* joked that the roly-poly fellow in the admiral's uniform might easily have been mistaken for a fourth elephant. Boris didn't mind. His hunger for attention made him impervious to embarrassment or shame, it seems. But his irrepressible urge to see his own name in the newspapers also led him into situations that Gutzeit didn't appreciate.

Boris again graced the Grand Ballroom of the Waldorf-Astoria in November 1934, this time for an event honoring Hugh L. Cooper, the president of the Russian-American Chamber of Commerce. Boris spent much of the evening hobnobbing with famed Russian revolutionary Maxim Litvinov, whose successful efforts to have the United States recognize the Soviet Union had led Stalin to name him people's commissar for foreign affairs. One would think that Boris, who was by then deeply entangled in the tentacles of the Soviet intelligence services, should have been downplaying his relationship with the Soviet Union. But Boris doubled down on the connection soon after, when he volunteered to serve as a translator for a visiting delegation from the Russian film industry. The fact that he once again played the buffoon, translating a long answer by Soviet film head Boris Shumyatsky to a question about the future of color in the movies as simply "No!," distracted anyone who might have thought twice about Boris's loyalties. As long as Boris kept up his correspondence with Berlin, Gutzeit left him alone.

Boris was living the high life, spoiling his wife and son in their luxurious doorman building just steps away from Riverside Park. The neighborhood was a favorite of Jews in the entertainment world, such as George and Ira Gershwin, who lived just a few blocks away. At Paramount by day, Boris was still turning talented amateurs from the sticks into marquee attractions in Times Square, and by night he consorted with the rich and famous, reading about both in the next day's papers. In the midst of it all, he never stopped worrying about his family back in Russia, especially because he was less consistent than he ought to have been in his correspondence with Zarubin in Berlin. He was mistaking benign neglect on Gutzeit's part with approval, which he ought to have known could be a deadly error.

Confident that his family back in Russia was safe, Boris had little desire to visit until one day in mid-July 1935, when he was called into a meeting of Paramount executives to translate a cable that had arrived in Russian. As he scanned the message he was amused and then concerned to see that it was meant for him. Would his Soviet spymasters be so indiscreet as to communicate with him in Russian at his workplace? Then he saw what it was about, and his concern turned to shock: It was a message from his father telling him that his mother was dying in Zaporozhye. If you want to see her alive again, come now, his father wrote.

Because he was now an American citizen, Boris needed a visa to visit the Soviet Union. He contacted Gutzeit, who informed him that Moscow not only approved of the visit but would arrange everything via the Soviet travel agency Intourist, including a suite at Moscow's Savoy Hotel, a grand, pre–World War I hotel, once a favorite of Moscow's theater world, now reserved for visiting dignitaries.

Boris sailed from New York on July 20, 1935, to Southampton, England, and then made his way by ferry and train to Paris. He flew to Moscow, schlepping eleven steamer trunks filled with food, clothing, medicine, and eight 78-rpm discs of the very latest in American jazz. Gutzeit had ordered customs in Moscow to leave Boris alone, but the discs ended up causing quite a fuss, because of concerns that such musical liberties might undermine the revolutionary discipline that Stalin demanded Soviet artists display. After tense negotiations, Boris was allowed to keep the jazz records, but only if he promised not to leave them behind when he went back to America, a requirement they actually noted in his passport.

Boris spent eleven days in the Soviet Union, beginning in Moscow and then making a quick side trip to Leningrad. Boris had heard from friends who had visited the USSR that they had been tailed by the secret police, so he considered keeping a low profile. It was a sign of how little he understood his standing as a Soviet operative. Still, he couldn't resist the urge to reconnect with his homeland and discover for himself what communism had accomplished, or failed to accomplish. The poverty and privation that he saw was less of a shock than the fact that he couldn't get anyone to talk about their lives, much less freely discuss "the regime that had enslaved them in the name of freedom," as he later recalled. The Russian man on the street's curiosity about America was voracious, though communicated in furtive whispers: Does everyone really have their own car and their own house, with a radio and a washing machine?

Boris travelled by train to Kharkov, in the Ukraine, where his parents were now staying. Things were even worse there than in Moscow. The town had turned into a virtual prison because of the famine Stalin created to punish peasants who refused to join collective farms and the ensuing persecution of Ukrainian nationalists and intellectuals in general. Boris was particularly disturbed to learn that Stalin even had the town's famous blind street musicians arrested and shot as vestiges of nationalist culture.

Boris's mother was very much alive, but it wasn't much of a life. Mendel and Malka were "hopeless people in a frozen prison," Boris recalled. They lived in the past because they feared for their future. Malka experienced night terrors, which were eased only by the sight of Boris's old quarter-size cello, which she had mounted over her sick bed. It was a bittersweet experience to hear her hum for him the first tune he had ever played, Brahms's impossibly clichéd lullaby "Good Morning, Good Night." Neither his mother nor his father would talk about their lives since he'd left, and the fact that they wouldn't discuss the fate of his trouble-making brothers Isaak and Aleksander was surely a sign that they'd been caught up in Stalin's purges. One night, Malka felt well enough to join her husband and son at a restaurant. The food and decor weren't much by New York standards, nor was the music: a dreary little band churning out patriotic tunes approved by the Ministry of Culture. But then a power outage plunged the place into darkness, and the musicians seized the opportunity to ply Boris with questions: What is the popular music of America like? What is life like for American musicians? Boris regaled them with stories of the wealthy and famous musicians he knew back in New

York. When they appeared first impressed and then depressed, Boris urged them to play their own music, by which he meant the popular old melodies that the government could forbid, but not eradicate, as vestiges of the bad old days under the tsar. He led the way by treating them to a performance on cello of "The Song of the Minstrel" by Alexander Glazunov, his old teacher at the St. Petersburg Conservatory.

Back in Moscow, Boris was put up at the National Hotel, a massive, luxurious hotel facing the Kremlin that dated from the time of the last tsar and had served as the first headquarters of the Bolshevik government. The Kremlin might have seen the importance of leaving Boris alone, but Gutzeit had his doubts. Boris missed a rendezvous that Gutzeit set up with an intelligence officer, claiming to be too busy. That transgression might have meant the end of Boris's career as a spy, or even the end of Boris. But powers higher than Gutzeit had long-term plans for him. Boris boarded a flight back to Paris empty-handed, leaving all eleven trunks behind, including the jazz records. This time, Gutzeit's superiors had warned customs officials not to make trouble. Boris made his way back to Le Havre and then Southampton, where he boarded the brand-new SS *Normandie*—the OGPU had paid for him to travel on the largest, fastest, and most luxurious steamship in the world. He headed back to New York and was greeted by Ed Sullivan's nationally syndicated Broadway column, which cuttingly announced: "Boris Morros back from Russia and twelve pounds heavier."

Once home, Boris made a decision: If he was going to relocate to the West Coast, as Zukor had promised, it shouldn't be as a mere administrator but as a full-fledged filmmaker. Zukor didn't see things that way, but after rumors reached the Paramount lot that Boris had been talking to Metro-Goldwyn-Mayer Studios, Zukor was willing to offer the possibility of Boris making his own films at some point in the future. That wasn't enough for Boris, who boldly began negotiating with Zukor in the columns of *Film Daily*. Then suddenly on October 17, at a luncheon held by the American Motion Picture Association at Jack Dempsey's nightclub, Boris announced that he had accepted an offer from Paramount and would be leaving that weekend. What Boris didn't tell the press was that Zukor had called his bluff and Boris had backed down: He would be heading west to become the head of Paramount's music division, the position he'd originally been offered, which suggests that Boris would have much to learn in Hollywood when it came to business negotations. The next night, Zukor threw a farewell party for Boris at the New York Athletic Club, and the next week he hustled Catherine and Dick onto the Broadway Limited Streamliner train at Pennsylvania Station and began a new chapter in his life, once again.

CHAPTER SEVEN
GATEWAY TO HOLLYWOOD, 1935–36

By the mid-1930s, Southern California was no longer the Wild West that had enchanted filmmakers when they arrived in 1907. Back then, Los Angeles was barely urban, and Hollywood was mostly unsettled. Just a decade later, Los Angeles was no longer a village situated between the desert and the ocean, but a thriving port and an agricultural powerhouse, with Hollywood counting more than seventy movie studios. In the 1920s, the rest of the American film industry, attracted by the low land prices and mild weather that allowed for year-round shooting, moved to the West Coast. The industry became not only one of the most powerful players in the American economy but a major influence on America's sense of self. While Warner Brothers specialized in gangster films with tough guys and tougher dames, Twentieth Century Fox became best known for adventure, comedy, and historical drama. Columbia showed off an optimistic, do-it-yourself vision of America, and MGM focused on family-friendly fare. Paramount was less predictable, putting out comedies, westerns, detective pictures, and literary adaptations. No matter what the genre, Paramount's world was populated by witty, urbane heroes and glamorous, often risqué heroines.

The world that was on display in Paramount's films was the vision of its founder, Adolph Zukor, who was born in a tiny Hungarian shtetl in 1873. Orphaned as a child and raised by his Orthodox Jewish uncle, Zukor believed in little but himself, and at the age of sixteen he made his way to the United States with forty dollars in his pocket, which made him a comparatively rich man. In New York, he remade himself as an American, trying his hand at professional boxing and baseball before making a fortune in the fur business and founding the Famous Players Film Company, which would eventually become Paramount Pictures.

Zukor did for the movies what Henry Ford did for the automobile, turning filmmaking from a slapdash way to make a quick buck into a smooth-running, efficient, collective business enterprise. By the late 1920s, Paramount was known as "the movie factory," churning out seventy or more films per year that featured upscale stars such as Douglas Fairbanks, Mary Pickford, Wallace Reid, and Gloria Swanson, in addition to popular animated characters like Betty Boop and Popeye. The quiet, cautious, and predictable Zukor was also an enormously resourceful and hard-nosed businessman, the first to realize the advantage of showing Paramount films in Paramount theaters. He also realized that audiences came as much for the live acts between the films as for the films themselves, though the arrival of sound put an end to the American film industry's dependence on vaudeville acts to fill seats.

All of the studios suffered during the early years of the Great Depression, as Americans found it harder and harder to come up with the price of admission: forty cents for an evening show and twenty-five cents for a matinee. Those were not trivial sums, back when the average American's weekly wages were thirty-five dollars and falling fast. Things were especially bad for Paramount, which suffered from shrinking audiences, even as the company was expanding the number of its own cinemas. Paramount's profits fell from $18 million in 1930 to $6 million in 1931. A year later, the company was $21 million in debt, though it didn't officially declare bankruptcy until early 1935.

Eventually, Paramount and the entire film industry began recovering from the troubles of the early Depression. Despite a federal antitrust ruling that forced Paramount to legally separate the division of the company that made the movies from the division that showed them in its own theaters, the business emerged from bankruptcy in 1936 with the help of a new generation of Paramount actors, among them Bing Crosby, Gary Cooper,

Marlene Dietrich, the Marx Brothers, and Mae West. Zukor was something of a snob, having gone from Poland to polo in a single generation, as the old saying went. Zukor brought to Paramount old-world artists and intellectuals such as Sergei Eisenstein and Josef von Sternberg in an effort to "class up" American culture. Under Zukor's leadership, Paramount even ran a finishing school for its actors that was part liberal arts college and part spa.

Paramount's comeback was also helped by the advent of color films, which arrived just in time to provide a much-needed boost for the entire industry. Zukor was convinced that sound technology had improved to such an extent that better film music, and in particular classical music, would play a major role in the studio's further recovery. Whereas the other big studios hired popular songwriters, such Irving Berlin at Fox, the Gershwins at RKO, and Cole Porter at MGM, Paramount Pictures was banking on classical musicians, among them Frederick Hollander, Erich Korngold, and Victor Young, who had conservatory training and legitimate, if not stellar, careers.

Even before he found a home for Catherine and Dick in Los Angeles, Boris took possession of a suite of offices, recording studios, and soundstages on the twenty-six-acre lot fronting Melrose Avenue where Paramount's studios were located. It was there that he met with Paramount's production manager, the legendary Ernst Lubitsch, and finished negotiating his job title: Head of Paramount Studio's Music Department. If Boris was disappointed that he was still stuck in the world of music instead of making his own pictures, he was gratified to see the news of his promotion not only in *Film Daily* and the *Los Angeles Times* but in every major newspaper in the country.

Boris fit in easily in Hollywood. Like so many transplants from the East Coast, he marvelled at the way doors that were closed on Wall Street, Main Street, Madison Avenue, in the Ivy League, and even on Broadway were open in Hollywood. The fact that Hollywood's aristocracy was composed of Jewish immigrants—fifty-three of Hollywood's eighty-five major producers were Jewish when Boris arrived—made things even easier.

Despite their wealth and prominence, William Fox (born Wilhelm Fuchs), Louis B. Mayer (born Lazar Meir), and Samuel Goldwyn (born Szmuel Gelbfisz), not to mention Jack Cohn, Harry Warner, Jesse Lasky, and Carl Laemmle, were determined to be seen as real Americans, a sentiment that Boris implicitly understood. Their patriotism was a matter not just of eating pork, working on the Sabbath, marrying their children off to gentiles, and voting Republican but of making as much money as possible. Hollywood's religion was social mobility, and Boris got moving, starting with the purchase of a luxurious home at 915 North Beverly Drive, off Sunset Boulevard. The thirty-five-hundred-square-foot stucco house, which had seventeen rooms and a swimming pool out back, was just around the corner from the Beverly Hills mansions of Edward G. Robinson, Samuel Goldwyn, and Louis B. Mayer. But Boris was rarely home.

Because Boris was such a hard worker, it took Zukor five people to replace him in New York: a head of deluxe operations, a stage-show producer, a musical director, a talent booker, and a managing director for the theater. In Hollywood Boris was busier than ever. While Catherine slept late and had nothing to do all day, having handed the responsibility of raising Dick to nannies, Boris got up early seven days a week and was often the first employee through the famed Paramount gate. A short walk across the massive complex, which had its own hospital and fire department serving thousands of employees, brought him to his suite of offices. Most of Boris's time was spent at his desk with his ear glued to the telephone, hiring and firing composers, arrangers, and musicians. He was infamous for avoiding memos, no doubt because his written English was so poor. Still, despite being celebrated in the press as one of "more than a score of nationally known composers" who were bringing Paramount back to profitability, Boris wasn't writing much music, though he did insist, unlike the music directors at most other Hollywood studios, on conducting the scores himself at Paramount's enormous scoring stage.

The national press marvelled as Boris, within weeks of his arrival, supervised the composers Frederick Hollander, Leo Robin, and Ralph Rainger in a fifty-six-song writing marathon that resulted in the score for

Bing Crosby's new picture, *Rhythm on the Range*. Boris served as music director for no fewer than thirty-eight films in 1936, and it wasn't unusual for him to be simultaneously supervising three full orchestras, plus a choir or two. He later recalled: "Everybody needed me. Everybody wanted my advice." On a typical day, Bing Crosby or any number of actors, singers, musicians, composers, directors, or producers might drop by for conversations that would inevitably be interrupted by phone calls summoning Boris to the soundstage to fix a song, or to a shooting set to coach a singer. No matter what the occasion, Boris could be seen playing with the amber worry beads supposedly given to him by Rasputin.

When the workday, which might be as long as sixteen hours, was over, it still wasn't over. Boris hurried home, where Dick would be relaxing by the pool after his daily round of golf at the Hillcrest Country Club. Having inherited his father's negotiating abilities, if not his work ethic, Dick had convinced Beverly Hills High School that golf fulfilled his physical education requirement. Catherine, uninterested in the shopping, socializing, or philanthropies that filled the days of so many wives of Hollywood executives, had spent yet another day on the sofa with her gossip magazines. She hadn't even made dinner: The Danish cook who lived with them did that. Mealtime was often uncomfortable in the Morros household. Catherine made sure that Boris knew how unhappy she was that he was gone most of the time, but she also didn't want him around. Unable to articulate her resentment at Boris, who after all had given her a child, a house, and the free time to make a life for herself, Catherine was becoming bitter and angry.

Boris was happy to change into his evening clothes and leave Catherine behind again. After-hours, in nightclubs such as the Clover Club, the Mocambo, the Players, and La Boheme, or at the fundraisers or testimonials that were such an important part of the Hollywood social scene, Boris ate, smoked, danced, and mingled with the stars until late in the evening. Sometimes there was more work than play. As in New York, no gala, it seemed, was complete without Boris's baton, especially when it came to Jewish causes. Boris directed the music at the June 1936 West

Coast premiere of *Land of Promise*, the film about Zionist struggles to settle Palestine that he'd scored back in New York. The lavish show at the Biltmore Hotel, the fanciest space in the city, attracted Hollywood's Jewish aristocracy, including David O. Selznick, Edward G. Robinson, and Paul Muni.

Boris wouldn't have been able to take his place among Hollywood's elite had he not been so good at his job. Just a few months after he settled into his routine at Paramount, Isabel Morse Jones's Words and Music column in the *Los Angeles Times* was calling him a "new luminary in orchestra circles." But the longer he stayed at Paramount's music department, the more his classical music reputation suffered and the more his old reputation as a "fixer" followed him. At Paramount, he introduced a number of innovations, such as scoring pictures while they were still in the shooting stage and even having the actors speak their lines to the accompaniment of the score. But working on other people's movies left him feeling unsatisfied. The weather in Southern California was beautiful, and he was making very good money at Paramount, but Boris wasn't any closer to making his own movies. Still, he never lost the sense of thrill he experienced at seeing his name regularly in both the gossip columns and the trade journals. That's not to say the press always took him as seriously as he would have liked. The most widely read syndicated newspaper columnists of the day, not just the "unholy trio" of Hedda Hopper, Louella Parsons, and Sheila Graham but also Ed Sullivan, Walter Winchell, and Dorothy Kilgallen, followed his every move at Paramount, from his meetings with talent and business trips back to New York to his acquisitions of individual songs. They followed him on his nightly rounds of the Sunset Strip clubs, and when by dawn's early light he soberly scanned the morning papers—never much of a drinker, Boris was known to fill a vodka bottle with water and chug it all night long—he could count on seeing his name in bold letters, which was a mixed blessing.

There were many who saw Boris as Falstaff in Southern California. They laughed at his egg-shaped figure and mocked his taste in fashion, which ran toward patterns, stripes, dots, and checks, in every color of the rainbow, usually all at once. Still, Boris willingly collaborated with the press, which insisted on portraying him as a Jewish immigrant who would never fit in, never become properly Americanized, and whose horrendous accent inspired equal parts pity and laughter. Within three months of his arrival on the West Coast, Boris was already standing out in the crowd, with his orange silk shirt, light green suit, purple necktie, and plaid handkerchief, an outfit that was said to be a gimmick to promote Technicolor, but there was more than a grain of truth in the joke he used to deflect the ridicule: "How else would anybody ever notice me in this big place?"

Though Boris was now enjoying a level of success that he had often only dreamed of, it didn't always come with the kind of professional legitimacy he hoped for. One of the very first projects he worked on in Hollywood, a Gary Cooper vehicle called *The General Died at Dawn*, won him an Oscar nomination for Best Score, a triumph tempered by the fact that the actual composing was done by someone else. Still, he knew how to stand up for himself. He convinced the famed conductor Leopold Stokowski to appear in Paramount's *Big Broadcast of 1936* and was unafraid to cross swords with the maestro regarding artistic matters: "What are you going to do," Boris asked Stokowski, "argue with me about music?"

Zukor had his own ideas about what Boris was best at. When the Paramount chief celebrated his silver jubilee, a late 1936 event that was broadcast nationwide on Paramount's radio affiliates, Boris reluctantly led the fifty-piece orchestra while Carole Lombard, Fred MacMurray, and hundreds of Zukor's other close friends danced the night away. Boris was also less than delighted when Zukor asked him in February 1937 if he would like to produce, direct, and host a promotional thirty-minute radio show about Paramount behind-the-scenes that would be nationally syndicated via a deal with NBC. Boris thought he might make "Paramount on Parade" into a serious, almost journalistic series, but Zukor knew that Boris's hilarious accent would be the real reason to tune in. As W. C. Fields joked on the front page of the *New York Post*: "Heard your program, Boris, and it was great. But why did you do it in dialect?"

Executives at ABC tuned in to "Paramount on Parade" and recognized a natural performer when they heard one. Impressed by Boris's ability to connect to listeners, they gave him his own weekly syndicated program of classical music, featuring something called the Boris Morros String Quartet, an ensemble drawn from the ranks of the local classical music community. Clearly a bid to burnish Boris's classical music credentials, the Sunday afternoon show ran throughout the first half of 1938. Of course, Boris's continuing efforts to legitimize himself in the classical music world were undermined by his almost weekly participation in the musical portion of fundraisers and awards dinners. His attempts to recruit "real" classical composers, including Schoenberg, Rimsky-Korsakov, Prokofiev, and Stravinsky (who, like many Russian classical musicians visiting Los Angeles, stayed at Boris's home), to write music for Paramount failed. Boris had ways of compensating: He planted an item in *Film Daily* that said the French government was planning to make him an "Officier d'Académie," also known as the Silver Palm, for his contributions to French culture. The problem is that there's no record of Boris ever receiving that distinction. Boris, it seems, could convince anyone of anything, except the Soviet secret police.

CHAPTER EIGHT
A DOUBLE LIFE, 1936–38

"For many years," Boris bragged to a reporter, "my 'serious' musician friends looked down their noses at me, and said, 'Boris, you have sold your soul to the devils of Hollywood.' Now it is different." It certainly was, though not in the way that they imagined: Boris had sold his soul, or at least part of it, to the devils of Moscow. On top of the demands of his day job and his many extracurricular activities, Boris was living a double life as a Soviet spy. For now, all that involved was sending Zarubin his monthly stipend in Berlin, though Boris wasn't even very consistent about doing that. He got away with it not only because Soviet intelligence was willing to keep one of its best prospects on a long leash but because they were still in a state of upheaval. In late 1935, Stalin was in the process of reorganizing his secret police, which would now be called the NKVD, or People's Commissariat for Internal Affairs. During the reorganization, most current operations were suspended and hundreds of active agents were purged.

In fact, Moscow only found out that Boris had relocated to California when Gutzeit read about it in the New York papers. An agent with the code name "Archimedes" was sent to Los Angeles in late November of 1935 to get Boris back on track. When Archimedes, whose real identity has never been determined, called the Paramount switchboard for Boris's telephone number, he was confused to learn that far from being head of Paramount's Hollywood studios, Boris was merely its new director of music. The confusion turned to concern when Boris's secretary rebuffed

Archimedes, telling him that Boris was extremely busy and wouldn't be seeing anyone. When Archimedes telephoned again later that day and received the same response, his concern with Boris's deception turned to the kind of cold anger that Soviet agents were trained to channel into results. "Rising doubts in my mind forced me to resort to cunning," he reported back to Moscow. Archimedes telephoned one more time, and assuming an English accent, said he was a Mr. Goldstein from New York with news of Boris's family back in Russia. The ruse worked. Boris called back within the hour and was surprised to hear a heavy Russian accent on the other line. Boris had been enjoying the benign neglect of his superiors in Soviet intelligence, but he agreed to meet the next day after business hours. As Archimedes reported: "By the tone of his voice, I could sense that he was none too pleased by my arrival."

The next day at five P.M., Archimedes was waved through Paramount's imposing front gate. He walked along the studio's campus, marvelling at the costumed actors strolling around Hollywood versions of New York's Lower East Side, Paris's Latin Quarter, and a Western ghost town, until he arrived at Boris's office building. It was certainly a step up from the warren of windowless rooms Boris had occupied back at Paramount's New York headquarters. Boris gave Archimedes a typical Russian welcome: a bear hug, a glass of vodka, and an inquiry into his visitor's health, the health of his family, and the health of his friends and colleagues.

Archimedes wanted to get right down to business. Why hadn't Boris been living up to his promise to write regularly to Zarubin in Berlin? Boris apologized and promised to try to do better. But he balked when Archimedes asked him if it might be possible to put an NKVD agent on the Paramount payroll in Hollywood. Boris claimed that he'd just arrived, and anyway, despite having bragged that he was being made head of the whole operation, Boris now claimed he was a lowly director of an unimportant production division, a job he said was called "minor and administrative." It didn't come with the authority to make such decisions, Boris noted. Archimedes kept his cool. He might have confronted Boris about his lie about becoming head of the studio, but he thought twice and decided to save that card for later. In the meantime, he handed Boris a wad of cash and told him to post fifty dollars of it right away to Berlin and to send the rest in monthly installments. Boris exhaled in relief and led Archimedes to the door, assuming that would be the last he'd ever see of him. Boris was surprised when Archimedes told him he'd be back the next day.

By Tuesday, Boris had thought things through and was ready to try a different approach: a better lie. He told Archimedes he might be able to place one or two Soviet operatives on his Hollywood payroll, but he'd have to check personally with New York, and he wasn't scheduled to go there for months. Boris of course could hire whomever he wanted and was in fact planning a trip in just a few weeks for a series of meetings with Zukor. Archimedes would have been merely annoyed at Boris's lack of initiative if he hadn't been shocked to suddenly realize that the door to Boris's office was wide open. Boris's secretary, Archimedes saw, could hear every word of their conversation. When he signalled to Boris that he didn't want her listening in, Boris laughed and asked her to bring him the file of his correspondence with Zarubin in Berlin. As Archimedes reported to Moscow, Boris acted not only with a complete lack of discretion but actually defended his indiscretion as a strategy. "The more open, the better," Boris explained. Hiding his contacts with Berlin from his secretary would only cause suspicion.

Archimedes didn't see it that way. When Gutzeit saw Archimedes's report in early December 1935, he wrote to Moscow that it was clear that the seduction of Moscow's man in Hollywood was going to be complicated: "All of F.'s intrigue since his return from the Soviet Union," Gutzeit wrote, was evidence that Boris "wished to sever ties with us." Gutzeit wasn't willing to let go of Boris that easily: "We do not intend to leave him alone. In 2–3 months we will meet with him again and try to get the help he promised." But Gutzeit was soon too busy trying to survive to keep chasing down Boris, who had made a trip to New York and even flown back with Zukor himself in late January. Boris heard nothing from his new friends for another eighteen months. The delay was largely due to the ongoing purges of counterrevolutionaries and suspected counterrevolutionaries that Stalin had been carrying out since 1934. Gutzeit, Archimedes, and the entire Soviet intelligence service had been living in constant fear, terrorized by the idea that every cable that arrived from Moscow might mean their being recalled and sentenced to death by a single bullet to the head somewhere in the vast basement of the NKVD's Lubyanka headquarters. And when that maddening insecurity had reached its peak, Stalin decided to purge the purgers in show trials that nominally targeted Trotskyites and Jews, but were often motivated by nothing more than the supreme leader's paranoia.

It wasn't until mid-July 1937 that Boris heard again from the NKVD. This time it was Paramount security on the telephone, asking what they wanted him to do with an "Edward Herbert," who was at the front gate demanding to see Boris right away. Boris, thinking that it was Zarubin, and remembering he'd heard that even some of Moscow's most venerable agents were being called to account, realized he had no choice but to let him through. As it turned out, it wasn't Zarubin, but a youthful, dapper figure with an eye patch who introduced himself as Samuel Shumovsky, a diplomatic officer based in Washington, DC, who was on the West Coast to honor a group of Soviet pilots that had just set a distance record, travelling from the Soviet Union over the North Pole to California. As Boris quickly surmised, Shumovsky was in fact a Soviet agent who, under the code name "Blerio," specialized in gathering intelligence related to aviation technology. Gutzeit had instructed him to make a special trip to Los Angeles to find out why Boris had failed to keep his end of their bargain.

Shumovsky walked through the door of Boris's suite and, with a glance at the secretary, entered Boris's office, closed the door, and exploded in anger, cursing and shouting that Boris had put the life of one of Stalin's most honored spies in danger from the Nazis. Boris had known on some level that he would eventually have to account for stranding Zarubin in Berlin without enough money or proper cover, which is why his answer was well prepared. Boris couldn't keep his promises to Moscow anymore, he claimed, because Paramount was finally planning to pull out of Germany altogether—which would not in fact happen for years—and keeping people on the payroll there just looked too suspicious. Failing to maintain contacts with Zarubin in Berlin might put one man's German assignment in danger, but getting caught sending letters and cash every month would put all of Moscow's American operations in jeopardy, Boris maintained. If Shumovsky appreciated the logic behind Boris's argument, he seemed convinced beyond any doubt when Boris pulled out his wallet and handed over the hundred dollars that he still hadn't sent to Berlin. It was a gesture that satisfied and impressed Shumovsky, making an even bigger impression than if Boris had claimed to have sent all the money. Boris might have been slow to understand who his new friends were, but he was learning fast: Communists were often more in thrall to *kapital* than the most committed capitalist, unable to imagine why anyone would ever voluntarily return money, unless they were either incredibly rich or ideologically committed. Still, Shumovsky left Boris's office with a warning: You don't have to send any more money, but you must continue to write to Berlin; the life of the man you know as Edward Herbert depends on it. And so does yours.

Soviet agents had suggested before that Boris was playing a deadly game, but he'd never taken it quite seriously until now. Boris was so terrified by Shumovsky's threat that he fled. Within a few days, Boris and Catherine boarded a train at Pasadena's newly opened Mission Revival–style passenger train station, the legendary "Gateway to Hollywood," and headed east. Boris had sold the trip to Catherine as a surprise vacation that would take them to London, Paris, Vienna, and Leningrad, but she knew better, if for no other reason than that the papers had announced that Paramount was sending Boris to Europe to look for someone for the title role of the new production of *Carmen*. It wasn't clear how a visit to the Soviet Union fit into the agenda, but Moscow not was pleased to have one of its most valued American contacts gallivanting across Europe and making plans to visit the Soviet Union without letting them know first. That was the point: Boris was trying to extricate himself from the grip of Soviet intelligence by showing them that he was too indiscreet, too unpredictable, too busy to serve their purposes.

Boris and Catherine remained in Europe for two weeks, with Boris taking meetings while Catherine shopped. Berlin was quite purposely not on the agenda, and not surprisingly, they never made it to Russia. After a brief stopover in New York, they were back in California, where Boris returned to his usual overstuffed agenda—that year he supervised the music for forty-eight films—and kept searching for a way to get out of a situation that he was no longer in control of. Failing to make good on his promises hadn't worked, so Boris tried something new: Perhaps he could come up with some sort of intelligence, something significant enough to convince them to leave him alone. It was the kind of logic that had gotten him into trouble in the first place, but in early November 1937, Boris reached out to Gutzeit with the message that a German-Hungarian conductor and NKVD contact named Georgy Karlovich Sebastian, who had a successful concert career in the Soviet Union before finding work in Hollywood, was in fact a German double agent. This was the only formal report that Boris wrote for the Soviets that has ever come to light, and it seems less like a professional intelligence briefing than a personal attack motivated by jealousy:

> Not long ago, someone by the name of Sebastian came to Hollywood from NY.
> According to available information, S——n is a foreigner, who lived for a long time in the USSR, where he was in charge of either one of the broadcasting departments or a music company. Married to a Soviet citizen. His wife came with him to the USA. Both of them left the Soviet Union recently, and plan to return soon. During their stay in Hollywood, S——n said the nastiest things about the Soviet Union and told dreadful stories about the horrors in the USSR. On the whole, as you can see, S——n has extremely anti-Soviet views. We are sending you this report to be used as you see fit.

For anyone familiar with the sorts of communications that passed between NKVD headquarters in Moscow and its agents in the United States in the 1930s, this is a bizarre document, more gossip column than secret and fatal denunciation of an enemy of the revolution. Gutzeit was pleased at Boris's sense of initiative, especially after Moscow confirmed that Sebastian had in fact started working for the Germans, but they did nothing more than bar Sebastian from entering the Soviet Union. It was an odd decision, given that they would be free to interrogate and liquidate him there, but they didn't dare touch him while he was in the United States; or perhaps Sebastian was worth more alive in America than dead in the Soviet Union, and they hoped he would continue to operate so that they might learn more about his contacts. It is also possible that Sebastian was a double agent, pretending to work for the Germans while in fact secretly serving the Soviets. No matter what the reasoning—and there is nothing in the Soviet archives that clarifies it—Boris's scoop, far from convincing Moscow to set him free, seems to have only confirmed the NKVD's sense of his loyalty and usefulness.

Boris now found himself in a tricky position, because the feeling among many Americans that the Soviet Union was their best hope against Hitler was tempered by rising anti-communism in Congress, a sentiment resisted by a committee co-chaired by Samuel Dickstein that had been investigating foreign subversives since 1934. Dickstein—who was in fact a Soviet agent—tried to keep the committee focused on threats posed by Nazis on American soil, but even as late as 1937 there was surprisingly little opposition to Hitler in the United States, and Hollywood was no exception, despite Jewish dominance in the film industry. Germany was after all the film industry's largest foreign market. When the Nazis came to power, the American Jewish Congress proposed boycotting Germany, but the American Jewish Committee and B'nai B'rith supported maintaining economic relations with Hitler. When Hitler demanded the firing of Hollywood's Jewish representatives in Germany, the studios complied, on the condition that essential workers in distribution and sales were allowed to keep their jobs.

Hollywood's shameful accommodation of the Nazis was plain to see on the screen. Before the war, only one movie critical of Hitler, *I Was a Captive of Nazi Germany*, was released. The Production Code Administration, which exercised veto power over the release of any films that didn't meet Hollywood's moral standards when it came to representing sex, crime, drugs, violence, and the rule of law, stopped all other such efforts under pressure from Hitler's full-time liaison to the film industry in Los Angeles's German consulate. In fact, the studios were so afraid of losing their German market that they allowed Nazi representatives in Hollywood to screen and vet more than four hundred films before their release from 1933 to 1940.

Among the Paramount connections forced out of Germany was Boris's man in Berlin. Zarubin returned to Moscow and received the Order of the Red Banner from Stalin for his role in organizing an anti-fascist underground in Berlin. Despite not having received regular letters from Paramount for months, Zarubin had nothing but praise for Boris. An official communiqué from Zarubin to Moscow on June 8, 1938, written under the code name "Betty," described Boris as an essential component in Soviet intelligence's American operations, one whose "worldwide reputation within the film industry" was not to be underestimated and whose politics were impeccable: "F. is completely loyal and pro-Soviet," Zarubin wrote, recommending that Moscow step up efforts to use him. "F. worked extremely carefully, carrying out all our workers' instructions and directives down to the smallest detail, never allowing for interruptions to either the supply of money or the business correspondence." But Zarubin went a step further than Gutzeit, Melamed, Ovakimian, Shumovsky, or Archimedes had done: "We can trust this man completely," Zarubin wrote. "Everything this man says or promises, he does."

Any shortcomings in his performance, Zarubin offered, were due to the fact that Boris was simply a very busy and important man. If Boris was in any way a less-than-perfect agent, Zarubin wrote, it was because Moscow had no significant presence on the West Coast: "Because in recent years, he has been living far from our centers of work, we have met with him very infrequently and neglected his education." That might start, Zarubin suggested, with "gifts of various inexpensive but interesting objects of Soviet origin, e.g., wooden crafts, embroidery, etc." Perfume, chocolates, or handkerchiefs for Boris's secretary couldn't hurt either.

Moscow might also, Zarubin suggested, need to adjust its tactics when it came to handling their special American source: "Our people need to use their meetings with him efficiently, to set concrete problems and solve them in the American fashion, and to use only the remaining time for conversation."

Zarubin's report is difficult to interpret. Far from being a productive and dependable agent, Boris had been an unreliable correspondent, often avoiding and misleading his spymasters. Perhaps Zarubin was trying to protect Gutzeit, who had been unable to turn Boris into a more productive agent. If so, the effort failed. Gutzeit was among the three thousand Soviet agents who were recalled, interrogated, and shot by their own superiors during this period. The stakes were quite a bit lower in Hollywood, where all too often Boris was an also-ran. Nominated for another Academy Award for his contributions to the score of the 1937 film *Souls at Sea*, Boris lost out to Universal's now-forgotten *One Hundred Men and a Girl*.

Not long after returning from a Hawaiian vacation with Catherine and Dick in September 1938—yet another attempt to keep up the appearance of a happy family life—Boris left his office for a working lunch at Lucey's, a swanky restaurant popular with Paramount's directors and actors. As he passed through the studio gate, he was accosted by a diminutive, down-at-the-heels fellow who struck him at first as a hobo. He'd apparently been trying to get through to Boris for days, but the guards took one look at his disheveled appearance and decided that there wasn't any need to inform Boris. He called out to Boris and announced that he was a friend of Edward Herbert. Boris kept on walking, but this little man unleashed a rainbow of expletives in Russian, German, English, and French. No matter how rude they were, Soviet agents were not to be ignored, yet Boris put his head down and hurried off to his appointment. The man, whom Boris was never able to identify, and about whom the Soviet archives are also silent, stalked Boris all the way to the front door of the restaurant, where bouncers blocked his way and let Boris in. The man waited outside, peering through the foliage that protected diners in the restaurant's outdoor garden from the attentions of fans. When it became clear that Boris was going to make lunch last as long as it took for the police to arrive, the man left. But Boris had a bad feeling. Had his failure to follow instructions finally caught up with him? Did Stalin's long arm reach all the way to Hollywood?

CHAPTER NINE
DECLARING INDEPENDENCE, 1938–42

It was just a tiny item buried on an inside page of the November 29, 1938, edition of *Film Daily*, below the stock quotes and above an ad for a stock footage house: "Boris Morros, head of Paramount's music department, announced yesterday that he will leave the studio at the termination of his contract in January." What the announcement didn't mention was that Boris wasn't leaving the film business but starting one of his own. The news came as a surprise for anyone who had seen Boris strutting through the studio lot with his conductor's baton tucked under his arm and Rasputin's beads wound around his forefinger, or hobnobbing about town, lavishly tipping the bouncers, posing for the cameras, or button-holing the journalists. Why would he willingly leave the protective nest of Adolph Zukor, who had plucked Boris from a desk job on Broadway and made him a national celebrity in Hollywood, with a salary to match? In 1937 he was identified by the US Treasury as one of the highest-paid workers in America, with an annual salary from Paramount of $52,333, which was more than Jimmy Cagney or Bette Davis made that year—the equivalent of almost $1 million today. Boris's colleagues, his friends, even his wife couldn't understand why he would want to give up Paramount's regular paychecks to try to make it in the film industry as an independent producer. If *Film Daily* didn't at first do justice to Boris's departure from Paramount, they soon made up for it, no doubt after an angry telephone call from Boris, by calling it one of the signal events of the year in the film business.

Boris's decision was motivated in part by the changes he saw coming in the film business. Hollywood was recovering from the depths of the Depression, rebounding from $56 million in losses in 1932 to profits of almost $30 million in 1939. Still, despite increasing ticket sales, the major Hollywood studios were losing influence, power, and revenue to independents like United Artists and smaller players like Universal Studios. The star system that had served Hollywood so well, locking America's most beloved actors into exclusive, long-term contracts, was fading. Roosevelt's National Industrial Recovery Act, which had allowed the film industry to retain some of its monopolistic practices in the name of supporting one of the most country's most important industries, had run its course, with the legal ruling that the studios' control of both distribution and exhibition violated fair business practices. As if giving up their own exhibition venues weren't enough, Paramount, Warner Brothers, MGM, Twentieth Century Fox, and RKO were also struggling with the increasingly powerful and vocal unions that represented everyone from carpenters, electricians, and makeup artists to writers and cameramen, and they decided to start making fewer pictures.

Boris's decision was also personal, a matter of raw ambition. The Hollywood mogul Jack Warner once described the lives of the Eastern European Jews who had made their fortunes in the film business: "We were free to climb as high as our energy and brains could take us." It hadn't been that easy or simple for Boris, who felt that he been lured to the West under false pretenses. Zukor not only refused to let Boris make his own movies as he had promised, he didn't even always give Boris credit for the work that he did do. Boris's musical contributions to *Hollywood Boulevard*, for example, went entirely uncredited. What little glory the Paramount music department attracted went to its composers, not to its chief administrator. If he stayed with Paramount, Boris reasoned, he would remain a baton for hire for the rest of his life and would never achieve the kind of prestige he'd been dreaming about since childhood—not to mention the kind of money he believed he was worth.

There was another reason behind Boris's decision, but he couldn't tell anyone about it, because it would mean admitting that he had been lying to his family and friends, fooling his employer, and betraying his adopted country for years. If, as Boris suspected, the only reason the Soviet spy apparatus was interested in him was his position at Paramount, Boris was hoping that by starting his own company, he would be freed from his Soviet puppet masters—among many other benefits. The NKVD did leave Boris alone from late 1938 until early 1940, but not because he left Paramount. Rather, the neglect was mostly due to Stalin's Great Terror (1936–38), with its show trials and purges, arrests and defections, internal exiles and secret liquidations, which left decimated Soviet intelligence's overseas operations. If agents were replaced at all, it was by with rookies who had little field experience. Stalin's August 1939 Nonaggression Pact with Hitler, which led Hitler to gloat that "now I have the world in my pocket," turned the USSR into an undeclared enemy of the United States and made it almost impossible to send Soviet agents to America. Those who were allowed into the country were severely restricted in terms of their ability to operate, because the Communist Party could no longer offer the material or political support that it had early in the decade.

Because Boris Morros Productions—which would be based partly in offices on Santa Monica Boulevard and partly in New York, in a suite of rooms on the twenty-third floor of the Sherry-Netherland Hotel that would double as Boris's pied-à-terre—would at first focus on distributing or remaking foreign films for the American market, there were plans to open a branch of the company in Paris. As soon as Boris wrapped up his final projects at Paramount, including the music for John Ford's *Stagecoach*, he booked passage to France. Boris remained in Paris for only a few days, but it was enough time to meet with French film producers looking to squeeze more money out of their products by selling the rights to foreign-language adaptations. Boris was beginning his career as a producer by peddling secondhand goods, but it was a start. Then he steamed back to New York aboard the RMS *Aquitania*, a once-luxurious express liner formerly favored by Hollywood stars but lately a bit shabby. Boris was after all paying his own way now. Upon arriving at Manhattan's West Side piers on March 3, 1939, Boris announced to the press that he'd secured the rights to remake no fewer than twenty-two French films and that he was in talks with Hollywood studios to film eight of them. Then it was back to Los Angeles to sign the incorporation papers for Boris Morros Productions and to make peace with Catherine, who was not happy to have been left behind while Boris enjoyed Paris to the fullest.

By the summer of 1939, the twenty-two films that Boris had boasted of making had turned into just one, but one was enough: an adaptation of *Les Deux Légionnaires*, a 1931 French comedy about two bumbling members of the French Foreign Legion. Boris renamed it *The Aviators* and helped adapt it to suit American tastes, along with a team of third-rate and therefore very inexpensive scriptwriters. Nor was the producer Boris teamed up with quite top-shelf. William LeBaron was a Paramount veteran whose career had peaked years before when he produced Mae West in *She Done Him Wrong* and *I'm No Angel*. The director also came cheap: A. Edward Sutherland was a British-born fixture on the Hollywood scene who had gotten his start as an actor, as one of the original Keystone Kops, but since the mid-1930s he had been bouncing from studio to studio as a director of forgettable films.

The Aviators eventually got a new name, *The Flying Deuces*. Boris didn't mind skimping on the behind-the-scenes talent, but he was determined to play it safe when it came to the actors. He approached the already legendary and very bankable comedy team of Stan Laurel and Oliver Hardy. They were expensive, but Boris was able to assure the group of New York bankers who were financing the film to the tune of $300,000—in addition to the $200,000 of his own money that Boris told them he was committing—that the names Laurel and Hardy alone practically guaranteed a hit.

The Flying Deuces was essentially a series of gags in an exotic location. Laurel and Hardy play two American fishmongers visiting Paris, where Oliver Hardy's character falls for an innkeeper's daughter, who is in love with someone else. To forget their troubles they join the foreign legion, only to find that they have essentially signed on to a lifetime of hard labor in North Africa. After they desert their posts, they are caught and sentenced to the firing squad by an officer who turns out to be the daughter's fiancé. A madcap chase ends with them behind the controls of a stolen plane, which then crashes. Stan's character survives, but Oliver's character dies, ascending to heaven and then returning to earth, reincarnated as a horse. *The Flying Deuces* wasn't a masterpiece, but Boris reasoned that people needed some relief from the grim news from Europe: "These are troubled times, and there is in the world enough sadness already," Boris told Paul Harrison, whose In Hollywood column was carried in newspapers from coast to coast. "So I am not making a picture with a message and with everybody dying in it."

The shooting of the film began in mid-July 1939, with Boris betting he could do it cheap and fast. Boris told any journalist who would listen that most of Laurel and Hardy's scenes were shot without dialogue because pantomime and slapstick were the actors' strong points, when in fact, less dialogue would make the film easier to market to foreign audiences. The cast and crew were working for union scale—the industry's minimum standard wage—because Boris promised them a piece of the profits, an arrangement that he described as "cooperative." He made up for it by treating them like a big family: They all ate lunch outside together every day on long picnic tables, and at the end of the day he invited them to watch the daily rushes. Boris wasn't shy about soliciting advice on the costumes from the set's carpenters and electricians and asking the makeup girl for her comments on the script.

Boris may have resented his years behind a desk at Paramount, but it taught him how to get things done. Shooting for *The Flying Deuces* ended a week early and $30,000 under budget. Boris arranged sneak previews in which he counted the number of times audiences laughed: 317 times over the course of the seventy-minute film, an average of more than four laughs per minute. That was more than good enough for someone who claimed his only goal was "to have fun making fun, for people who want to have fun."

Boris managed to attract plenty of publicity for *The Flying Deuces*, but it wasn't always the right kind. A nationally syndicated article from August 27, 1939, just days after the agreement that made the USSR and Nazi Germany allies and permanently ended whatever sympathy most progressive Americans had for communism, shouted A RUSSIAN REVOLUTION'S AFOOT IN HOLLYWOOD. The story, which appeared on the front page of the *Washington Post*, was nominally about *The Flying Deuce*'s unusual production methods. However, the writer couldn't resist suggesting that the congressional committee then investigating Soviet influence in Hollywood have a closer look at "round-faced, happy Boris Morros." That kind of publicity should have worried Boris, but with Moscow having been silent for almost a year, he felt he could rest easy.

The article helped put a damper on what was supposed to be Boris's triumphant return to New York the next month as a full-fledged moviemaker. As his train pulled into Pennsylvania Station, he carried under one arm a newspaper with the news of the Nazi invasion of Poland and England's declaration of war on Germany. Under the other arm was a print of *The Flying Deuces*, which still lacked a national distributor. But Boris was hopeful. He held a sneak preview, though New York audiences seemed less amused by the film than West Coast viewers, laughing only 236 times. Nevertheless, RKO Pictures agreed to take on the film.

RKO was no doubt influenced by a long feature in the *New York Times*, headlined THE "LITTLE BEAR" WITH BIG IDEAS, that marked Boris's official entry into Hollywood's upper echelons. Just a week after the Soviets invaded Poland and kicked off World War II, the newspaper announced: "The gentleman so named wishes to tell the whole world, or what's left of it, that he is now in business for himself." Portraying Boris as an outsider who brought something new to the business, in contrast to the film world's movers and shakers, who had been "desk bound for too many years," the story argued that Boris knew what people wanted: to laugh. But no writer, it seemed, could resist commenting on Boris's image: "An ebullient, rotund little dynamo with a thick czarist accent, Mr. Morros offsets his lack of stature by an abundance of self-confidence."

Boris was used to journalists having fun at his expense, so the autumn 1939 trip to the East Coast was a great success in his eyes, and on the way back to Los Angeles, Boris was ecstatic, fantasizing about dollar signs and Academy Awards. Having recently started teaching film music and cinematography at the University of Southern California, he was due back in the classroom, but his mind was less on his students than on other film projects. Boris was especially looking forward to making an American version of *The Grand Illusion*, Jean Renoir's already-classic 1938 French drama about World War I. Given Hollywood's reluctance to make war movies during wartime, it was a risky move, but Boris believed that the quality of the film was more important than its relation to current events. Asked by the *New York Times* how he could possibly top the magisterial original, he had a ready answer: "I'll just imitate it."

There was still plenty of work to be done on *The Flying Deuces*, and in late October 1939 he was back in New York to prepare for its premiere at Broadway's Rialto Theatre. Boris generally didn't mix family and business, but this time he brought along Catherine and Dick for the publicity leading up to the premiere on November 3, 1939. It was the climax of his entire career so far. His name might not have been on the marquee, but as he walked up the red carpet with Catherine on his arm, his name was on everyone's lips, or so it seemed.

The reviews that appeared across the country didn't pretend that *The Flying Deuces* was a work for the ages, but that had never been Boris's goal. He was happy to see newspaper after newspaper announce that it was perfect fare for moviegoers looking for a respite from the news in Europe. *Film Daily* called *The Flying Deuces* "an auspicious debut," and the box office receipts proved it. Even if Boris's claim that his $500,000 movie grossed $2 million in its first few weeks was dubious, the success of his first film meant that a second one was possible.

By mid-December 1939, Boris was back in Hollywood, having dropped his idea to remake *The Grand Illusion*. He started a new production company, National Pictures, and set his sights on a treatment of the life of swing jazz clarinetist and bandleader Artie Shaw, whose 1938 recording of "Begin the Beguine" had made him a pop star. Boris called the project, which was to star Shaw playing himself, *Second Chorus*, which in the music world means the elaboration on the melody line heard in the first chorus of a song. The title was just as fitting for Boris's own career as a film producer, but in some respects, the project was an odd choice because Boris despised popular music and swing jazz in particular. He changed his tune, quickly and publicly: "Swing is a legitimate form of musical expression," he told the press, "recognized by such great classicists as Toscanini and Stokowski." With this lukewarm attitude, it was no wonder Boris couldn't attract a top-name director to the project, which soon went from being the Artie Shaw story to a romantic comedy featuring a bandleader based on Shaw, who would now be playing a character based on himself. Boris went with the second-tier director H. C. Potter and relatively unknown writers because he was again planning to spend his money on big stars. When Jack Warner refused to loan John Garfield out to Boris, Boris arranged an "accidental" meeting with Fred Astaire—whose string of hits with Ginger Rogers were among Hollywood's biggest moneymakers in the 1930s—on the golf course of the Bel Air Country Club. Boris convinced Astaire to join the cast by revealing that he would be playing opposite Shaw. That was an optimistic gesture on Boris's part, since Shaw, who had been turned off acting by what little experience he'd had in Hollywood, made it clear that he wasn't interested in the movies anymore. That didn't stop Boris.

After one of Shaw's sets at the Chateau Marmont Hotel, Boris buttonholed the clarinetist and tried to convince him to join the film by reminding him that he would be playing opposite Fred Astaire. "I got a *staaah*," Shaw remembered Boris saying. Boris then told Shaw that the film would be an artistically and historically accurate depiction of the jazz world. Shaw, who had doubted the seriousness of the film, was only convinced to commit when Boris promised him that he would have full control over his own dialogue.

Making *Second Chorus* was turning out to be a juggling act for Boris, who was desperately trying to arrange financing, distribution, and production facilities. Eventually, he was able to get RKO to host the production, and he signed a deal with his old friends at Paramount to release the film. Both studios were encouraged by Boris's idea to again work "cooperatively," which meant less money up front. In the end, the film only cost $500,000 to make, a relatively small amount for a major Hollywood feature. But the making of the film was marked by sad news. In mid-June of 1940, Boris was in a conference with Paramount when a messenger came into the room bearing a mysterious cable that had arrived in Russian. Would Boris mind translating? He wasn't surprised to learn that the cable from the Russian branch of the Red Cross was addressed to him, but the contents shocked him: His mother, Malka, had died.

The news was devastating, but Boris found work was the best therapy, and there was plenty of that as the *Second Chorus* shooting date of July 1, 1940, approached. For the female lead, Boris had signed Paulette Goddard, whose marriage to Charlie Chaplin, virtually a persona non grata in Hollywood due to his openly leftist sympathies, had damaged her reputation. As usual, Boris was buying low.

During the filming of *Second Chorus*, the *New York World-Telegram*'s H. Allen Smith paid a visit to the RKO studios, writing one of the lengthiest and most revealing sketches of Boris that ever appeared in print. Boris pulled out all of the stops for Smith, starting with the infamous Rasputin beads, which he casually took out of his pocket and began twirling around his finger, clearly an invitation for Smith to ask about them. When Smith declined, Boris told him anyway: "You knowing Rezzputin?" he asked Smith. "I am knowing Rezzputin in Roshia. I am conductor from the Moscow Seemphony. Rezzputin and me, ve are the spiritzel-type men." Smith, whose transcription of Boris's English would have been insulting if Boris was capable of being insulted, was looking for good copy and didn't have to work hard to find it when it came to the Rasputin beads: "If the interviewer does not ask about it at once Mr. Morros whirls it faster and more vigorously, until he has it going like a lasso and finishes up by getting it fouled around his ears."

By October 1940, *Second Chorus* was done. Industry insiders who caught early glimpses weren't enthusiastic, and Astaire and Shaw refused to go on a publicity tour. Boris took it upon himself to drum up some publicity. He went on the road for a month with a print of the film. At least that's what he told Catherine and Dick. In fact, Boris was again escaping the NKVD, which had tracked him down and reactivated him after more than two years of silence. Boris had wishfully thought that their silence was a signal his spy career was over. But the NKVD was by no means done with Boris. They had simply put him on hold while they put their house in order, a house they now shared, uncomfortably at best, with Hitler.

As the alliance between Berlin and Moscow began to fray, Stalin became increasingly and correctly convinced that World War II and whatever global conflict that followed it would be won or lost not only on the battlefields of Europe but in the factories and laboratories of the United States. Something had to be done to revive the Soviets' American operations, something more than just replacing the agents who had been purged. Declining membership in the Communist Party of the United States meant that the Soviets could no longer depend on a large pool of ideologically motivated recruits. This was when Moscow turned to its "Hollywood Hustler."

But before reaching out to Boris, Soviet intelligence began its first serious inquiry into whom exactly they were dealing with. The fact that they had never done even the most rudimentary background check shows how astonishingly amateurish and chaotic the Soviet intelligence operations could be. A Russian joke from the time had it that Moscow was almost ready to smuggle a nuclear bomb in a suitcase into the United States—all they had to do was perfect the suitcase.

Thinking that late was better than later, Moscow commissioned a series of secret intelligence reports on Boris. They were glad they did, because they confirmed doubts and unearthed troubling new information about his family, information that even Boris didn't have. According to these reports, Boris's brother Aleksander, a local official in the Ukrainian town of Starobelsk, had been arrested along with his wife in late 1937 and convicted of membership in a Trotskyite group. Punishment for their crimes meant an eight-year prison term for his wife and a death sentence for Aleksander. Soviet intelligence had also learned that another of Boris's brothers, Isaak, a government functionary in the Russian city of Yoshkar-Ola, had been arrested in 1938 on suspicion of counterrevolutionary activity and convicted of treason, but he died in a prison hospital before his death sentence could be carried out. The agents investigating Boris had also tracked down Boris's father in Zaporozhye, where they found "incriminating evidence" that Mendel had engaged in unspecified counterrevolutionary activities, which might have meant simply providing his sons with shelter.

Soviet agents made sure to keep these revelations from Boris by censoring the letters that passed between the various members of the family, but they brought their concerns about Boris to Lavrenti Beria, the newly appointed head of the NKVD. He stopped them before they could finish. Beria was one of the most notorious figures in the history of the Soviet Union, infamous for his brutal efficiency and long memory. He recalled knowing someone by the name of Boris Morros in Azerbaijan back in the early 1920s, a staunch and dependable revolutionary who had worked as an exporter connected with the Baku-based firm that had assumed control of the recently nationalized Azerbaijan oil industry. Boris had indeed been in Baku in that period, but a sub-investigation Beria commissioned didn't find anyone who had worked at the firm that remembered him.

Beria's apparently faulty memory of Boris remained a mystery for decades, when the whole subject became even more curious. Shortly before her death, Elena Stasova, one of the highest-ranking female spies in Soviet history, claimed that while she was organizing the Congress of the Peoples of the East in Baku in September 1920, she recruited the head of the event's translating services, a chubby, prematurely bald musician named Boris Morros, into the nascent Soviet spy machine. According to classified Soviet intelligence files that were only made public decades after Morros's death, Stasova recalled that she ordered him to make his way to Constantinople and then to the United States, where he would Americanize himself and await further instructions. There's no independent evidence to corroborate this alternate version of Boris's career as a spy, nor did Beria seem to be aware of it. Knowing what we now know about how Boris became a Soviet spy, it seems that Stasova was either wrong or engaging in some deathbed rewriting of history. As for Beria, it is likely that his memory was playing tricks on him when he recalled Boris. But Beria came from an earlier generation of Bolsheviks that put a premium on personal relations over mere facts. Beria told his underlings: Boris Morros was one of us and still is. Find him and put him back to work.

A series of secret memos from September 1940 ordered the Soviet *rezidentura* in New York City to send someone to Los Angeles to find Boris. Within a month, Samuel Shumovsky, the spy from Washington, DC, who had frightened Boris back in July 1937, was calling Boris's office and leaving messages at the Paramount gate, and though there is one cryptic sign that the two met, Boris left the incident out of his memoirs. What we do know is that Boris left town immediately on an unplanned, solo publicity tour for *Second Chorus*.

Boris travelled solo across twenty-eight states, wearing a red shirt and black tie on which Fred Astaire had hand-painted "Boris Morros and Second Chorus" over lines of musical notation. Doing his best to win over film critics, he generated plenty of publicity, but as was so often the case, writers found Boris a more interesting subject than his movies. Nonetheless, Boris thought that publicity was a matter of quantity, not quality. If all of those articles that mocked his accent and his wardrobe also mentioned *Second Chorus*, his mission had been accomplished.

Of course, *Second Chorus* was no longer Boris's only mission. When he arrived in New York to set up a private lunch for journalists at the 21 Club, Boris was unexpectedly contacted by Gaik Ovakimian, who had replaced Gutzeit as head of the New York *rezidentura*. The two men met twice, once on November 2 and once on November 4, 1940, after which

Ovakimian reported that Boris was amenable to a new assignment, and that he had been ordered to return to Los Angeles and wait.

Second Chorus premiered in early December 1940, going head-to-head with *High Sierra* and *The Philadelphia Story* and attracting mostly dreadful reviews. The ever-supportive *Film Daily* gave the movie a positive review, and the *Hollywood Reporter* announced: "In the box office bag. . . . A show to thunder from the roof-tops!" But those were exceptions. The *New York Times* found that "seldom has a first-class talent been less effectively used." Years later, both Astaire and Shaw admitted that *Second Chorus* was the worst film they'd ever been associated with. Shaw said it convinced him never to work in Hollywood again. The film did well at the box office, however, and it eventually got two Academy Award nominations, for Best Score (by Artie Shaw) and for Best Original Song ("Love of My Life" by Shaw and Johnny Mercer). It's hard to say whether Boris considered the film a success. When asked what the most important thing about *Second Chorus* was, he answered: "It rhymes with Boris Morros."

Boris later recalled that he was so busy over the next few months with teaching at USC and developing new projects that never came to fruition—including a movie about the writer O. Henry and a film about American efforts to rebuild England's shattered Royal Air Force—that he almost forgot that it was only a matter of time until Moscow reached out to him again. It happened in February 1941, when Ovakimian reported to Moscow that he'd reconnected with Boris, who had agreed to use his production company to help arrange American visas for several Soviet agents located in the Baltics. Boris was less enthusiastic about a plan that Moscow hatched to have him travel to Japan under the cover of studying Japanese music, while in fact making contact and perhaps turning the Japanese prime minister's brother, Hidemaro Konoye, a classical composer and conductor. Boris declined, citing commitments in Hollywood. As unusual as it was for an agent to turn down an assignment, Ovakimian knew that Boris's value to Moscow was his reputation in Hollywood and so he let it go. Meanwhile, yet another shakeup of the Soviet intelligence services was underway. The NKVD was reorganized and renamed the

People's Commissariat for State Security, or the NKGB. All assignments were suspended or postponed while Beria formulated an intelligence strategy that would suit Moscow's deteriorating relations with Berlin. That process was certainly obstructed by the FBI's arrest of Ovakimian as a Soviet agent in May 1941. He was sent back to Moscow in a prisoner exchange, leaving Boris free once again to focus on his film projects.

Boris's next film, *Tales of Manhattan*, had its origins in a conversation with a friend, the director Billy Wilder, who suggested that it might be interesting to make what was called an omnibus or anthology: a film composed of a number of short films. But an idea wasn't enough. They needed a story. Inspired both by a decade-old Wilder screenplay written in Berlin and a 1930 Mexican novel named *Story of a Tailcoat*, Boris wondered: What about a movie that follows the fortunes of a cursed tuxedo that passes from hand to hand, bringing trouble to everyone who wears it, including an actor, the dupe in a love triangle, a classical musician, an alcoholic lawyer, and a thief who robs a gambling party, until finally the coat brings good luck to a poor, black sharecropper?

Boris approached the project with his usual sense of thrifty ambition. At first he wanted to have the different episodes directed by Hollywood's top directors, including John Ford, William Wyler, and Ernst Lubitsch. Boris's co-producer, the notorious Sam Spiegel, convinced him that they couldn't afford more than one director, so they hired Julien Duvivier, a legend in France but a relative stranger in Hollywood, which meant that he'd work for cheap. Having a single director simplified things, but with a projected seven episodes written by two dozen screenwriters (among them Wilder, Buster Keaton, Herman Mankiewicz, and Clifford Odets) and a cast that was to include Eddie "Rochester" Anderson, Charlie Chaplin, W. C. Fields, Henry Fonda, Rita Hayworth, Edward G. Robinson, and Orson Welles, *Tales of Manhattan* promised to be a glorious, expensive mess. It took Boris the better part of a year just to assemble the cast, and he did so without spending a cent, using his now-infamous "cooperative" approach. As he told the syndicated columnist John Truesdale, who, like everyone in the press, delighted in mocking Boris's already unique syntax:

"For these people, I didn't have some money enough, so enthusiasm I used to buy them." Soon Boris was "being called man of the year" by the *New York Times* and was "being looked on by Hollywood in awe" because of the scale of *Tales of Manhattan*, which now had a budget of $860,000 and a distribution deal with Twentieth Century Fox. Filming started in early November 1941. Despite the pall cast over the production by the news from Pearl Harbor, it was finished by the year's end.

When he first began producing movies, Boris prided himself on his efficiency, but by the time he made *Tales of Manhattan*, his working methods had grown more chaotic. He dropped Twentieth Century Fox for United Artists, then left them for Paramount, a deal that Zukor celebrated with a huge party that also marked Boris's eighteenth anniversary at the studio. Then Boris got a better offer from his original distributor, Twentieth Century Fox, and took it, Zukor be damned.

CHAPTER TEN
TURNABOUT, 1942–43

The cocktail party on North Beverly Drive in February 1942 was nothing out of the ordinary for Beverly Hills, except for the presence of the Russians. When Boris arrived, the neighbors and celebrities, in some cases one and the same, were streaming in and heading for the bar. There were also a number of prominent Russian diplomatic officers and functionaries who were visiting California. Ever since Hitler's invasion of Russia in June 1941, which ended the German-Soviet Nonaggression Pact, such figures were being welcomed again by the left-wing film industry types who packed the place. So Boris felt right at home as he hugged and back-slapped his way through the crowd—and tried not to spill his usual glass of water, which he hoped everyone thought was vodka. Boris had never stopped associating with the Russians who had settled in or were just passing through Los Angeles, greeting them like old friends. But there was one Russian guest, a barrel-chested fellow with thinning blond hair and glasses, who reeked of vodka, that Boris pretended not to recognize when he approached.

It was Vasily Zarubin. Boris, who quite reasonably assumed that Zarubin had perished at the hands of either Stalin or Hitler, shook his hand and moved away, but Zarubin followed him, slipping his chubby arm firmly but discreetly through Boris's. "Don't you know me?" he asked in a low voice with a heavy Russian accent. "After all, you should. You saved my life, you know." Zarubin then pulled Boris toward the backyard, where Boris suddenly pretended to remember who he was. Strolling across the grass, just out of earshot of the other guests, Zarubin switched into menacingly perfect English: "You could have done better, you know. You should have written me more often while I was in Germany." Boris, who of course had never seen the reports in which Zarubin praised him so enthusiastically, tried to deflect the accusation with a joke: "What could I do, when all you recommended to me was acrobats? Japanese acrobats are bad enough, but German acrobats, Nazi German acrobats at that."

Zarubin wasn't amused. He pressed Boris's arm more tightly as they strolled deeper into the garden. "Forget that I was ever Edward Herbert," he ordered. "I am now with the Soviet embassy. My name is now Zubilin. Vasily Mikhailovich Zubilin." Boris was desperate to disentangle himself from Herbert, or whatever name he was using, and get back to the party, but Zarubin was in the mood to talk. How was Boris's family back in Russia? Not so good, Boris answered. His mother had died, he hadn't heard from his sisters in years, and he suspected that the worst had happened to his brothers. Zarubin confirmed that it was probably too late to help two of them, Aleksander and Isaak, but perhaps there was still hope for the other two, Savely and Serge, who, he informed Boris, were apparently both wasting away in a Siberian prison, where disease, exposure to the elements, starvation, and torture were the rule. He tried to move back toward the house, but Zarubin kept firm hold of Boris's arm and led him further into the garden. "And my father," Boris asked. "What about him?"

"Maybe you would like me to get your father over here for you," Zarubin suggested, suddenly sympathetic. "This time for good." The look on Boris's face told Zarubin they were back in business, and negotiations started then and there. Zarubin could indeed make it happen, but Boris had to be more discreet. There could be no more fundraisers for Russians, no parties where other Russians would be present, and needless to say, no more treating visiting Soviet dignitaries to dinner. Boris objected, saying that his patriotic credentials were impeccable: He had even registered for the draft. Zarubin was unmoved. Then he was gone.

Boris, who hadn't heard from Moscow for months, later claimed that the February 1942 meeting with Zarubin came as a total surprise, but he might have expected it. Germany's invasion of Russia, known as Operation Barbarossa, was the most ambitious military operation in the history of warfare, and it had changed the entire Soviet-American intelligence landscape once again. Soviet's agents would no longer be dedicated to undermining "the imperialist war" being waged by England and France, but were to join together with those countries in the anti-fascist cause, which after Pearl Harbor included the United States. The revitalization of Moscow's demoralized and decimated American front would be led by none other than Zarubin.

Much had transpired in the life of this legendary spy since Boris had last been in contact with him. After his return to Moscow, where Zarubin taught at the Special Purpose School, the training academy for Soviet agents, came assignments in Yugoslavia and China. Zarubin was then stationed in Poland, where in 1940 he was implicated in the Katyn forest massacre of twenty thousand Polish officers who found themselves on the wrong side of the conflict when the Soviet Union invaded Poland. Zarubin was called to back to Moscow, and in October 1941 he met with Stalin in an eerily empty Kremlin, the rest of the government having already fled to the east as Nazi troops closed in on the city. Stalin told Zarubin he was sending him back to the United States to rebuild Soviet intelligence's American operations, replacing Ovakimian as the chief legal resident in Washington, DC. His portfolio included rebuilding the Communist Party of the United States, developing political sources in the nation's capital, and leading the intelligence-gathering operations looking into the development of an American nuclear weapon, known as the Manhattan Project. It is evidence of how important this intelligence initiative, called "Enormoz," was to Stalin, and how secret it was, that he risked his own life—the German artillery fire was within earshot—to give the orders directly to the only man he thought could make it happen. Half a century later, Zarubin's biographer found evidence that Stalin also had a special request, one that shows how central the Soviets' man in Hollywood had become to their most important long-term goal. Find Boris Morros, Stalin told Zarubin, and put him to work. Or put him to death.

The threatening encounter between Zarubin and Boris at the Beverly Hills cocktail party in February 1942 set a new tone for their new relationship. A month later, Zarubin was back on the West Coast, where he read in the newspaper that Boris would be taking time off from assembling the circus of actors and writers that was to become *Tales of Manhattan* to help produce a concert in Los Angeles to raise money to send food, clothing, and medicine to the Soviet Union. It was a clear violation of Zarubin's instructions to stay away from anything that would connect him with the USSR. Zarubin snuck backstage several hours before the benefit and in a drunken fury accosted Boris, screaming in Russian as he pinned him to the wall: "Didn't I tell you not to be seen with Russians at affairs like this one? Do you want the whole world to know that your sympathies are with us?" Boris, who had little by little come to realize how dangerous his double life had become, could only think: "Why is he screaming at me in Russian if he wants us to be as discreet as possible?" Then Boris couldn't think at all, because Zarubin was suddenly jamming a pistol into his belly: "You are not to mix with any Russians," he shouted, warning Boris that unless he changed his ways, he'd never see his father again.

If Boris was worried by the way Zarubin behaved a month before, now he was terrified for his life, and his father's life, and with good reason he was willing to say or do anything to get away from this man. Then, just as suddenly as Zarubin had appeared, he was gone. But Boris had the feeling he would never be far enough away. In fact, two weeks later, Boris's secretary at Twentieth Century Fox knocked on his door and told him there was a Vasily Zubilin on the line. Boris's Soviet handler was now playing good cop: Should he stop by North Beverly Drive tonight to pick up some boxes of clothing that Boris wanted to send back to Russia? Boris couldn't think of any reason to refuse that wouldn't cause more problems than it solved.

When the doorbell rang, Catherine, whose hatred of communists was longstanding and very personal, opened the door, introduced herself, exchanged a few words with Zarubin, and disappeared. Boris didn't know which Zarubin to anticipate. He had turned on the charm for Catherine, and Boris now expected the mask to fall. But Zarubin was friendly and helpful, bringing up the matter of Boris's father immigrating to America in return for Boris's help in setting up cover for several Soviet agents scheduled to arrive in the coming months. When Boris, who had letters from his father practically begging Boris to bring him back to America, asked if it were really possible to get his father exit visas and send him halfway across a world at war, through seas infested with U-boats, Zarubin replied: "I can do anything."

Over the course of several meetings with Zarubin in Los Angeles in March and April 1942, Boris consented to providing at least four NKVD agents with cover jobs. One of these agents, known in secret cables as "West" and still unidentified, would go to Switzerland, ostensibly to fight the government's decision to ban *The Flying Deuces*, because it apparently belittled the French Foreign Legion. Another Soviet spy, named "Evgeny," who also remains unidentified, would work for a friend of Boris's in the diamond business. Boris consented to finding a Hollywood-based position at Boris Morros Productions for a female agent named "Nora" and also to put an agent known as "Mer," now identified as Isaak Akhmerov, on his payroll. All the details were to be arranged at a May meeting in Washington, DC.

Boris later portrayed himself as a guileless, terrified victim of Zarubin. In fact, little by little he was realizing he was actually in a position to make demands of Zarubin and the Kremlin. In return for providing cover for Zarubin's four agents, Boris demanded that Zarubin find out for sure where Serge and Savely were and take care of their families. Within days, Zarubin had learned that the two brothers had been sent into internal exile in Siberia, accompanied by their families. Two weeks later, Zarubin told Boris that he'd arranged to have them receive 3,000 rubles (about $8,000 today). Zarubin had also arranged for locals to help them find an apartment big enough for all of them, and he made sure they would get a very generous monthly stipend of 500 rubles.

Boris had no reason to believe any of it, but it was time for him to do his part. He told Catherine in May 1942 that he was travelling east to meet with potential backers of *Tales of Manhattan* in New York, and to visit their son, Dick, whose wayward career at Beverly Hills High School had been cut short. He was now enrolled in a military-style boarding school in Annapolis, Maryland. Of course, the real reason for Boris's trip was the rendezvous with Zarubin. As soon as Boris had satisfied himself that Dick was surviving, if not enjoying school, Boris drove the forty miles to Washington, DC, and checked into the luxurious Willard Hotel on Pennsylvania Avenue, just two blocks from the White House. Boris took a brief taxi ride to the Soviet embassy on Sixteenth Street NW, and against Zarubin's explicit instructions, walked in the front door announcing that he was looking for Vasily Zubilin. If it looked like carelessness on Boris's part, it was actually a well-thought-out strategy to take charge of the situation—to handle his handler. The embassy secretary told Boris that no one by that name worked there, but when Boris walked out, she followed him and gave him a slip of paper with a telephone number. When Boris got back to his room at the Willard and called the number, Zarubin answered, surprised and then enraged by Boris's breach of protocol.

Even when sober, Zarubin was congenitally indiscreet, and he hated timid types who played by the rules, but he insisted that Boris's behavior reflected poorly on the entire *rezidentura*. If word got back to Beria that the operation was being run so sloppily, things could get ugly. Eventually, Zarubin regained his composure and told Boris to meet him on New Jersey Avenue between K and I Streets, a neighborhood close to Union Station known as Film Row because so many studios had distribution offices there. If anyone saw them, Boris was to say he was there on business. From there they took a taxicab to a shabby apartment house in a run-down neighborhood nearby. They walked into a ground-floor apartment, and Boris met a slight, beautiful woman in her forties with an elegant, polished bearing and a seven-year-old boy. It was Zarubin's wife and child in real life, though in a typical Soviet twist, they were also playing the role of Vasily Zubilin's family.

Despite their years of long-distance collaboration, Boris knew almost nothing about Zarubin besides his uncontrollable temper, heavy drinking, and foul mouth. Boris had never entertained the idea that this boorish bully was one of the Soviet Union's highest-ranked, most trusted intelligence agents, someone who had only recently sat face-to-face with Stalin and taken on the job of reviving Soviet intelligence efforts in America. Nor did Boris know that "Helen," as she was known to her American acquaintances, was a legendary Soviet spy who had been ordered by Stalin to try to "turn" no less a figure than Eleanor Roosevelt.

"Liza," as Zarubin's wife was referred to in classified cables, was officially on assignment as Zarubin's assistant, but it was common knowledge in Moscow that she had the upper hand in both the professional and personal relationships, except when her brutal, philandering, and alcoholic husband got violent, which according to Boris's later recollections was not infrequently. On the day Boris met her in that virtually empty apartment, "Liza" had been assigned to play the role of mild-mannered wife of a minor diplomatic official and loving mother. She did it well, making sure Boris heard her warn her little boy that he could go play outside, but that he had to be back soon, in time for dinner.

The conversation didn't last long, but as usual, Zarubin seemed to run through the entire range of human emotions, from irritation and rage to sadness and humor. They began with the matter of bringing Boris's father to America, which Boris still seemed to doubt would be possible. Zarubin waved his muscular arms and slammed his fists against his chest: "I can do that. I can do a great deal more," he shouted, claiming that he was the head of the American operations of the NKGB, which gave him absolute power over his agents. "I feel as free here to do exactly as I want as anywhere else in the world!" Boris fought the urge to get up and leave, but he realized that this was the only way to get his father out of the Soviet Union. Zarubin seemed to be thinking the same thing. "For such favors I must be paid," he roared. "You *have* to do what I say! There is no way out for you! For I have long arms, long enough to reach anywhere in this country." Eventually, Zarubin brought the meeting to an end, but not before reminding Boris that he had not yet come up with cover jobs for the agents in Switzerland and in Los Angeles. Zarubin then explained to

Boris that from then on, whenever he wished to make contact, he should put the time and place at the end of a fake love letter signed with a double G clef and addressed to an agent named Leah Melament, a music teacher whose code name was, not very creatively, "Teacher." Her Upper West Side Manhattan apartment was used by the New York *rezidentura* as a mail drop, and as Boris soon learned, it was also Zarubin's love nest.

Boris nodded, but he had no intention of going out of his way to help Zarubin any more than he had to. It wasn't simply that he feared exposure in Hollywood or was reluctant to help anyone involved in the persecution of his family back in the Soviet Union. Rather, Boris felt that the best way to get what he wanted out of the Kremlin was to keep them off guard, which he knew was a risky game with deadly stakes. That is why in the summer of 1942 he repeatedly rebuffed Zarubin's attempts to reach him by telephone, even going so far as to burn the messages Zarubin left with his secretary at Twentieth Century Fox. Boris realized that he might have simply arranged cover for Zarubin's agents, but once Zarubin had what he wanted, he would have no incentive to follow through on his half of the bargain. Boris knew that holding back was the best way to motivate Zarubin to bring Mendel to the United States and to protect his family, not only in the Soviet Union but also in America. The strategy worked: That summer Mendel requested and received official permission to visit the United States.

If Boris was a less than fully committed spy, it was also because he had a full-time job as a movie producer. *Tales of Manhattan* had its West Coast premiere on August 5, 1942, at Grauman's Chinese Theatre in a star-studded benefit. The lobby lights remained low due to wartime regulations, but Boris's million-dollar smile more than made up for it. Demand for tickets was so strong in Los Angeles over the coming days that all five theaters showing the film sold out the entire run, even at increased ticket prices. Boris was looking forward to the New York premiere, but first he planned to make a publicity stop in Boston, where he had almost made a name for himself two decades earlier. It was a bittersweet homecoming: Marjory Adams's profile in the *Daily Boston Globe* of "the most amazing producer in Hollywood" seemed to take special delight in mocking his wardrobe and his accent. Triumph and humiliation came together for Boris once again.

Then it was on to New York for glory. What he got instead was Zarubin banging on the door of his suite at the Sherry-Netherland. Boris hadn't bothered to notify Zarubin via Leah Melament that he would be coming east, but now he realized he was being watched. It was a disturbing realization, made worse by Zarubin's outburst: Why have you done nothing in the way of providing those cover jobs in Switzerland and Los Angeles? Why didn't you arrange your visit through Leah Melament? Don't you want to make sure your family back in Siberia is taken care of, and not "taken care of"? Then the predictably unpredictable Zarubin calmed down and invited Boris to lunch. When Boris demurred, saying that he had an important business meeting, Zarubin laughed: "For you and me, Boris, there is only one business that counts."

They rode in a taxi downtown while Zarubin explained to Boris that in addition to the cover jobs they had already spoken about, Zarubin would be sending a group of Soviet agents to Los Angeles to become employees of Boris Morros Productions. They would pretend to work as camera operators, carpenters, electricians, and musicians. Apparently, Zarubin had no idea that the film industry's labor unions had these sorts of jobs locked up and that it took years of effort and significant connections to get one of them. At first Boris was baffled by how clueless Zarubin seemed to be about the situations he was putting his agents into, but then he realized Zarubin was well aware of such things. He simply considered them problems a Hollywood big shot like Boris could solve with a few strokes of his fountain pen. The cab pulled up in front of Lüchow's, a restaurant that had once been in the center of New York's entertainment district but that was now mostly empty except for the tourists looking for hints of the days when operetta was America's most popular music.

Even before they were seated, Zarubin ordered vodka, switched to beer and vermouth while they ate, and then switched back to vodka. Accustomed since childhood to seeing Russians put away astonishing amounts of alcohol, Boris had never seen Zarubin sober, but on this day he was appalled at how much Zarubin drank. Zarubin drank his way into another tantrum, giving Boris three months to find places for his agents. When Boris again tried to explain it wouldn't be easy, Zarubin warned him: "You *better* come through. Here in the United States, where people think they are so safe from us, we manage to catch up with those who try to forget what they owe us." Boris fled to a cab to head uptown, where all he could think was "What have I gotten myself into?"

Tales of Manhattan opened at Radio City Music Hall, the country's premier cinema, on September 24, 1942, part of a "Salute to Our Heroes" initiative that urged New Yorkers to buy war bonds. With Soviets pushing back against the Nazis at Stalingrad, US Marines occupying the Solomon Islands, and Allied planes bombing German-controlled train lines in France, it was the least that Boris could do, especially because such patriotic activities would distract anyone who suspected his allegiances.

If the Hollywood publicity machine had been cruel to Boris in the past, now its generosity knew no bounds. Or perhaps the syndicated columnists didn't dare criticize a film that managed to feature so many of America's most beloved and gifted talents. Hedda Hopper, whose column specialized in society news and anti-communist vitriol, called the film "one of the best pictures I've seen," while Louella Parsons found it "the fable of the year." Walter Winchell, who not long before was helping America laugh at Boris's rotund figure, was the most impressed, launching what looked like a one-man publicity drive. In addition to calling it "one of the greatest films I've ever seen," he lent his words to advertisements that called *Tales of Manhattan* "as thrilling as New York's skyline." The critics were only slightly less impressed, praising the film as an unprecedented, even brilliant achievement. They lauded Boris and his co-producer, Sam Spiegel, as "two of the most fabulous and resourceful personages in the film capital."

Though *Tales of Manhattan* faced stiff competition, playing opposite landmark films like *Pride of the Yankees, Holiday Inn, Yankee Doodle Dandy,* and *Bambi,* not to mention the patriotic war films *Battle of Midway* and *Wake Island,* and the war comedy *To Be or Not to Be,* the crowds wouldn't stop coming. Its two-week run at Radio City Music Hall was extended to three and then four weeks. In fact, *Tales of Manhattan* was Twentieth Century Fox's most profitable picture of 1942.

Tales of Manhattan was a big enough success to survive a controversy that erupted over its fifth episode, in which Paul Robeson and Ethel Waters play ignorant, good-hearted sharecroppers that find the tuxedo jacket, discover wads of cash in its pockets, and bring it to their preacher, played by Eddie "Rochester" Anderson, who uses the money to buy land to build their own church. Morros knew Robeson socially from liberal Hollywood cocktail party and fundraiser circles and brought him into the project in part to strike a blow for racial progress. It hadn't been easy to sign Robeson, who had vowed never to work in Hollywood again as long as the only roles available for blacks were demeaning and degrading. It was the reason Robeson had turned down a role in *Gone with the Wind*. It was Robeson's friendship with Boris, along with the promise that Robeson would be able to revise the script to excise any racial stereotypes, that convinced him to sign on to the project. But Boris, as always, was playing the game his way, paying Robeson only a fifth of what Edward G. Robinson was getting.

Moreover, like Artie Shaw when he signed on to *Second Chorus*, Robeson had no experience with a Boris Morros promise. When Robeson began to make suggestions, for example, that the film might show the black community in the future, when their good fortune and hard work had lifted them up out of poverty, Boris suddenly countered that Twentieth Century Fox only took on the project if it had control over the script, so there was nothing he could do. Robeson swallowed his pride and read his lines, but when he saw the final result, in which he and Waters are portrayed as docile and superstitious, he attempted to stop distribution with an ultimately unsuccessful plan to buy up all of the prints. *Tales of Manhattan* began attracting harsh criticism in the black press, and picket lines started forming at Manhattan's Loew's State Cinema.

Boris argued that he had fought to include the episode against the urging of friends and colleagues who believed that American filmgoers wouldn't pay to see a movie that climaxes with an all-black sequence. He reminded critics that *Tales of Manhattan* showed its audiences life the way black sharecroppers actually experienced it, and that the episode was, by virtue of its all-black cast, one of the few Hollywood productions that refused to show passive blacks genuflecting before dominant whites. Eventually, the racial controversy petered out. But *Tales of Manhattan* was the last Hollywood film Robeson ever made.

Tales of Manhattan's treatment of race wasn't its only controversial aspect. Even before the film's official release, John Truesdale's In Hollywood column was calling it a "socialized movie." That wasn't necessarily an insult or a warning; after all, the Soviets were now America's allies in the war against fascism. Still, Robeson's reputation as America's best-known communist, one of the few who stayed in the party even after August 1939, posed a publicity problem for the film. If the Robeson episode's plea for collectivism sounds less like a progressive New Deal bromide and more like Popular Front propaganda, that's because the film's script writers were either communists like Donald Ogden Stewart or fellow travelers like Ben Hecht and Alan Campbell. Then there was Boris's public explanation about the "cooperative" way he signed his stars, in which "they all took their socialized medicine and came back for another spoonful." Indeed, after the honeymoon period with the film critics was over, the press began to turn against the film on political grounds. The New York *Daily News* eventually called *Tales of Manhattan* "a hefty piece of Communist propaganda," while *PM* deplored its "communist sentiments."

Not long before, Zarubin would have been mightily displeased to see that one of the Soviet Union's most potentially significant operatives in the United States was being so open about his left-wing sentiments. Then again, Boris's most important asset, from Moscow's perspective, was his fame, and avoiding communists and cleansing his public statements of anything that sounded like socialism would only make him look suspicious. After all, what kind of Soviet spy would openly associate with communists? Apparently, Moscow was beginning to see the wisdom of Boris's "the more open, the better" approach.

Tales of Manhattan made Boris $200,000, the equivalent of more than $3 million today, and that was before overseas sales. More importantly, it raised Boris's reputation in Hollywood, showing up doubters like a Twentieth Century Fox publicity man who privately said, "Morros was legitimate as a musician, but what the hell was he doing making a movie?"

Boris was delighted to find that though the film won no Academy Awards or even nominations, Tales of Manhattan was included in most lists of the ten best films of 1942. He was quickly brought down to earth when a "love letter" arrived at his offices from Leah Melament. Boris's eyes went directly to the last lines, which politely warned that the three months Zarubin had given him to prepare cover jobs for his agents had passed. Boris, emboldened by the success of Tales of Manhattan, burned the letter in his trash can. Zarubin complained to Moscow that they'd been far too lenient with Boris, but Beria's belief in Boris was absolute. Zarubin, despite Boris's less-than-cooperative ways, or perhaps because of them, was ordered to set in motion Mendel's permanent trip to America. Boris soon received a cable from the State Department with some unexpected news: His father was on his way!

The eighty-two-year-old Mendel arrived in Seattle on January 20, 1943. Boris managed to book a flight up the coast the next day, which was not easy to do, given the military's wartime requisitioning of much of the aviation industry. He rejoiced to see his father, who was exhausted from the six-week journey that had taken him by train to Vladivostok and by steamer across the U-boat-infested Pacific, but he was nonetheless jubilant to be reunited with his son.

The joy didn't last. Back in Los Angeles, Boris settled his father into North Beverly Drive, but Mendel, who saw Tales of Manhattan and wasn't impressed, didn't approve of Boris's career and just didn't feel at home in America, yet he wouldn't talk about what things were like back in the old country. Zarubin showed up in February to see how things were working out. Mendel, who understood better than Boris that Soviet agents didn't pull off miracles for nothing in return, merely downed a glass of vodka and returned to his room. Zarubin didn't mind. He spent the evening with

Boris, finishing the bottle, and now that they'd given Boris what he wanted, figuring out what Boris would do in return.

During lunch the next day at Perino's, the most elegant restaurant in Hollywood, Zarubin had some new ideas. Perhaps Boris could put agents on the payroll of the sheet music and music publishing subsidiary of Boris Morros Productions that he had set up in a suite of offices at the corner of Sunset and Vine? Boris had started the music publishing company as a vanity project for his son, Dick, who had gone from being a spoiled, lazy teenager who barely made it out of high school to a chronically under-achieving adult. He didn't like Zarubin's idea, not only because it would draw Dick into Boris's dealings with Moscow but because the business was too small to take on extra employees.

But Boris was having a hard time concentrating, because the fellow in the next booth seemed to be working very hard to show that he wasn't listening to their conversation. When Boris looked the man's way, the man stared straight back, and at one point he even winked at Boris.

Struggling to focus on Zarubin's proposal, Boris hinted that the only way it could happen was if they could attract the right investors. Zarubin could hardly believe his ears. Was Boris offering to help only if Moscow funded the venture?

When Zarubin returned to Los Angeles in May, he had a new proposal for Boris: Moscow was interested in investing in the publishing subsidiary of Boris Morros Productions if it could provide cover for a whole new generation of spies that Moscow was preparing to send to the United States. Boris, who was at the moment searching for financial backing for *The Waltz King*, an operetta about the composer Johann Strauss Jr., was delighted at the timing of Zarubin's offer. But then Zarubin revealed that he knew exactly how much of an investment Boris was looking for. Zarubin might have gotten those figures from the pages of *Film Daily*, but he had also somehow found out how much money Boris had in the bank, to the penny, and that was deeply troubling. Either someone had been reading Boris's mail and going through his garbage, or Zarubin had a source at Boris's bank.

American troops had landed in North Africa earlier in 1943 and by the summer were making their bloody way north, through Italy and eventually to the heart of the Nazi empire. All of America was watching, except, it seems, for Boris, who was focused on business. He travelled to New York in August to look for financing for *The Waltz King* and a variety of other projects. He was settling into his room at the Sherry-Netherland when Zarubin called from the lobby. Boris hadn't bothered to notify Zarubin via a "love letter" to let him know he was travelling east. It hardly seemed necessary anymore, now that Boris knew Zarubin had him followed. This time, things went differently. When Zarubin entered the room, he signalled to Boris not to say anything. He then went about methodically inspecting the room for, as he indicated to Boris, hidden FBI microphones inside lampshades, under the telephone, inside the light switches, and in the closets and bathrooms. Satisfied that they could speak freely, Zarubin gave Boris the details for a rendezvous the next evening at Leah Melament's apartment.

When Boris arrived at the apartment, he was surprised to find that no one answered the doorbell and the door was unlocked. He went inside and waited. There was plenty of time to think, and his thoughts were not pleasant. How did Zarubin know how much Boris had in the bank and how much he needed? How did Zarubin know exactly when and where he would be travelling? Which of his acquaintances—his mailman, his garbageman, a bank teller, a bellboy, one of his employees, maybe even his own wife—was betraying him? Why was Zarubin suddenly being so careful about the possibility that the FBI might be recording them?

Eventually the door opened and in walked Zarubin's wife. Boris asked where her husband was, but she only gestured for him to follow her into the elevator and down to Broadway, where they stopped in front of the Beacon Theatre. All of a sudden, Zarubin appeared, with stunning news: He had had found a backer for the music publishing company that would provide cover for his agents. They were ready to do business.

CHAPTER ELEVEN
CHORD AND DISCORD, 1943—44

Four months after the meeting, on December 17, 1943, a call came from Zarubin summoning Boris to New York to meet the mysterious investor who was willing to put $200,000 into his publishing company, secretly bankrolling what was intended to become the most extensive and ambitious cover operation in the history of Soviet foreign intelligence, one that would hopefully protect Soviet agents in the field from Alaska to Argentina.

Boris was tempted to hop on the next plane and meet his still-unnamed investor, but wartime aviation restrictions made that impossible, so he composed a romantic missive to Leah Melament, ending with the information that he would be arriving by train in Manhattan sometime between Christmas and the New Year. By now, Catherine was used to Boris's mysterious business trips, but this time was different: Boris would be off enjoying himself in New York for the holidays while she was looking after his father back in Beverly Hills. Boris and Catherine rarely fought, preferring to carry out a sort of marital Cold War. Now Catherine wanted to have it out, but Boris, believing he was on the verge of finally making espionage pay, refused to get distracted. He booked a train ticket to New York and left the next day.

Boris arrived on December 21, giving himself plenty of time to enjoy his favorite restaurants with old friends, see the latest Broadway show, and maybe even work on his film projects without worrying that Zarubin knew he was in town. He was annoyed but not surprised when the telephone in his usual suite at the Sherry-Netherland rang just minutes after the bell-hop set down his luggage. It was Zarubin, who was following Boris more closely than he had realized. Zarubin was all business on the telephone: "Walk over to Columbus Circle at eight tomorrow morning and start heading north on Broadway. I'll find you."

Boris spent a mostly sleepless night wondering about the change that had come over Zarubin. In addition to continuing to insist on the silly formalities of the love letters to Melament and checking hotel rooms in a fit of paranoia, Zarubin had been making his calls from telephone booths and arranging public meetings that would allow him to observe Boris approach from afar before making contact. Did Zarubin suspect Boris's loyalty? Or was he trying to protect both of them from the FBI?

Boris showed up at exactly eight the next morning at Broadway and West Fifty-Ninth Street and started walking north while the Wednesday morning rush-hour traffic headed downtown. He was approaching West Seventieth Street when he spotted Zarubin spotting him. Saving the traditional Russian greetings for later, they crossed Broadway and walked toward a parked car. A driver whom Zarubin greeted as Leonid invited them in, started the car, and headed over to the Henry Hudson Parkway. As they drove north, Zarubin said nothing, too busy checking the side mirror to see if they were being followed. It wasn't until they'd left the city limits and were cruising up the Merritt Parkway in Connecticut that Zarubin finally relaxed.

As they sped past the snowy, heavily wooded scenery, Zarubin began boasting about the people Boris was about to meet: "Famous people, rich people," Zarubin bragged. "Boris, in fact you already know them: The husband's politically connected, and the wife's father was one of Roosevelt's diplomats before the war." Boris searched his memory for such a couple but came up empty. In Westport, they got off the parkway and headed north to the sleepy village of Ridgefield. They stopped at the local Western Union office, where Zarubin got out and made a telephone call. After a few minutes, a car pulled up and out stepped a rangy man with bad skin, who was dressed in heavy boots and a leather jacket. "Here is our treasury, Boris, our millionaire, my good friend," Zarubin said. Boris didn't recognize the face, but the name was familiar. He had often read in the society columns about the notorious "Pink Tycoon," America's richest radical: Alfred K. Stern.

After the introductions were over, they piled into Stern's station wagon and drove another seven miles to his country home, a white-shingled, colonial mansion on Kitchawan Road, in the neighboring town of Lewisboro, New York. A pretty, petite woman with a familiar face was waiting in the front doorway. It was the writer and socialite Martha Dodd Stern, who greeted Boris enthusiastically. They'd met the year before, on the Twentieth Century Fox lot, when she was turning one of her books into a script and he was looking for a follow-up to *Tales of Manhattan*. Martha then demonstrated the kind of enthusiasm she was really capable of, grasping Zarubin around the waist and giving him a long, deep kiss, full on the mouth, in plain view of her husband. Boris had seen his share of Hollywood Babylon, and he'd heard the rumors about Martha's tendency to mix sex and politics, but he was nonetheless shocked. It was only when Alfred saw that the scene was making Boris uncomfortable that he nudged Zarubin and whispered: "Now, Vasya, that's enough." With these sorts of people, Boris thought, he might be out of his depth.

Zarubin wriggled out of Martha's grasp, laughed, and clapped Alfred on the back with brotherly affection. Then they all went inside and got down to business in the luxuriously appointed library. By lunchtime, they had struck a deal, one that Boris wasn't totally happy with. The Sterns would put not $200,000, but $130,000 into the Boris Morros Music Company. Boris decided not to object. Alfred, whose money had gained him entry into communist society but who longed for more active involvement in the cause, was promised an executive position in New York taking care of finances, while Boris would handle the content side from offices on the West Coast. Zarubin would get out of their way, limiting himself to dealing with the Soviet spies he would place in the firm. Posing as talent scouts and music publishing rights agents, they would fan out across the hemisphere gathering information for the Soviets. The operation would be called Chord.

It took a few weeks for Boris, Alfred, and Zarubin to put their plans on paper, which gave Boris time to look into his new business partners. He came away with mixed feelings. The Sterns were salon socialists blinded by a naive romance with communism that might make them easy to manipulate. But there was much about the couple that Boris didn't know, starting with the fact that Martha Dodd Stern was by 1943 already an accomplished Soviet agent.

Born in 1908 in Ashland, Virginia, Martha grew up in Chicago, where her father, William Dodd, was a politically liberal history professor at the University of Chicago. She was a spoiled socialite with brains, reading Nietzsche in finishing school, and she kept that independent streak for her whole life. Upon graduating from the University of Chicago, she got a job as assistant literary editor of the fervently anti-communist *Chicago Tribune*, the most conservative newspaper in the country. In 1933 she followed her father to Berlin, where Roosevelt had appointed him ambassador to Germany. There this tiny, lively, girlish beauty with a wild imagination took the Berlin social scene by storm. Intoxicated by the "constructive work" that Hitler was doing, she recalled: "I 'Heiled' as vigorously as any Nazi." Martha sailed through a whirlwind of state dinners, receptions, evenings on the town, and weekends in the country. She was invited to high teas and low-down drinking parties and was thrilled to discover that the Nazis were tapping her telephone lines and reading her mail. She and the head of the Gestapo, Rudolf Diels, became lovers, and she gladly took up his invitation to help the Nazi cause. By fall 1934, Martha was proving as promiscuous in politics as she was in her intimate life, on the receiving end of what was tastelessly being called "the first Nazi penetration of America." But Diels fell afoul of Hitler's unpredictable loyalties and was arrested and jailed. Disillusioned, Martha pledged herself to the communist future. She became close to members of the anti-Nazi "Red Orchestra" circle led by Mildred Harnack, and she struck up a passionate love affair with Boris Vinograd, the Soviet press attaché in Berlin, who had been instructed to use his considerable romantic powers to recruit Martha. Soon she was stealing documents from her father's office and reading his classified mail and his confidential cables. She shared all of it with Vinograd, but when he was recalled by Moscow and her father resigned his post, Martha settled in New York City where she began writing a memoir of her Berlin years. Spying for Moscow was now, however, her primary focus. She received orders from Moscow via its chief resident in New York City, Isaak Akhmerov, the same agent Zarubin had placed in Boris's offices back in 1942. Her main assignment, recruiting new agents, was just right for her, because her real value was her list of contacts. She also threw herself into left-wing politics, becoming a celebrity subversive who worked with a dozen communist and communist-front organizations, which Moscow did not appreciate. Moscow considered Martha, referred to in classified cables between New York and Moscow by the code name "Liza"—which was of course also the code name of Zarubin's wife, yet more evidence of how amateurish Soviet intelligence could be—to be "a gifted, clever, and educated woman," but Akhmerov was warned that she "requires constant control over her behavior." Akhmerov's superiors agreed: "She considers herself a Communist and claims to accept the party's program. In reality, Liza is a typical representative of American bohemia, a sexually decayed woman ready to sleep with any handsome man." She was a bit more selective than that, setting her sights on Alfred K. Stern.

Stern was born in 1897 into a Jewish family in Fargo, North Dakota, and attended Harvard before serving in World War I. Upon his return, Stern, an irresolute, lazy, and not very bright dandy, married into the Sears Roebuck fortune and unsuccessfully dabbled in banking and real estate, but he longed to do something more important, and eventually he found a place for himself in various New Deal projects in Chicago. After a divorce, he moved to New York, where he served as an advisor to New York's socialist congressman, Vito Marcantonio, though he still found plenty of time to throw his money away on various communist-front organizations. At one of them, he met and wooed Martha Dodd, whom he married in 1938.

Friends thought it must have been a marriage made in the Kremlin, and in a sense it was. Martha and Alfred were genuinely in love—with communism. Together, they turned their gorgeous apartment on Central Park West into a posh left-wing salon, attracting the likes of Paul Robeson, Lillian Hellman, and Henry Wallace. Their country house in Lewisboro, with its swimming pool and twenty-three acres of fields and forest, became a well-known gathering place for socialist writers, including Marc Blitzstein and Clifford Odets, as well as the entire Soviet diplomatic corps. The Kremlin had doubted the value of the unpredictable, indiscreet, excitable Martha, but their opinion changed once it became clear that she had married a ready source of cash.

Things had gotten off to a good start at the Sterns' country home on December 22, 1943, so Zarubin was more than optimistic when he met Boris for breakfast the next day at the Sherry-Netherland. They walked down Fifth Avenue to Alfred's office at 30 Rockefeller Plaza, one of the cathedrals of capitalism then known as the RCA Building, where the lawyers started hammering out the organizational details of the Boris Morros Music Corporation. On New Year's Eve, Zarubin and Alfred came to Boris's hotel room to sign the contracts. Zarubin, as usual fueled by vodka, regaled them all with lusty renditions of patriotic Russian tunes, only interrupting himself to chide Alfred for actually reading the documents. Then Alfred handed over two checks to Boris, one for $100,000 to cover expenses in California, and one for $30,000 for the New York offices. In return, Alfred became vice president of the company and received from Boris, the president of the company, two nonnegotiable promissory notes agreeing to a 40 percent return on Alfred's investment. As Boris later recalled, he took the train back to California convinced that he'd finally been able to reverse the terms of his relationship with Zarubin by effectively persuading Soviet foreign intelligence to invest in his newest venture: "I considered myself in the happy position of a man who feels quite safe while enjoying all the fun of playing a very dangerous game."

In California, Boris took advantage of Alfred's distance and inexperience and changed direction. Even before Zarubin set him up with

Stern, Boris knew that there wasn't much money to be made in his music publishing company, which was, after all, mostly a way to keep Dick out of trouble. The real money was in the recording industry. After the hard times in the 1930s, it had bounced back, in part due to the white-hot war economy. Then came the 1942 strike by the American Federation of Musicians, which would have caused a complete shutdown of the industry, had figures like Boris not set aside their qualms about using non-union labor in the recording studio. Zarubin and Stern might have accepted Boris using their money to make a fortune for himself as long as Zarubin was able to get cover for his agents. But these two committed communists wouldn't let Boris do it by strikebreaking. So Boris simply set up a subsidiary company called American Recording Artists, or ARA, located at 5655 Wilshire Boulevard, right in the middle of Miracle Mile, and decided not to tell Zarubin and Stern.

While he tutored Alfred long-distance about the ways of the music publishing world, Boris set about building a recording studio, buying presses to manufacture records, hiring an agent to distribute records to disc jockeys and jukeboxes, and recruiting talent. Duke Ellington and Benny Goodman were reluctant to tarnish their reputations by strikebreaking, but Boris was convinced that he could make a killing off lesser musicians with more flexible ethics, such as Bing Crosby's brother Bob, and the one-armed trumpeter Wingy Manone.

But Alfred wasn't satisfied with being a glorified accountant. He began writing lengthy daily letters to Boris, letters that far too often crossed the line from suggestion to criticism. Things came to a head when Alfred objected to Boris's intentions to buy the rights to the song "Chattanooga Choo-Choo," which had recently been a hit for Glenn Miller, Cab Calloway, and Carmen Miranda. Alfred felt that Boris should focus on more ideologically correct material, like Russian folk songs. Most infuriating of all for Boris, Alfred held the purse strings, and he wouldn't budge. As far as Boris was concerned, Alfred wasn't putting in enough money to keep the company afloat, much less turn a profit. Eventually, things got so uncomfortable that Boris and Alfred stopped talking to each other.

Zarubin spent most of his time managing Alfred and little time hiring spies and sending them out under the cover of talent scouts and rights agents. Zarubin's dream was going nowhere.

Boris knew that Zarubin's long silences were inevitably followed by angry, drunken confrontations, so Boris wasn't surprised when on March 20, 1944, his secretary walked into his office and told him that he had a call from his New York publishing company. Boris expected Zarubin, but it was Alfred on the line, telling him that Zarubin's wife needed to speak to him: The Zarubins were being recalled to Moscow and wanted one final meeting. Boris was to get on the next available plane to New York, at Moscow's expense.

Two days later, Boris said goodbye to Catherine, who was now used to seeing her husband suddenly disappear with the most meager of explanations, and flew to New York Municipal Airport. There, Alfred, with his sharp suit and hangdog look, was waiting at the arrivals gate. Alfred was the last person Boris wanted to see at this point, and the drive into Manhattan was tense. They managed to avoid talking about the company, and neither knew much about the fate of Zarubin, but Alfred was worried: "I don't know where we'll ever find another leader to take his place," he told Boris. For his part, Boris wondered what Alfred meant by "we."

As usual, Zarubin knew exactly where Boris was at all times. It was no surprise when a few minutes after Boris settled into his room at the Sherry-Netherland, there was a knock on the door. It was Zarubin, who had a strangely troubled look on his face for someone, as he now explained, being promoted to the rank of general. After the usual check of the room for listening devices, he explained that there were a few things he needed to wrap up in New York. He instructed Boris to show up that evening on Broadway, just below Columbus Circle, to meet his new handler. Then Zarubin was gone. He left Boris with much to think about. After almost a decade of searching for a way to escape the clutches of his Soviet spymasters, Boris had finally found a way to make espionage pay, in part through Zarubin's benign neglect. Could Boris count on the same from Zarubin's successor?

The nuclear secrets that Zarubin and his agents had illegally harvested from the various locations of the Manhattan Project hadn't yet had much of an impact on the course of the war. Indeed, the atomic weapons that Soviet scientists were developing with the help of that intelligence wouldn't be viable until after the war. It was conventional warfare that turned the tide against the Axis in 1943. Germany's industrial strongholds were reeling from Allied bombing, and Nazi forces were fleeing the Americans as they liberated Italy, starting in the south of the country, while the Red Army was forcing the Germans to retreat from territory they had occupied in the Ukraine. That meant Moscow's attention was anywhere but America. Indeed, there were voices in the Kremlin, very quiet ones, that questioned the wisdom of putting any resources at all into running agents in the United States. Boris was worried that Moscow would send a clueless amateur to replace Zarubin, but Stalin and Beria were looking past the end of the war and instead chose one of the most experienced and decorated spies in the history of the Soviet Union.

Later that evening, Zarubin's wife was waiting at the prearranged place. Together they walked up to Columbus Circle. Zarubin was standing under the awning of a Chinese restaurant called the Far East. Zarubin and Boris headed up the stairs and found themselves in a low, dark room. With the exception of a few businessmen silently eating in one corner and a balding, middle-aged man nursing a martini in the opposite corner, the place was empty.

When the man in the corner saw Boris and Zarubin enter the restaurant, he got up, walked over to the jukebox, put a coin in, and selected a song, to the annoyance of the businessmen sitting across the room. Though no one was within earshot, the man, whom Boris remembered as having the look of "a garment worker dressed up in his Sunday best," obviously wanted to make sure no one overheard their conversation. It started with the introductions. "This is my successor, Jack Soble," Zarubin told Boris. "From now on, he's your boss." Zarubin made sure that Soble knew exactly whom he was dealing with, or at least Boris had the sense that Zarubin was trying to impress Soble: "Our Comrade here is completely devoted to the motherland," Zarubin said, clapping Boris on the shoulder, "and is one of our most trusted and loyal agents."

Soble knew all about Boris, but Boris knew almost nothing about his mysterious new handler. In time he would learn that Soble was one of the most accomplished operatives in the history of Soviet intelligence, as quick-witted as he was untrustworthy, which Trotsky learned the hard way back in the early 1930s. Soble was a high-strung master of fictions whose weak spot was his attachment to his wife, Myra, and their son, Larry, whom they had named after Lavrenti Beria. He was an unlikely partner for Boris, who had so little experience in espionage and so little interest in politics, but together they would change the course of twentieth-century history.

Soble was born Abromas Sobolevicius in 1903 in Lithuania, where his Orthodox Jewish family owned a successful brush-and-bristle exporting firm. As a student in Leipzig in 1920, he joined the Communist Party along with his older brother, Ruvelis, who took the name Robert Soblen. Jack Soble worked for left-wing newspapers in Leipzig and then moved with Robert, who had studied medicine, to Moscow, where in 1927 they were recruited by Trotskyites at the Tenth Party Congress. After Trotsky was exiled in 1928, the brothers served as a liason between Trotsky and his clandestine supporters in the Soviet Union and supervised publication of his *Opposition Bulletin*, which led to their formal ejection from the party in 1928. But Stalin knew that having Soble on the inside was better than having him on the outside, and he knew that threatening his new wife, Myra, was all it would take to convince him.

Soble, together with his brother, started reporting to Moscow not only on the activities of Trotskyites in France and Germany but on the plans Trotsky himself was hatching from his exile in Turkey and then Denmark. That arrangement lasted only two years before Trotsky caught on, telling Soble, "You will one day regret what you are doing. I never want to see you again!" The brothers returned to Russia and formally rejoined Soviet intelligence, which eventually sent them to the United States. There, in addition to spying on Trotskyite, Zionist, and Jewish organizations in the United States and Canada, they were to work under Zarubin gathering classified information on politics, technology, and the military. The six agents that Soble supervised collected information about the personal lives of politicians, intellectuals, and celebrities, focusing especially on their sex lives and their drinking and drug habits, to be used for blackmail. Even more important, Soble's agents followed up on Zarubin's so-far success-ful efforts to infiltrate American naval ports, army bases, and air force facilities. Soble was in large part responsible for the extraordinary intel-ligence asymmetry between the United States and the Soviet Union in the late 1930s. While the United States had virtually no overseas intelligence presence, Soble's agents kept Moscow up to date on the size and nature of America's military preparedness and weapons capabilities. But Zarubin paid only Soble $150 per month, nowhere near enough even for a family living in a humble six-story apartment building in Washington Heights. Soble considered the cover job that Zarubin arranged to help make up the difference downright humiliating: He managed a tiny midtown snack bar, the S&V Cafeteria, along with his nephew, a Soviet agent named Ilya Wolston. Soble especially resented his cover job when he learned that in 1941 Zarubin had been given the most important assignment in the history of Soviet intelligence: to steal the recipe for America's atomic bomb.

Zarubin ordered a round of martinis for everyone, and while they waited, he explained that Boris would no longer use Leah Melament as a go-between. Instead, he would deal directly with Soble, who had a publicly listed telephone number, though Boris was to use his discretion when it came to calling because one never knew who might be listening. The waiter returned with the drinks and Zarubin fell silent until the waiter returned to the kitchen. Soble would still be reporting to Zarubin: "There will be no trouble, of course, Boris, but if there is, I assure you I will be able to reach you. I will know, Boris, whether you are or are not carrying out the original plans we agreed upon."

In the 1930s, Boris had heard rumors about the grisly fate of Soviet agents who failed to complete their assignments in America and had been recalled to Moscow and purged. In recent years, there had been whispers that Beria had given up whatever restraint he had ever exercised when it came to agents who disappointed him, putting hundreds of them to death without so much as an investigation, much less a trial. But Zarubin knew what Boris was thinking: "And, when I am in Russia, I will be able to reward your family with privileges—if you obey my dictates. And if not—I leave what will happen to them to your imagination."

Boris had plenty to think about on the flight back to California, starting with the threats to his family back in Russia. Never much of a family man when it came to Catherine and Dick, he harbored a deep affection for his Soviet relations, no doubt partly out of a sense of guilt. Here he was living the good life in America, while they were cold and starving back in Russia, if they were alive at all. Contact with them had been spotty before the war, and since then Boris had heard almost nothing, so upon returning home, he decided to press his father for information. The news wasn't good. Mendel had always refused to talk about the fate of the family back in Russia. Now he unburdened himself of a terrible secret, confirming what Zarubin had hinted at years ago: Aleksander and Isaak were both dead at the hands of the secret police, and Serge and Savely, both suspected of counterrevolutionary activity, were probably dead as well. Boris had no illusions about what the Soviets did to their own people, but what Mendel had to say was a shock he never recovered from. If Boris's attitude toward that thing Zarubin called "the motherland" had always been ambivalent, now he was filled with rage. Boris vowed to redouble his efforts to make the Soviets pay.

CHAPTER TWELVE
SPOOK'S BALL, 1944–45

Anonymous letters denouncing Soviet spies as double agents were common in Moscow in the 1940s. Few made it all the way to Stalin, but the one that his aides passed along to him in mid-August 1943 was different, because it was so unbelievable. Zarubin, one of the most decorated figures in the history of Soviet espionage, was at the top of the letter's long list of Soviet agents in America said to be betraying the revolution, accused of having a series of clandestine meetings with FBI agents and Nazi spies. Zarubin's wife, Elizabeth, whom Boris had met as "Helen" in Washington, DC, in 1942, and who was revered in the Soviet intelligence community as the "Red Joan of Arc" for her pure and innocent faith in the cause and her daring acts of teenage revolutionary heroism, was second on the list. The names that followed were mostly unfamiliar to Stalin and included a number of Soviet diplomats and trade officials across the United States and Canada. Then came a line that caught his attention: "Everything of value" that the Soviets working for the Nazis could uncover "passes on to the Germans through Boris MOROZ (HOLLYWOOD)."

The notion that some of the most important Soviet spies in America, in particular Moscow's man in Hollywood, were German agents sounded preposterous. Stalin ordered Lavrenti Beria to get to the bottom of it, and fast. It wasn't long before internal investigators found that at least some of the letter was worth taking seriously. Zarubin had been grossly indiscreet in his personal and professional life, drunkenly making scenes in public places and calling agents by their code names on the telephone, but he was certainly not a double agent working for the Nazis or the FBI. Nor was there any evidence that Zarubin's wife or any of the other figures mentioned, including Boris, were under suspicion. The question that Beria now had for his investigators was: Who had written the letter?

Very few people knew enough about Soviet intelligence's American operations to put together that list of names, and only someone very close to Zarubin would have been able to tail him on his supposed meetings with Nazis and G-Men. It had to be Zarubin's assistant, Vasily Mironov. In recent months Mironov had been telling anyone that would listen how much he hated Zarubin, whom he had worked for in 1940, when Zarubin was involved in the Katyn massacre in Poland. Stalin had his answer. Mironov was recalled, arrested, tried, and found to be mentally unbalanced; he was sentenced to five years in a combined mental institution and work camp. He was released in an effort to allow him to redeem himself, but then he was caught trying to pass on information to the Americans about Zarubin's role in the Katyn atrocity. The punishment was execution by firing squad.

The repercussions of Mironov's denunciation were far from over. Despite the preposterousness of the contents of Mironov's Anonymous Letter, as it came to be known, it led to yet another shakeup in Soviet foreign intelligence strategy. Stalin had no way of knowing who else had received a copy of the letter, but he wisely assumed the worst. The mess at the Soviet embassy in Washington, DC, and at the consulate in New York City convinced Stalin to reduce the size of the various networks and rings operating in America and to rein in the more worrisome agents. Among the latter was Zarubin, whose indiscretions could not be allowed to endanger his assignment to deliver the secrets of America's nuclear weapon to Stalin. Moscow instructed Zarubin to sideline his agents involved in political espionage and instead get close to the scientists working on the various Manhattan Project initiatives spread out across America, from upper Manhattan to Oak Ridge to Los Alamos to Berkeley. One of his most promising prospects was an agent named Margarita Konenkova, who was romantically involved with Albert Einstein, and who had been ordered by Zarubin to pry loose the secrets of the bomb from the man who had made it possible. Zarubin was also allowed to move forward in his ultimately successful efforts to place Julius Rosenberg into a spy ring run by Soviet Purchasing Commission official Semyon Semenov. And Zarubin continued to manage efforts by his wife, who was close friends with Robert Oppenheimer's wife, to have Oppenheimer secretly hand over classified reports from the Berkeley Radiation Laboratory and from Los Alamos.

Moscow's sudden reluctance to remain involved in anything but nuclear espionage left Martha and Alfred Stern in a difficult situation. Soble was ordered to regain some control over Martha and Alfred Stern, who were committed in theory but unpredictable in practice. It was an almost impossible task. When Soble first met them at their Central Park West apartment, Martha opened the door, and after hearing Soble's "parole," or coded greeting, of "I am Sam," gave him her usual comradely greeting. As Soble later remembered: "The beautiful stranger threw her arms around me in a tight embrace and gave me a long, passionate kiss." Soble, like so many committed communists who lived year after year in straitened circumstances in the midst of capitalist plenty, was seduced more by the Sterns' money than by Martha's affections.

Eventually, Soble became very close to Boris, though at first he wasn't very impressed by the chubby movie mogul in the loud suit whose stories didn't quite add up. When Soble sat down with Alfred to try to find out why Boris's music publishing company was burning through Alfred's money so quickly, they got nowhere. Rent on the offices was affordable, the only employee other than Boris and Dick was a secretary, and even Boris couldn't spend enough money on dining and travel to put the company in financial danger. Then an item in the newspaper clarified things: Boris had started a record company. The fact that he hadn't told them was bad enough, but Soble and Alfred were sure that ARA was a bad idea: They worried about the higher costs involved in making records and the ethics of supporting a business that capitalized on a legitimate strike by a union that included many Communist Party members and sympathizers. But Soble and Alfred trusted Zarubin, and Zarubin trusted Boris. Consulted by Soble, Zarubin wrote: "We can trust Frost; he won't take off with the money." So they let Boris go his own way, which was, to their distress, a very public way.

As usual, Boris was indifferent to the secrecy in which he was supposed to be operating. Soble was especially disturbed to hear rumors that Boris had recently attended a party at the Soviet consulate in New York. Soble also heard from other agents how Boris had been openly boasting to them about who was really funding his various businesses. Classified reports to and from Moscow around this time emphasized Boris's "indiscretion and imprudence," but no one dared to touch someone protected by Beria. Moscow did send Boris a message about the consequences of carelessness. After word spread that Boris's father, once so reticent, had been telling anyone who would listen about the deal that had brought him to the United States, Soble ordered Boris to put his father into an isolated rest home, where no one would pay attention to an old man raving about Russian spies.

Boris wasn't totally justified in blaming Alfred Stern for Chord's shortcomings. The record company hadn't made any money yet in large part because Boris was inexperienced in the business. He had thought he might save money by manufacturing his own records on secondhand presses, but the machines required extensive and costly repairs. He needed a new infusion of funds from the Sterns, so he repaired his relations as best he could with Alfred and made several trips east to consult with him. Boris enjoyed socializing with the stars at the Sterns' parties on Central Park West, but he always paid it for the next day when Stern would lecture him on how the Boris Morros Music Company and ARA could better serve "the cause." During these trips, Boris would also catch up with Soble, who had begun acting strangely. He openly criticized his superiors in Moscow, complaining that a legend like himself deserved better than being reduced to bossing around burger flippers in a humble Times Square snack bar. Hadn't he done heroic service fighting Trotskyites across Europe and America and beyond? Hadn't he run a Soviet agent inside the United Palestine Appeal? Hadn't he helped his own brother penetrate the

Office of Strategic Services? Hadn't he delivered information to Moscow about America's weapons-testing programs?

Eventually Boris realized it was the FBI that Soble was worried about, not Moscow. Boris was by now used to the habit Zarubin had of checking hotel rooms to make sure they weren't bugged—it was standard Soviet intelligence procedure—but Soble was obsessed, especially after news spread that an official at the Soviet Purchasing Commission, Victor Kravchenko, had defected and was secretly cooperating with the FBI. Before Soble would begin any conversation, he would check every side of every piece of furniture in the room and pat down all of the upholstery and curtains. According to Boris's later recollections, Soble would not only turn every light switch or appliance on and off, but he would take apart the wiring and follow it all the way to the wall sockets, which he also took apart and checked. He inspected the sink and the toilet and went through each closet inch by inch, shaking out every piece of Boris's clothing. Only then would he turn up the radio and begin the meeting, always in a whisper, always switching languages mid-sentence.

Boris wanted to write off Soble's concerns as paranoia, but he had his own reasons to worry. In the spring of 1944, while out driving with Dick, who was on leave from a stint in the military, Boris became convinced someone was tailing them. Boris had gotten used to being followed by one of Zarubin's underlings, and he assumed that Soble would continue the practice, but the tail had never before been so obvious—if in fact it was the Soviets. On a visit to Alfred and Martha Stern's apartment, Boris heard from the doorman that several men wearing the fedoras and baggy black suits that G-men favored had been hanging around the lobby and making inquiries about a "little fat fellow." Boris's fears that he had come to the FBI's attention became so acute that he chose to miss a July 1944 rendezvous with Soble in New York because he was convinced that agents were following him.

By the summer of 1944, Allied soldiers were making their way across Normandy and southern France on their way to Paris, British bombers were targeting western and central Germany, and the Red Army was retaking Lithuania and Poland and heading toward eastern Germany. But the fact that the United States and the Soviet Union were so strongly united in their battle against fascism did little to ease Boris's mind about the dangers of being exposed as a Soviet spy. He was too deep into Chord to back out, even though the business was causing nothing but trouble for everyone involved. No one involved had seen any profits, nor had the business served as cover for a new generation of Soviet agents as Zarubin had hoped.

Alfred Stern had the patience and confidence of many people born into money, and he shrugged off Boris's and Soble's concerns about the FBI. But now he was bursting with frustration. Boris was rapidly going through Alfred's investment, throwing away money on record presses that were supposed to save expenses and paying his good-for-nothing son $200 per week as vice president of the publishing company. Boris was even making noises about another round of financing. So in August 1944, Alfred convinced Soble that it was time to make a visit to Los Angeles to see Boris in action. They were not happy about what they discovered.

The ARA recording studio was a shabby warren of dank, tiny rooms, while Boris had set up himself and his son in a grand suite of offices. Soble described it as "a big, showy, elaborate place, in keeping with his flamboyant personality and expensive tastes." Boris's employees were incompetent, the administration was amateurish and chaotic, and the records were so poorly manufactured that many of them broke even before they left the pressing plant—not that Boris noticed. He was too busy buying clothing and treating himself and his friends at Hollywood's fanciest restaurants and nightclubs. When Alfred began lecturing Boris as to the proper way to run the business, Boris responded with uncharacteristic rage, complaining that if Alfred and Soble had given him what he originally wanted, he would have been able to run the business correctly. It wasn't Boris who had been burning through Alfred's money irresponsibly but Alfred himself, who as the New York head of the music publishing company did little more than take his friends to expensive lunches, according to Boris. As it was, Boris explained, only $6,500 remained of the initial investment Alfred had put into the West Coast branch, and without another $150,000 from Stern they might lose everything. Alfred was flabbergasted at Boris's chutzpah, his apparent lack of commitment to the cause, and his incompetence in running the business. He flew home, disappointed and dejected.

Soble thought that Martha might succeed where he and Alfred had failed. Martha was no fan of Boris, but Soble convinced her to try to get Boris and her husband to come to terms, if for no other reason than the cause for which they all worked. Even Martha saw the point: The struggle against fascism would soon be won, and the Soviet Union could not afford to have any infighting in the final battle against capitalism that was supposedly coming. Soble brought Boris to New York, and over a long evening with Alfred and Martha at Central Park's luxurious Tavern on the Green restaurant, he tried to make peace among his three agents and to make sense of Boris's business plans. The meeting was a failure on both accounts. Alfred was willing to do anything Martha told him to do, even if it meant making nice with Boris, but Boris refused to admit that he needed to start trusting Alfred's business sense. It was money Boris needed, not advice.

Soble realized that his initial sense that Zarubin had placed too much confidence in Boris might have been correct. The visit to California had revealed that Boris had registered one of the record plants not in the name of the company but in his own name, which hardly inspired confidence in his honesty. He wouldn't take advice, he continually made empty promises, and he was more indiscreet than ever, telling all of Hollywood about how he knew Beria and Soviet foreign minister Vyacheslav Molotov personally. Even if Boris's personal spending could be reined in, he didn't seem to understand the bigger picture. As Soble, writing under his code name "Czech," reported to Moscow: "Boris, having fallen for music, almost forgot about the main idea. Music is only a means of fulfilling our central goal, that is penetration by providing cover identities to Soviet operations into a number of countries neighboring the U.S." Soble admitted to his superiors that this "bizarre situation" was "a big mistake." Since Chord had accomplished virtually nothing in terms of providing cover for Soviet agents and was even beginning to alienate Stern, whose bank account was so important to Moscow's efforts in America, Soble began looking for a way to cut his losses.

Soble made some harsh recommendations. He told Moscow that Boris should be relieved of all administrative tasks and be confined to musical decisions, and that any further investments would have to come from Boris's own pocket or from company profits. If Boris didn't agree to those terms, the only solution, Soble recommended, was to shut down the businesses and try to recoup Alfred's investment from Boris over time. Instead of responding to Soble right away, Moscow reached out to Zarubin, who told them that as far as he knew, Boris and Alfred had patched things up and that Chord would be ready to provide cover within a few months, or even sooner if necessary. Most important, Zarubin told Beria, Soble and Alfred needed to remember that Boris was an invaluable element of the Soviet global intelligence network, and not only by virtue of his prominence and apparent wealth: "You have to trust B———s completely; he is honest and loyal." But it's impossible to escape the conclusion that whatever their doubts, Zarubin, Soble, and the Sterns loved being close to a Hollywood celebrity, even one who wasn't quite trustworthy.

Ever since Zarubin's return to Moscow in August 1944—with $5,000 that Stern had given him, written off as a record company expense—his authority had grown enormously. Crucially, Zarubin also carried two thousand pounds of classified documents relating to the atom bomb that he had gathered from his sources at the various laboratories, research centers, and factories involved with building the world's first nuclear weapon. Zarubin was awarded another Order of the Red Banner and promoted to commissar of state security, given the Order of Lenin and made a major general, and then promoted again to deputy chief of foreign intelligence. Zarubin's rise was good news for Boris, who had learned that Kremlin politics outweighed the complaints of field agents like Soble. And since Boris's film career seemed to be on hold for the foreseeable future, any help that Zarubin could offer to turn around Chord was important.

But Soviet intelligence also valued Stern, and they took it seriously when Alfred went over Soble's head and reached out to Moscow for help.

On November 15, 1944, at the urging of Martha, whose dislike of Boris had blossomed into distrust, Alfred composed a report, under the code name "Louis," that painted a dire portrait of the business. He maintained that his original investment had dwindled to nothing because of Boris's "poor business management and misguided artistic temperament." Even so, Alfred treated Beria's darling gingerly: "Of course relations between myself and my partner remain cordial and this criticism does not affect his devotion and political stability." Alfred was walking a fine line. Admitting to Moscow that the operation had failed reflected poorly on Alfred himself, not to mention on Zarubin, which is why he tried to avoid blame and focus on the future: "He knows that on the present operation basis I do not intend to put in any additional money," Alfred said of Boris. "I want to emphasize that money alone cannot solve his personal and other problems . . . I am convinced that unless a reorganization is carried out quickly we will not give what is expected of us. I want to reaffirm my desire to be helpful. My resources are sufficient for any solid constructive business but I don't intend to maintain silence when my resources, time, and efforts are being spent for nothing."

Stern would never make much of a spy, but he knew that the mere mention of his fortune would attract attention. Still, the timing was off. The very same December 27, 1944, cable in which the New York residence noted that "LOUIS is complaining about FROST and emphasized that unless prompt drastic measures of reorganization are taken the whole business is doomed to failure" also announced that Boris was involved in a game with much higher stakes: "FROST received a letter from SKRIB from ALASKA in which he says: 'Ivory is cheap. If you want I can get.' In FROST'S opinion this means that SKRIB is ready to work if we want."

"Skrib" was the code name of a Soviet agent named Clarence Hiskey, one of Zarubin's spies, who worked as a Manhattan Project physicist until he was fired on suspicion of espionage. Hiskey was then drafted into the army and stationed in Alaska. Zarubin, who was still involved in Soviet efforts to penetrate the Manhattan Project, seems to have realized that it wasn't possible for him to take up Hiskey's offer—"ivory" appeared to refer to documents from the Manhattan Project that Hiskey took with him to Alaska—but Boris could, so Zarubin apparently instructed Hiskey to reach out to Boris.

The timing of Boris's entry into the world of atomic espionage was unfortunate. Under normal circumstances, Moscow would have been pleased at Boris's sense of enterprise. But a Soviet agent, William Weisband, who had recently been placed in the US Army's Signal Intelligence Service, reported that American cryptographers working on a code-breaking project with the secret name "Venona" had made significant progress in deciphering secret Soviet cable traffic, including the message about Hiskey. It is unclear whether Boris completed the deal and passed the notes along to Zarubin before Hiskey's superiors, inspired by the deciphering of the December 27 message, renewed their suspicions and had his belongings searched. The fact that they found nothing incriminating might only have been a sign that Hiskey had already passed his notes on. There the trail goes cold.

Despite the initiative that Boris showed with Clarence Hiskey, Moscow decided to cut its losses with Chord. In early 1945, Moscow issued instructions to Soble: "Dissolve." Doing so wasn't going to be simple. Soble realized that shutting down the company would have meant leaving Alfred with a $130,000 debt and nothing to show for it, and Moscow wanted to keep Alfred happy. Soble began pressuring Boris to close up shop and find a way to repay Alfred. Boris resisted, in part because he knew that the $30,000 Alfred was to use for the New York office had suspiciously disappeared, having been spent on everything from tennis balls and fancy restaurants to vodka for every occasion. Boris now claimed to have put more than $60,000 of his own money into his joint ventures with the Soviets and objected to paying back Alfred on principle.

Unable to convince Boris any other way, Soble played his last card: "I'd hate to feel responsible for the extermination of your relatives in Russia. Wouldn't you?" That ploy no longer worked on Boris. His mother was dead, his father was safe in the United States, two of his brothers were dead at the hands of the secret police, and he quite reasonably presumed that two others had also been executed. Boris knew there wasn't much hope for anyone else in the Morros clan back in the old country.

So the Boris Morros Music Company and ARA not only stayed in business but actually made a go of it. With his secondhand presses finally functioning properly, Boris recorded and released dozens of records by second-string popular music talents who would work for cheap. The most successful of them was Eddie Cherkose and Jacques Press's "There's Nobody Home on the Range," which improbably became President Roosevelt's favorite tune, later recognized as one of the songs that helped win the war, as Boris liked to brag. In fact, the song was so popular that Boris built a new plant that could produce thirty thousand discs per day to meet demand, and the money started rolling in.

"There's Nobody's Home on the Range" subsidized jazz records by bigger names like Hoagy Carmichael, Peggy Lee, and Art Tatum, and in yet another stunning example of Boris's imprudence when it came to his espionage activities, he recorded Earl Hines and Wardell Gray performing Gray's composition "Spook's Ball." The phrase nominally referred to a Halloween party, but Soble wasn't happy to see Boris releasing a record whose title was a synonym for a gathering of spies, even if it made money. *Downbeat* magazine's judgment that ARA was "rapidly becoming an important factor in the industry" emboldened Boris even further. He planned to open two new pressing plants on the East Coast and acquired an experimental factory in Michigan that made discs from unbreakable plastic instead of fragile shellac, a move that seemed risky at the time but turned out to have been prophetic. He branched out into hillbilly music and announced a deal to release an album of religious music by the Vatican Choir, with liner notes by New York archbishop Francis Cardinal Spellman. ARA products were now being exported to Canada, South America, Australia, and England. Boris even helped popularize the genre of the "original soundtrack recording" when he released the Academy Award–winning soundtrack to Alfred Hitchcock's *Spellbound* by Miklós Rózsa.

By April 1945, Boris finally had enough money in the bank to start closing the chapter on his relationship with Alfred. The $100,000 that Boris paid Alfred back over the next three months was perhaps the most important financial transaction of his life. Moscow had been hearing less-than-flattering things about Boris for years from Alfred and Soble, but money spoke louder than words. The fact that Boris was willing to return such a huge sum meant not only that he hadn't been corrupted by capitalism but that he could finally and truly be trusted. Even better, he was now both famous and rich, a combination Moscow couldn't resist.

Martha Stern, who had always been more skeptical about Boris than her husband was, didn't care how much money Boris paid back: He simply wasn't to be trusted. When she heard rumors about Boris being followed by the FBI, she didn't buy it. Far from being a target of the FBI, Martha claimed, Boris was probably working for them as a double agent. The thought had also crossed Soble's mind. Boris had more than once called and spoken quite openly on the phone about what Soble really did for a living. Boris had even mentioned Soble's real name, cover business, and home address. Was he really talking the whole time to the FBI?

In June 1945 Soble opened up to Moscow about his concerns that the FBI was following Boris and that they had identified him as a Soviet spy. He received an unequivocal response from Moscow: "Deactivate F., because any further contact between him and Cz is dangerous." It's not clear why the deactivation never happened. It wasn't only because Boris was seen by some in Moscow as less than fully trustworthy. According to Zarubin, Soble himself had been exhibiting erratic behavior that went far beyond checking hotel rooms. Despite the reports to Moscow critical of the members of his ring, Soble had let his affection for Boris and the Sterns get in the way of his better judgment when it came to Chord, according to Zarubin.

While Boris wasn't deactivated, his adventure in the record business was over. After he paid back Alfred, he found he had enough money to get back into making movies. The recording ban came to end in 1944, and the major record companies were back in business. ARA would no longer be in a position to compete, so Boris shut down the recording studios, closed the pressing plants, and sold the company. Boris never saw Martha or Alfred Stern again, but he wasn't quite finished with his American Mata Hari and her Pink Tycoon.

CHAPTER THIRTEEN
GETTING TO CARNEGIE HALL, 1945–47

Before the war and well into the 1940s, the Soviets had focused on political espionage, with a shocking degree of success. Despite the current sense of tragic overreach by the House Committee on Un-American Activities and Senator Joseph McCarthy's misguided crusade against communists, hundreds of Soviet agents were in fact operating in the United States, compared to a handful of American agents in the Soviet Union. Indeed, no government in modern history was as thoroughly penetrated by foreign spies as the United States was at mid-century. In addition to counting on Samuel Dickstein in Congress, Soviet spies infiltrated virtually every federal agency, including the State Department, the Department of Justice, the War Department, the Office of Special Services, the Commerce Department, and the Treasury Department. Even "The Temple," as the White House was called in secret cables, had been penetrated: The president's senior administrative assistant, Lauchlin Currie, was a Soviet agent, and the same charge has been made, though not definitively proven, about one of Roosevelt's top advisors, Harry Hopkins, who actually lived in the White House throughout the war. Then of course there was the matter of Soviet penetration of American interests abroad—the US embassy in Moscow, for example, contained 120 hidden Soviet microphones.

As a result, Stalin apparently knew everything Roosevelt knew when they met to discuss military strategy in Tehran in 1943—Zarubin's daughter was at his side as a translator there and also at Yalta in 1945 and Potsdam a few months later. But in 1941 when Stalin and Beria learned from their agents that America was building a nuclear bomb that would dwarf the destructive power of conventional weapons, they realized that the coming conflict with the nation that the Soviet would call "the main adversary" would require their spies to stop worrying so much about ideology and start worrying about science, to put the obsession with Trotskyites behind them and focus on the technology of mass destruction. Zarubin had led the way, successfully supervising the Soviet infiltration of America's nuclear program, not simply the infamous Rosenberg circle but dozens of spies at virtually every laboratory and factory where the bomb was being developed, including Los Alamos, which the Soviets infiltrated just weeks after it opened, eventually planting twelve agents there. Among them was Ethel Rosenberg's brother, David Greenglass. When he wasn't boring his coworkers silly with speeches about the superiority and inevitability of communism, Greenglass was stealing classified documents that were often left out in the open. As a result, Stalin knew about America's atom bomb before Vice President Truman did. Boris had also played his part in Beria's plan to start focusing on science and technology, setting up Chord to provide cover for Zarubin's nuclear spies and even reaching out, it seems, to bring in Clarence Hiskey's intelligence from the Manhattan Project.

Despite the setbacks represented by the Kravchenko defection and the intelligence provided to the Americans by William Weisband, as well as the halt in research when the war required that Stalin's scientists invest their time in less speculative projects, Moscow was well on its way to catching up with America's nuclear weapons program by the end of the war in August 1945. The problems with generating sufficient uranium were all but solved, and the Soviets turned their attentions toward harnessing the power of a nuclear chain reaction and actually constructing their own version of America's "superweapon."

But Soviet plans for winning the peace were dealt a serious blow just a month later, when a cipher clerk in the Office of the Military Attaché in Ottawa, Igor Gouzenko, defected. Gouzenko was hardly a central figure in Stalin's intelligence strategy, and Ottawa wasn't exactly the roiling center of Soviet spycraft. But Moscow couldn't know what kind of damage

Gouzenko's desertion might do; indeed, it soon led to eighteen criminal convictions in Canada. Then in November 1945 came an even more damaging blow: One of the most crucial figures in the Soviet Union's American intelligence operations, Elizabeth Bentley, defected. Known to Moscow as "Teacher's Pet" and eventually known to the tabloids as the "Blonde Spy Queen," Bentley belonged to the American League Against War and Fascism, a communist front that put her into contact with two major Soviet spy rings. She was able to give the FBI the names of more than eighty Soviet spies operating on American soil, among them operatives in the White House; the Departments of Justice, Treasury, and Agriculture; the War Production Board; the OSS; the Foreign Economic Administration; and the Senate Committee on Military Affairs. The FBI could not yet corroborate the information that Gouzenko and Bentley had provided, much less make it public, but Moscow didn't know that and again assumed the worst, folding the NKGB into the Ministry for State Security, or the MGB, which essentially put foreign intelligence under the control of the Soviet secret police. Once again Soviet spies in America were ordered to lay low.

Lying low was not Boris's specialty, despite plenty of practice, and he was determined to find a way to make Moscow pay, literally and figuratively, though he was only gradually realizing how dangerous that would be. What made Boris Morros an unlikely Soviet spy was ironically what allowed him to survive that dangerous profession: He was ideologically uncommitted, constitutionally indiscreet, addicted to fame and money, and oblivious to the distinction between truth and fiction. Still, as World War II drew to a close, Soble wondered if Beria would finally retire Boris, whose adventure in the record business had been so problematic from Moscow's perspective. Boris made plenty of money, but the original goal of blanketing the hemisphere with agents covered by a tiny Southern California music publishing house and record company was never accomplished.

Soble had become as close to Boris as anyone ever had, or so he thought. In truth, their friendship was less a matter of socializing than of a shared sense of existential precariousness. So Soble was both discouraged and encouraged to hear that Beria had big plans for Boris, who had the one quality that Moscow demanded above all else: the ability to adapt and improvise. As the Soviet intelligence community faced the postwar future, it became clear that Boris, who could buy his way into almost any deal and talk his way out of almost any situation, would be essential to their strategy. Though Boris had once longed for the day when he no longer mattered in Moscow, he was becoming more and more determined to remain in play as a spy, partly to avenge his brothers and partly out of greed.

A December 1945 memo to Moscow from Soble noted that Boris was giving up the record business and returning to the film business, which had been quite successful for him: "If we want to work with him, he is ready to set up together with us a movie firm." Boris had apparently named his price: $200,000. Soble thought it could be done for half that, and he cautiously endorsed Boris's notion that a film company would provide excellent cover for agents throughout the world and even make money for the MGB. Soble was less pleased to note a new, assertive tone in Boris, who had been emboldened, not chastened by the Chord experience. Boris insisted on an answer from Moscow within a month: "If there is no answer by the middle of January, he will consider himself free," Soble wrote. Soble got no answer to his proposal, perhaps because Moscow knew that Boris's freedom wasn't for him to determine.

The only thing better than being funded by Moscow was being left alone by Moscow, so Boris was at once disappointed and relieved when there was no response. Using his old ARA offices, Boris teamed up with his partner from *The Flying Deuces*, William LeBaron, and remembered one of his old ideas whose time had come: a drama that would star Carnegie Hall itself, to be made by the two new independent film companies he established with LeBaron, Federal Films and Liberty Pictures.

As a classical musician, Boris had wanted to get to Carnegie Hall since childhood, and if practice wouldn't take him there, the movies now would. It was back in 1942 when Boris first had the idea of a picture that would tell the story of the then fifty-year-old legendary concert hall at Seventh Avenue and West Fifty-Seventh Street in Manhattan, "from Beethoven to Benny Goodman," as he told the syndicated columnist Virginia

MacPherson. His original plan was to offer a history of the hall from the perspective of a subscriber who starts out unable to afford anything but the cheap seats but who eventually ends up with his own box. If that wouldn't entail enough drama, there would be gimmicks, as there always were with Boris. Boris arranged to televise Francis Cardinal Spellman blessing the production and Mayor William O'Dwyer directing the first scene. The film would also be shot in Technicolor and stereo sound, which were both new at the time. Of course, the biggest draw was Carnegie Hall itself. Boris was able to rent out the building for six weeks in the summer of 1946 in return for 1 percent of the gross receipts. United Artists, which had underestimated Boris back in 1941 and lost *Tales of Manhattan* to Paramount, signed on early as the distributor.

When it came to the talent, Boris aimed high. At first he announced that Benny Goodman, Arturo Toscanini, Duke Ellington, Vladimir Horowitz, the Boston Symphony Orchestra, and the Vatican Choir had all committed to appearing. As summer approached, the cast somehow changed, for the better. Now Boris had signed Jascha Heifetz, Arthur Rubinstein, Vladimir Shostakovich, Sergei Prokofiev, Walter Damrosch, Jan Peerce, Fritz Reiner, and Lily Pons, with the New York Philharmonic directed by the triumvirate of Artur Rodziński, Bruno Walter, and Leopold Stokowski. Boris was also able to sign his old student from St. Petersburg, Gregor Piatigorsky. LeBaron, who had seen Boris impress many people over the years with such connections, was dubious and decided to make Boris prove he knew Piatigorsky when he came to play at the Hollywood Bowl. Sitting with Catherine and Dick in the audience, LeBaron good-naturedly dared Boris to take them backstage and introduce them all to the famously brooding cellist. Boris first sent Dick to the greenroom to scout out the situation. Dick came back with an all-clear sign, and minutes later Piatigorsky greeted Boris warmly in the Russian style, with kisses and bear hugs.

Once something worked for Boris, he stuck with it. Just as with *The Flying Deuces*, *Second Chorus*, and *Tales of Manhattan*, he kept costs down by getting his actors to work cheap, paying them the same rate that they would charge for performing at a regular concert. That would never have been possible in Hollywood, where the actors unions were powerful. As luck would have it, Hollywood's editors, developers, and printers had gone on strike, so Boris decided not only to shoot the film in New York but to do post-production there too.

Everything fell into place at the last minute, including the script, which now told the story of an Irish maid who works at Carnegie Hall for four decades and meets the greatest musicians in the world. Her son is a talented composer and pianist, but her dreams of seeing him perform at Carnegie Hall are frustrated because his love is for jazz music. Mother and son are eventually reunited at the premiere of his trumpet concerto, a classical piece played by the jazz trumpeter Harry James. The film would be a combination of *Stella Dallas*, *Meet Me in St. Louis*, and *A Song to Remember*, Boris told *Film Daily*; but this tale of the power of music to overcome social and economic barriers sounds more like *The Jazz Singer*, or perhaps even the Boris Morros story, the first part of it anyway.

Putting together "the most majestic array of musical talent ever assembled for one picture," as the *New York Post* wrote, wasn't easy. For the overture, Boris commissioned the avant-garde composer Edgard Varèse, whom he had known in Hollywood back in the 1930s, to write a composition based on the idea of an orchestra tuning up. Boris was hoping for something humorous, but the famously dour Varèse came up with a hermetic, experimental work that Boris felt was simply out of character with the rest of the film. After Boris took all of fifteen minutes to radically rework the piece, a furious Varèse disassociated himself from the work.

It wasn't the only time in the filming of *Carnegie Hall* that Boris's lowbrow tastes led to trouble. Boris convinced his old pupil Piatigorsky to join the cast by promising that the renowned cellist could play "anything [he] wish[ed], providing it's not over two minutes long." Piatigorsky showed up on time and made an audio recording of Saint-Saëns's "The Swan," one of the most clichéd compositions in the entire classical repertoire, with a harp accompaniment. But when Piatigorsky came back the next day to film the scene, Boris wanted him to pretend to perform while six ornately gowned Hollywood starlets amateurishly pantomimed the music. When the virtuoso, mortified at such degradation of his art, objected, Boris answered: "I need them for the background."

Carnegie Hall consumed Boris's days and nights in late 1946 and early 1947. Even Dick's marriage in March 1947 was turned into a promotional event for the film, with the opera singers Jan Peerce and Richard Tucker performing for an audience dominated by cast members. Ads pronouncing the film to be THE GREATEST MUSIC PICTURE OF ALL TIMES and THE MIGHTIEST MUSIC EVENT THE SCREEN HAS EVER KNOWN! began appearing in April, but then Boris learned that the directors of Carnegie Hall wouldn't let him hold his premiere there. Never one to give up, Boris arranged to have a "double premiere" on May 4, 1947, to benefit the New York Philharmonic Pension Fund and the New York Foundling Hospital at the Winter Garden and the Park Avenue Theatre. Piatigorsky walked out in disgust after seeing his own scene, and some critics remarked on the perfunctory plot and bewildering variety of musical performances, which seemed more like a vaudeville show than a Hollywood film.

Carnegie Hall attracted controversy over Boris's failure to cast a single black figure, even in the jazz scenes. More worrisome was the sense some observers had that *Carnegie Hall* showed Boris's politics to be somewhat less than fully red, white, and blue. His casting of Marsha Hunt in the lead raised eyebrows—as if he hadn't learned his lesson from casting Paul Robeson in *Tales of Manhattan*. Hunt was blacklisted two years later, but she was already politically tainted because of her association with a variety of communist organizations. And though Boris could usually count on the *New York Post* columnist Earl Wilson for good publicity, a November 23, 1946, plug went a bit too far and in the wrong direction: "*Carnegie Hall* gave practically everybody in New York a day's work. Hurray for Stalin." After cuddling up to the Soviet Union in films like *Mission to Moscow* (1943) and *Song of Russia* (1944), Hollywood was now turning, like the rest of the country, against communism, so that kind of publicity could be bad for business.

But the initial responses to Boris's latest project were heartening. *Carnegie Hall* filled the Winter Garden and the Park Avenue Theatre for seven weeks before losing momentum. By then the film was showing not only across America but in London, Paris, Stockholm, Buenos Aires, and Manila.

Boris finally returned to California from a publicity tour in early summer 1947, feeling flush with success—despite some disappointing reviews, ticket sales were strong. That feeling turned to dread after both Catherine and Dick complained that they had suspected someone was following them. Two suspiciously well-groomed characters in cheap suits who were parked in front their home had followed Dick when he left in his car, and he'd been unable to shake them. Boris told Dick and Catherine not to worry, that Hollywood was filled with stalkers. Boris didn't tell them that he also had an uncanny feeling that he was being followed.

It was hard to know when to trust those feelings, but Boris had come to learn that when it came to the world of espionage, when there was any doubt, there was no doubt. But it wasn't only the FBI that seemed to be paying attention. Indeed, after a year and a half of silence, Soble had again reached out to Boris. As committed as Soble was to the cause, he had long felt unappreciated by the Soviet intelligence operations. One of their longest-serving and most devoted foreign agents, Soble could barely support his family, and he lived in fear of a knock on the door from the FBI. As a result, one of Soble's obsessions was becoming a United States citizen. He had applied years before in the hope that it would make it easier for him to work to supplement his spy's wages. In a December 1946 conversation with Boris, Soble indicated that he was apparently on the verge of getting his American passport, which he suggested would allow him to leave behind the life of a spy for good. But in June 1947, when Soble finally became an American citizen, he was summoned to Moscow. Ironically, his American passport made him an even more valuable intelligence asset than before. And as Soble rose in the ranks, he intended to take Boris with him. Soble's good fortune was a disaster for Boris, who was euphoric over the success of *Carnegie Hall* and looking forward to taking on new projects without worrying about Moscow. Now he realized that he would never be able to break away on his own. Unless something changed, he would spend the rest of his life looking over his shoulder, wondering who was intercepting his mail and listening to his telephone conversations. He would never be free of the fear that the car behind him was following him. He would never know for sure whether a new friend was in fact an old enemy.

Throughout his career as a Soviet agent, Boris had often thought about going to the FBI. He always rejected the idea, at first because of concerns about what would happen to his family back in the Soviet Union, and then because he didn't want to jeopardize relations with his best investors. Now that neither was an issue—there was little family back in the USSR, and his film career seemed to be self-sustaining—turning himself in seemed like a better and better idea, especially because the FBI seemed to be on his tail.

On the morning of July 14, 1947—Bastille Day, he noticed, hoping that it would mark his own declaration of *liberté*—Boris asked his secretary for a telephone book. He found the number for the local FBI offices, picked up the telephone, and then put it back down. All of the risks Boris Morros had taken to make a better life for himself had paid off. He had a house in Beverly Hills, a cook and a driver, and a successful career in America's dream factory, with the fame and bank account to match.

Had his luck finally run out? He mopped his bald dome, looked at the dial, and wondered: An American jail was surely better than the Soviet gulag, or an unmarked grave. Finally, he picked the phone back up, dialed the number, and announced: "I am Boris Morros, the Hollywood film producer. I would very much like to talk to some important person in your organization."

PART II

CHAPTER FOURTEEN
DOUBLE OR NOTHING: 1947

"Come right down, Mr. Morros," the voice on the telephone said. Boris called his driver, who took him downtown to the FBI's Los Angeles bureau, which was located in a nondescript office building. Two young, clean-cut men met Boris in the lobby.

"We have been waiting for you a long time, Boris," one of them said. The other agreed: "Yes, we have been waiting for you a long time. But it's not too late."

They sat Boris down and told him to start talking. It took a full week to tell the whole story to the FBI, from his childhood in Bobruisk to his time at the St. Petersburg Conservatory, from his days making music at the court of the last tsar to his flight to Baku and then Istanbul, one step ahead of the Bolsheviks, and from there to America, where he scaled the heights of the entertainment world, from Times Square's vaudeville era to the Golden Age of Hollywood. It was a story that had never failed to captivate friends, colleagues, and journalists. But the stony-faced agents sitting across the table from him in their charmless, run-down offices were more interested in the parallel life that Boris had been living for more than a decade. In fact, Boris told them little they didn't already know. As Boris and his Soviet counterparts had long suspected, the FBI had been following him for years, tailing his car, staking out his home, photographing his rendezvous, and recording his conversations.

According to the FBI's own declassified records, Boris first came to the attention of the FBI in the mid-1930s, not long after the Kremlin identified him as a potential recruit. The bureau was actually more interested in Zarubin, the way they were interested in all of the Soviets who worked in America in their embassies and consulates, or in various Soviet trade organizations. If Zarubin was worth watching, the reasoning went, so was anyone who met with him. It wasn't until Zarubin had returned from Berlin that Boris became interesting to the bureau. The diner who winked at Boris when he met with Zarubin at Perino's Restaurant in Hollywood in February 1943 was an FBI agent. The two men lunching at the Far East Chinese restaurant near Columbus Circle in March 1944 when he met Jack Soble were American agents. And in October 1944, J. Edgar Hoover's men were so sloppy in trying to cover up their break-in and theft of papers—which prominently featured Boris's name—from Alfred Stern's Rockefeller Center offices that Alfred immediately suspected the FBI. Boris's hunch was also correct that those young men in crew cuts and bad suits who had asked Alfred's doorman on Central Park West about "the little fat fellow" were federal agents. The strangers who had waited outside Boris's home in Beverly Hills and then followed Dick were from the FBI, and the men who tailed Boris and Dick's car were G-men, as were all of the trench-coated figures who seemed to be pretending not to follow Boris in California and New York during this period. But it wasn't until after the war that the FBI finally figured out that Zarubin was the same the "Edward Herbert" who worked for Boris in Berlin as a Paramount talent scout back in the 1930s, and the discovery immediately made Boris a priority. On a report on Boris's activities that Hoover received just three weeks before Boris's defection in 1947, Hoover scribbled: "How many other like situations exist in our files is what concerns me." Of course, there was only one Boris Morros.

Despite the FBI's familiarity with Boris's movements and meetings, it didn't become clear to the FBI that Boris was somehow connected to Soviet efforts to infiltrate America's nuclear weapons program until after Zarubin was recorded in Oakland, California, in spring 1943, paying off a local Communist Party official in return for a briefcase full of intelligence about uranium enrichment efforts at the University of California at

Berkeley's Radiation Lab, as well as developments in the Manhattan Project's locations in Oak Ridge, Tennessee, and Los Alamos, New Mexico. In fact, just two days after the handoff of the documents in Oakland, in a sequence of events straight out of *Tales of Manhattan*, the FBI was watching when Zarubin left the briefcase overnight at Boris's house in Beverly Hills. Zarubin correctly suspected he was being followed and didn't want to be caught with the evidence. They were also watching the next day when Zarubin picked up the briefcase and boarded a train bound for Washington, DC, where he sent the briefcase via diplomatic pouch to Moscow. Interestingly enough, the FBI first learned about the Manhattan Project from the surveillance of Zarubin's Oakland contact in April 1943, a good example of how the lack of communication between federal agencies in wartime allowed the Soviets to gain such a stark intelligence advantage. Even the FBI agents in charge of managing Boris's defection in July 1947 didn't know everything about him that J. Edgar Hoover did.

Hoover had received his own version of the notorious Anonymous Letter that had been sent to Stalin in August 1943. It was actually addressed to "Mr. Guver," a sign that it had been written by a Russian, because that language has no letter *G* and no corresponding key on the Cyrillic keyboard. For Hoover, of course, the assertions the letter made—that a network of spies was operating out of the Soviet embassy in Washington, DC, working with contacts at every level of American politics, business, and culture, including Boris—weren't really news. Hoover didn't share the information the letter contained or even its existence with the White House or the State Department, and his copy ended up in his secret files. Nor did Hoover let anyone else know about the wartime Venona project, in which Boris appears as "Frost," but also under a second code name, "John."

If Hoover was concerned about the FBI being outclassed by Soviet intelligence, he had only himself to blame. By 1947 he had been for a quarter-century the unchallenged monarch of America's intelligence-gathering efforts and its federal law-enforcement agency. Hoover got his start as a young Justice Department lawyer who became the federal government's point man in brutally successful but short-lived campaigns against foreign labor radicals in the Red Scare of the early 1920s. A more lasting obsession of Hoover's was his popular crusade against homegrown "public enemies" like Frank Costello, John Dillinger, Bonnie and Clyde, and Baby Face Nelson. By the time Hoover took charge of the newly created Federal Bureau of Investigation in 1935, it was the Nazis who increasingly claimed his attention, though Hoover was not above trying to bring down left-wing celebrities like Charlie Chaplin and Will Rogers. As a result of Hoover's obsessive focus on gangsters, Nazis, and celebrities, the Soviets were able to operate with a relatively free hand in the United States. Hoover only woke up to the reality of the danger posed by Soviet spies in 1938, when the FBI caught a Soviet spy who worked for the Office of Naval Intelligence. Following the Hitler-Stalin Nonaggression Pact of 1939, resident aliens in the United States were forced to register with the government, and the FBI was allowed to conduct surveillance on suspected subversives without a warrant and to jail anyone who belonged to a subversive organization (a euphemism for the Communist Party) or even talked about overthrowing the government. Ironically, Hoover's top-secret Special Intelligence Service, which provided cover for his spies through a fake import company, was located in the very same building where Boris's music publishing company had its New York headquarters: 30 Rockefeller Center.

When Hitler double-crossed Stalin in 1941, the United States and the Soviet Union were once again allies in the fight against fascism, so Hoover's anticommunist ambitions had to be curtailed. Nonetheless, between 1941 and 1945, the FBI quadrupled in size, to more than thirteen thousand agents and support staff engaged in the illegal evidence-gathering techniques that were the "holy trinity" of FBI strategy: wiretapping, bugging, and break-ins. No wonder Zarubin and Soble were so careful about checking hotel rooms for microphones, so obsessed with codes and paroles, so circumspect when it came to public rendezvous.

The United States may have started from behind in the Cold War, restrained by the notion that "gentlemen don't read each other's mail," in the words of Secretary of War Henry Stimson, but America soon led the world in signals intelligence and the technology of espionage. Nonetheless, Hoover's FBI lagged far behind the Russians when it came to human intelligence, which was less reliable but more effective. The FBI needed someone on the inside, someone who spoke Russian and who had connections back in the Soviet Union. The FBI needed Boris Morros, and in the summer of 1947 they finally had him.

After a week of listening to Boris tell his life story, it still wasn't clear to the FBI who exactly he was or why exactly he decided to come clean. During the Cold War, FBI agents used an acronym, MICE, to explain the possible reasons for defecting: money, ideology, compromise (often leverage gained through blackmail), or ego. When it came to motivation, Boris had a delicate and ever-shifting combination of all four.

Boris told the FBI that he was only a patriotic American doing his duty in his adopted country's time of need, but he was of course mostly immune to the ideology that drove spies like Zarubin and Soble. And while the FBI could offer Boris the biggest stage and the most respect he had ever known, in addition to the chance to avenge the death of his brothers, ego alone didn't motivate him in July 1947. Boris's decision to defect also had financial motivations: *Carnegie Hall* had turned out to be far less profitable than Boris had hoped.

The postwar period was in fact a good time to get out of the movie business. The film industry's growth peaked in 1946, after which television, protectionism in foreign markets, labor troubles, and the Paramount court decision—forcing the major studios to give up their ownership of theaters, stop the practice of block booking, and end their control over ticket prices—combined to give Hollywood its comeuppance. In contrast, Boris's partnership with the Kremlin in the record business had been troublesome though profitable. Might the Americans might pay even more? In this sense, Boris's defection was not a case of disillusionment with *The God That Failed*, as the famous 1949 volume of confessions by ex-communists had it, but The God That Failed to Pay Cash.

Boris's strongest motivation in putting his fate in the hands of the FBI was to avoid the possibility that he might be compromised and sent to the electric chair as a traitor. Just two weeks before Boris defected, Congress proposed replacing the old Office of Strategic Services (OSS), which along with the FBI had dominated foreign intelligence during the war, with a permanent organization that would operate overseas: the Central Intelligence Agency. Truman might have thought twice, however, about his new spy-catchers if he had known that the State Department analyst Alger Hiss had been present at the founding of the agency. Hiss had been a member of the Communist Party in the 1930s while working for the State Department, he reported to the Soviets while he was part of the US delegation at Yalta in 1945, and he later ran the United Nations Charter Commission.

In recent years Boris had felt safer in Europe than in the United States because of the FBI's limited presence abroad. Now he realized that the CIA's global mandate meant there was nowhere he could go to escape the reach of American counterintelligence. Another reason for Boris to switch sides was the changing political and cultural climate in the United States. During the war, American attitudes toward the Soviet Union and communism were a matter of grudging acceptance. Stalin was the enemy of an enemy. After the defeat of Germany, when "an iron curtain" descended across Europe, in Winston Churchill's immortal words, it became clear that the United States and the Soviet Union were going to engage in a struggle over the soul of Europe and of the whole world. President Truman authorized the Federal Loyalty and Security Program, which launched investigations into two million government employees suspected of "subversion," which was now defined as merely being connected with a subversive organization. Of course, the executive branch's passion for hunting down Reds in the postwar period was mild compared to that of the legislative branch. After the war, the House Un-American Activities Committee (HUAC) began focusing on rooting out communists, and it was starting to come perilously close to Boris. HUAC's chair, Representative John Rankin of Mississippi, called Hollywood "the greatest hotbed of subversive activities in the United States," and Boris, who had for decades associated with Russians and Soviet causes, who had made more than one trip to the Soviet Union, and whose films were repeatedly identified as almost communistic in outlook, wouldn't be able to put off an appearance before HUAC for long.

Boris didn't know it at the time, but American code-breakers monitoring cable traffic between New York and Moscow as part of the top-secret Venona project had made a major breakthrough in deciphering the communications encryption system that the Soviets thought was unbreakable. The very month that Boris became an FBI operative, the codebreakers informed the Justice Department of the existence of 349 suspected Soviet spies, Boris among them, operating on American soil, compromising the OSS, the Office of War Information, the War Production Board, and the Board of Economic Warfare, not to mention every significant sector of American business, industry, and culture. As was the case with the revelations of Igor Gouzenko, Whittaker Chambers, and Elizabeth Bentley, the information drawn from the decrypted cables was kept from the White House, the Secretary of State, and the Attorney General in order to build cases against the suspects implicated, though in the end few were ever tried and convicted. Still, Boris was determined to tell all before someone else did.

On the day he defected, Boris confided to his diary: "Nothing has happened so far, but it was a bad beginning and it may lead to bad things." He couldn't help but suspect that there would be a price to pay for betraying his adopted country for more than a decade. But a week later, things looked different. After Boris had finished telling his tale, far from putting him in handcuffs, the agents formally asked if he was willing to switch sides.

"When do I start?" Boris answered. They responded that he should take some time to think things over. Double-crossing Stalin would be a perilous undertaking, and Boris could tell no one of his decision, not his coworkers or friends or even his family. If Boris agreed to work with the FBI against Soviet intelligence, he would be courting an entirely new level of danger. A Soviet spy who failed to deliver often might redeem himself. A traitor was given no such chance. Boris would now be caught in the middle of what the historian Eric Hobsbawm famously called "the contest of nightmares."

Boris and his new friends at the FBI came to an arrangement, one that over the next decade would cost the FBI hundreds of thousands of dollars and require the full efforts of a team of agents and bureaucrats. Wherever he went, Boris would be accompanied by an FBI agent—he always kept the man's real identity secret, though he called him Bob Burton. The agent posed as a relative of an old friend, who was learning the ropes in the film business, officially earning fifty dollars a week as Boris's assistant, on top of his FBI paycheck. He would read every document and monitor every telephone call and report back to Hoover, building up a dossier focused on Boris that the FBI called "Mocase."

Official American policy admitted that since real peace with the Soviet Union was impossible and open war undesirable, the United States would step back and watch from across the Iron Curtain as the Soviets destroyed themselves. The FBI would focus its efforts on defending against domestic subversion. In fact, the man that the FBI called "our special special agent" would do whatever the Soviets asked and come back for more, informing the FBI every step of the way. Boris would eventually be actively gathering information, which was now the most important weapon in the Cold War, on Soviet political strategies, economic planning, and military readiness, in particular atomic weapons development, in addition to keeping the FBI up to date on the activities of the various operatives he came into contact with. Boris warned the bureau that he was planning on spending more and more time in Europe, scouting out films that might be remade for the American market. They responded enthusiastically: That's where the Cold War would be won or lost. Nonetheless, starting in 1947, with the establishment of the CIA from the ashes of the OSS, the FBI would be in principle forbidden from operating abroad. Clearly, Boris was a gamble for the FBI. Despite his experience with the Soviets, when it came to espionage, Boris was an amateur among professionals. Then again, one challenge for double agents was not to appear to be too competent or careful, lest they inspire suspicion. No one seemed less like a spy, much less a double agent, than Boris.

The first assignment the FBI gave Boris was to do nothing at all. That wasn't hard for a Soviet spy in America in the summer of 1947, given the state of virtual hibernation that Soviet intelligence was in. The Soviets had won the war. Surviving the aftermath was a different matter altogether. Victory had cost the Soviet Union dearly, with twenty-seven million dead, ten times as many as the United States, and its cities in ruins. Meanwhile the American economy was stronger than ever and beginning to exert what the Kremlin considered a dangerous influence in Europe via the Marshall Plan. Nonetheless, Stalin was convinced that the capitalists would be at each other's throats before long, his spies only there to hurry along the process. His intelligence experts, in contrast, saw a new Red Scare sweeping across America, further decimating the ranks of the Communist Party, which was the Kremlin's prime recruiting ground, and they worried that Stalin was underestimating the situation. Stalin's experts were even more worried when intelligence came back to Moscow with the news that Truman had authorized the building a new kind of bomb, one that would dwarf the weapons used against Japan. An official memo shortly after the end of the war went out to all of Moscow's intelligence stations worldwide, concluding: "There was no study or training of people, the most elementary principles of conspiracy were ignored, complacency and self-satisfaction went unchecked." Soble read the memo and thought it referred to Boris, but rather than making him disappear, Beria doubled down on the man who was now at once one of the Soviet Union's key assets in America and one of America's key assets against the Soviets.

CHAPTER FIFTEEN
BORIS LOVES MONEY!, 1947–48

Ordered by both of his spymasters to lay low, Boris did what he'd always done: try to make some money. Within days of defecting, he announced a $2.5 million film project, to be called *Woman of 100 Faces*, written by the novelist Thomas Mann, directed by Jean Renoir, and starring Greta Garbo. It was no surprise to the readers of the Hollywood trade papers, who were so used to seeing Boris announce the most ambitious of projects, which never even made it to the deal stage, much less to the screen, that the film never happened. In fact, the whole announcement was calculated to keep Boris and *Carnegie Hall*, which was just about to have its West Coast premiere, on the front pages. After its initial success on the East Coast, the film's box office receipts on the West Coast and overseas were disappointing, and some critics had been merciless. *Life* magazine called it "a dreadful movie." Even the *New York Times* film critic Olin Downes, who played himself in the film, was trying to distance himself from the production: "Morros accepted the flimsiest of second-class film yarns as the scaffolding on which to hang the composers' products." Boris didn't let the bad press get in the way. Instead he tried to put the blame for the film's lack of success somewhere else. The film may have been out of touch with the musical tastes of younger filmgoers, who preferred jazz and "race music," as rhythm and blues was then known, to classical music. Boris also sensed that "people are in a different mood now," looking for socially relevant films like *Crossfire* and *Gentleman's Agreement*.

With *Carnegie Hall* filling fewer and fewer seats and no new projects to take its place, Boris gave the FBI an idea: Jack Soble had recently been called back to Moscow and had asked Boris to keep an eye on his wife. Surely, Boris reasoned, the FBI would be interested in what the wife of the top Soviet spy in America had to say. If it gave Boris a reason to spend more time in New York, all the better, and in fall 1947 he made several trips east, treating Myra Soble and sometimes their son, Larry, to expensive dinners paid for by the FBI. Fitted with a secret recording device, Boris pumped Myra for information about Jack: where he was, who he was talking to, and what he was saying. Boris's insistent, even intrusive curiosity about Soble's activities struck Myra as odd, but Boris knew how to win her over. For all her commitment to communism, Myra's life as the wife of a top Soviet secret agent wasn't as exciting or as remunerative as it sounded. Myra often had to take in sewing piecework or work as a secretary to make ends meet, and the Sobles' apartment in Washington Heights was so small that Larry, no longer a baby, had to sleep in their bedroom. Myra escaped her humdrum life at the movies, seeing a film every day and devouring news about Hollywood celebrities from the gossip columns that so often mentioned Boris. A nagging suspicion about Boris's motives was a small price to pay for the touch of glamour he lent her.

Things got uncomfortable for Boris when in September 1947 Myra opened the door of her apartment and thrust a newspaper at him. Boris assumed she had seen his name in one of the gossip columns again, but the look on her face wasn't pride but fear. The syndicated columnist Westbrook Pegler had published a bombshell of an article connecting Alfred and Martha Stern with dozens of organizations identified by HUAC as communist fronts. It wouldn't be long before the trail led to Boris and Jack Soble, she worried.

Boris, who had placed so many dubious stories in the press over the years, wasn't nearly as concerned, not when one could hardly open a newspaper in the late 1940s without seeing some celebrity accused on political grounds. But Boris was unsettled the next month to learn that HUAC investigators were in Hollywood looking for communist subversives. Not surprisingly, they found them, as dozens of film industry figures, among them Walt Disney and Ronald Reagan, appeared as friendly witnesses and named names. On November 24, 1947, with the young California congressman Richard Nixon taking the lead, HUAC cited ten directors, writers, and actors for contempt of Congress for having refused to testify. "The Hollywood Ten," as they became known—Alvah Bessie, Herbert J. Biberman, Lester Cole, Edward Dmytryk, Ring Lardner Jr., John Howard Lawson, Albert Maltz, Samuel Ornitz, Adrian Scott, and Dalton Trumbo—were eventually celebrated for their heroic resistance to McCarthyism. But it was a difficult moment for Boris, who had worked with four of them at Paramount back in the 1930s and had originally signed up a fifth, Trumbo, as the original writer for *Tales of Manhattan*. Things got even worse when the next day the heads of Hollywood's major studios, speaking on behalf of the Motion Picture Association of America, issued the infamous "Waldorf Statement," which promised that the film industry would no longer hire suspected communists or anyone associated with groups or causes sympathetic to the Soviet Union. This act of political theater was not Hollywood's finest hour, and it shook Boris, many of whose friends and colleagues ended up on a blacklist that soon grew far longer than ten names.

Although the studios never kept a formal list of suspected radicals, Boris, as a Russian, occasionally associated with left-wingers and leftist causes that would have been a prime target of HUAC. He had never joined the Communist Party, but his political sympathies were suspect in some circles. The syndicated columnist Earl Wilson all but outed Boris in a piece that claimed Boris had worn pink shirts for years and knew plenty of Hollywood figures with the same "fashion" sense. Boris brought his concerns to the FBI, which had long resented the way the congressional committee was stealing its show and complicating further indictments. The bureau tried to protect Boris by reaching out to HUAC staffers, with little success. It took a personal call from Hoover to Nixon to make sure that Boris was left alone.

Boris assumed that these events would be the subject of his next rendezvous with Soble in late November 1947 in New York, but Soble seemed unconcerned. Instead, he had summoned Boris to explain to him that Soviet intelligence had been reorganized yet again. The MBG's duties were now being carried out by an organization called the Committee of Information, or the KI, which combined the duties of the MGB with the Soviet military intelligence agency called the GRU. That was not all. The new director of Soviet intelligence, the infamous Vyacheslav Molotov, had taken a personal interest in Boris, which certainly appealed to Boris's vanity. Soble soon set Boris straight: Molotov had wanted to know why such a potentially important asset like Boris wasn't being effectively used. Boris later claimed in his autobiography that Soble told him that he blamed poor supervision from Moscow, but a declassified report that Soble sent to Moscow tells a different story: "The trouble with him is that, because he lives in the Hollywood milieu, surrounded by luxury and abundance, he does not understand the value of money. Thousands of dollars are thrown left and right." Soble did add that Boris was not totally to blame, at least when it came to Chord: "One must be a man of steel to put up with Alfred Stern when doing business, especially in America, where risk, enterprise, and speed are the main elements of any commercial enterprise." Soble, who had survived so many changes of policy and personnel in the Kremlin, clearly knew how to explain the failure of Chord without taking any blame himself, and without giving Molotov the sense that the KI would be better off without Boris and the Sterns.

There was much that Soble didn't tell Boris about, starting with a report that Martha Stern had written in mid-1947 denouncing Boris as a double agent. Martha, who was convinced that Boris had fed Pegler the information about the Sterns' questionable associations, believed that Soble would bury such a document because of his friendship with Boris, so she sent it directly to Zarubin. As impulsive as Zarubin was vulnerable to Martha's charms, his first instinct was to order that Boris be "put on ice," as Soviet agents referred to the liquidation of their own agents. Soble, in an October 1947 meeting with Zarubin at the bar of Moscow's Metropol Hotel, the favorite watering hole of the city's Western journalists, tried with the help of plentiful cognac and vodka to convince Zarubin that Martha was wrong and that Boris was not only loyal to Moscow but someone worth holding on to. Zarubin, it seems, was won over when Soble reminded him that Boris had paid back Stern's $100,000 investment after Chord fell apart. With Zarubin's blessing, Soble reported to Molotov that Boris was "talented, energetic, and enterprising. He can undoubtedly keep a secret and is ready and willing to 'do things' for us." Boris's value, Soble wisely argued, was not in his business skills but in his connections, and that was what they needed to have him focus on.

Soble had also summoned Boris to New York to deliver the news that their relationship was about to change. Molotov had told Soble that he would no longer run the Manhattan cafeteria but would instead relocate to France, where Soble's cousins owned a company that imported and processed bristles for hairbrushes. Moscow was willing to invest $30,000 in the business, which was near Paris, to buy out Soble's family and turn the business into a front that would provide cover for Soviet agents operating in France.

When Boris relayed the news to the FBI, they were not pleased. The CIA had been given sole responsibility for overseas intelligence operations. But the two agencies hammered out a compromise in which the FBI would be able to continue to work with their own agents and sources, no matter where they found themselves. Still, the FBI was also concerned that Soble's new position meant that Boris was being sidelined, but Boris reminded them that Soble's relocation to France only gave Boris an excuse to spend even more time in Europe.

Soble's final message for Boris was a new assignment: Boris was to start digging into the past of one of his friends, General Lucius Clay, the commander in chief of US forces in Europe and, since March, the military governor of Germany's American zone. Clay, whose ancestor Henry Clay was a nineteenth-century politician from Kentucky known as "The Great Compromiser," was one of the earliest Cold Warriors, known as "The Great Uncompromiser." Boris, who had known Clay for more than a decade, was torn. Clay wasn't a gambler or an alcoholic or a sexual degenerate, so he didn't have vices that Moscow might have used to blackmail him; however, Boris knew that Clay's wife was unfaithful. Boris's FBI handlers reminded him that in order to remain in Moscow's good graces he would have to come up with something, so in an act of cold-hearted calculation, he reported to Moscow: "General Clay's wife cheats on him and does so with gusto."

Moscow had put Boris on Clay's trail, but the FBI began pressuring Boris to come up with some leads of his own. Boris opened his address book and started scheming against some of his best friends. He knew the Russians wouldn't be able to resist having someone close to Francis Cardinal Spellman, the sixth archbishop of the Catholic Church's New York Diocese and the man that many Vatican-watchers believed would be the next pope. Boris and Spellman had both lived in the same Boston neighborhood back in the 1920s, but they only became close in 1945, when Boris asked Spellman to write the liner notes for a recording of the Vatican Choir. Boris so impressed Spellman with his knowledge of music and musicians that he began depending on Boris to advise him when it came to hiring organists for New York's churches. In return, Spellman agreed to bless the set of *Carnegie Hall*, as long as the proceeds of the film's New York premiere went to Catholic orphanages. After the war, Boris's visits to New York weren't complete without an invitation to dine privately with Spellman in his opulent, almost decadent residence at 542 Madison Avenue, which was known as the "Power House," because so many deals, spiritual and temporal, were done there.

Spellman was a vocal and determined anti-communist who expressed special interest in issues involving Russian refugees, which gave Moscow more than enough reason to want to find something to use against him. Boris knew that Spellman's brother, Martin, a physician in Boston, was a hard-drinking atheist, a "good-for-nothing," as Boris reported to Moscow, who could be very embarrassing indeed to Spellman, especially because Boris helped out Martin financially from time to time. But Boris knew that it was the cardinal's own private life, in particular the rumors that he was a homosexual, that Moscow would find more useful.

The FBI was fully willing to deliver up Spellman to the Soviets, but Boris was uncomfortable with the assignment and spent more than one sleepless night thinking about how to solve the problem. Then in December 1947 Spellman made a visit to Los Angeles and invited himself over to Boris's offices for what turned into a three-hour chat about everything from politics to the movies. Spellman was actually shopping around a film project: Would Boris be willing to produce a film about a Catholic hero fighting fascists in World War II? Boris had to restrain himself from answering: Is the pope Catholic? Instead, he hesitated: What did he know about the Church during the war? Spellman answered that he could arrange for Boris to do research in the Vatican and even offered to type up a letter of introduction to the pope himself. Boris didn't have to think twice: It was good business, and it was even better espionage.

Blackmailing Clay and Spellman was just the sort of project Molotov had envisioned for Boris, and the development seemed to please his FBI contacts, who frankly hadn't expected much from Boris. The fact that he seemed to show little remorse in offering up his friends, to ridicule and humiliation in the case of Clay and dishonor and disgrace in the case of Spellman, certainly gives pause to anyone trying to understand Boris. For the FBI, it was a clue that they had underestimated Boris's survival instincts.

Soble heard about Clay and Spellman and was more enamored than ever with his celebrity friend, writing in a March 1948 report to Moscow: "Boris is not under suspicion, although as you know, there is an incredible 'purge' of Reds going on in Hollywood now. He travels everywhere, is on friendly terms with Cardinal Spellman, meets with the biggest cinema stars, and has countless acquaintances all over the world." Untroubled by Boris's connections to the Hollywood Ten and oblivious to Boris's miraculous immunity to accusations of communist sympathies, Soble suggested that Moscow was still underestimating his value.

Convinced by Soble's sense of how important a figure Boris might be, Moscow instructed Soble to rendezvous with Boris in Paris. It didn't take much to convince Boris to go, though he had to delay his departure to appear at a fundraiser in New York to support scholarships for young black singers at the Detroit Civic Opera, penance for having failed to cast any black characters in *Carnegie Hall*. It wasn't until April 14, 1948, that Boris, carrying a package that Myra had put together for Jack containing pens, ink, a typewriter, and his favorite kosher salami, and accompanied by an FBI minder posing as his attorney, boarded the *Queen Elizabeth* on Manhattan's West Side docks and steamed to France.

In Paris, Boris—now being exclusively referred to in classified Soviet cable traffic not by his old code name of "Frost" but by "John"—gave Soble exactly what he wanted. Boris, who always seemed to be surrounded by a crew of assistants, colleagues, business partners, and friends who flattered him shamelessly, took Soble to elegant Paris restaurants—they favored a Russian restaurant called Petrograd, which faced the Russian Orthodox Saint Alexander Nevsky Cathedral in the Eighth Arrondissement—nightclubs, shows, and parties, where he seemed to know everybody, all on the FBI's dime. Soble had always been in awe of Boris's Hollywood career and never questioned how Boris could afford it all, but he never felt quite comfortable in his world, so he was not afraid after a few weeks of capitalist debauchery to remind Boris that they were there for business. Soble explained that Moscow had two things in mind for Boris. Despite the disappointment that Chord represented—it had never provided the kind of broad cover for agents that Zarubin had envisioned—Soble suspected that Boris had walked away from the project with a considerable profit, which meant that he was in the position to set up businesses to provide cover for Soviet agents. Soble thought that a violin bow company would serve, but Boris, acting under the instructions of the FBI, thought bigger. At first, he proposed a company that would make films for the European market. Soble approved the idea, but Moscow balked at the figure Boris named: $250,000, the equivalent of almost $3 million today. Boris came back with a less expensive idea: $150,000 would be enough to start a television production company that would not only provide cover for agents but also serve as a convenient way for Moscow to transfer money to the

United States. Boris left out the fact that while the television production company would be good for Moscow, it would be even better for himself. The recent arrival of commercial broadcasting and the exploding number of television sets in American homes, from six thousand in 1946 to thirty-five thousand in 1948, meant that the medium was poised to challenge Hollywood. Boris wanted in.

Soble described Boris's plans in a report to Moscow that was somehow less than enthusiastic: "He is an honest man and obeys our decisions." The deputy chairman of the KI and the head of its foreign intelligence operations, Pyotr Fedotov, wasn't even willing to grant that much, writing back: "I am not entirely convinced of 'John's' selflessness in collaborating with us. Nevertheless, he is not someone to be spurned." Reading between the lines, Soble responded by admitting that Boris's motives were less than pure: "Boris loves money!" Soble then reiterated, in terms that indicate how much Soble had fallen under Boris's spell, that his "vast and diverse" range of connections, not just in the entertainment world but in the media, the military, business, and high society, made him someone that Moscow should consider a long-term asset: "He doesn't ask this 'elite' to invite him. On the contrary, this 'elite' begs him to visit them and hobnob with them."

Soble had always found Boris to be uninterested in politics. But now Boris was aping the Republican Party line coming out of the White House and Congress and even claiming that back in California he was about to be asked to serve as treasurer of the state Republican Party, a role that would put him in the position to inform on a wide range of political figures that he falsely claimed to be close to. The first chief of staff of the US Air Force, General Carl Andrew Spaatz, was Boris's "good friend," Soble reported, as was assistant secretary of state for public affairs and soon-to-be Connecticut senator William Benton, who had owned Muzak and was the publisher of *Encyclopaedia Britannica*. Soble even repeated Boris's story that he became close to New York State governor Thomas E. Dewey after curing his lisp back in 1943. Boris was also drinking buddies with UNESCO commissioner Milton Eisenhower, the brother of the former army chief of staff Dwight Eisenhower, whom Boris had met back in

1930 when Boris helped convert a theater in Abilene, Kansas. Soble wrote that Boris and General Hastings Ismay, who was then overseeing the partition of India with Lord Mountbatten, and who would soon serve as the first secretary general of NATO, "frequently go on the town together and try to find ladies they know." Just in case Soble and Fedotov thought it all too good to be true, Boris made sure they knew where Boris's allegiances really lay: "I cannot live in the USA and be a dispassionate observer of the outrages, atrocities, and terror committed by the American reactionary clique," he told Soble, in a pitch-perfect imitation of Stalinist rhetoric.

While in Paris, Boris couldn't resist indulging in the city's pleasures, especially if he could claim that it was a diversionary tactic. On the very day that the Soviets blockaded Berlin, June 24, 1948, the date many historians call the formal start of the Cold War—with airlifts organized by the man Boris was setting up for blackmail, General Lucius Clay—Boris attended a ball at the Louvre to benefit disabled French soldiers. The French magazine *Figaro* covered the event and reported that Boris had stolen the show, ordering ambassadors, ministers, and millionaires to sit on the floor of the museum, the idea being "to do away with formalities in the name of creating a 'free and easy mood,'" Soble noted. Around the same time, Boris ran a contest in which he would select French girls who would be given the chance at a Hollywood audition, an old casting-couch tactic that Boris seems to have indulged in from time to time when Catherine wasn't around, though usually he wasn't so public about it.

When Catherine heard about the contest, which was reported in the American newspapers, she was furious. Catherine and Boris were obviously bound together in ways that are difficult to understand. She was willing to accept Boris's dalliances as long as they remained private, but this was too much. Boris managed to calm her down by promising a summer together in Spain with the renowned Spanish conductor and pianist José Iturbi, whom Catherine adored. Their vacation was interrupted when Boris read that the US Justice Department had arrested twelve members of the American Communist Party's leadership (the number was eventually expanded to 140) and charged them with conspiring to advocate the violent overthrow of the government. The Soviets, who no longer depended on the US Communist Party the way they did in the 1930s, nonetheless correctly saw the arrests as a devastating blow to their American operations, since a trial would surely expose a number of their secret agents. But that was just the start of the bad news, at least from the Soviet perspective.

Boris and Catherine had just returned to Paris from Spain when they saw the headlines: The former Soviet spy, Elizabeth Bentley, who had quietly defected in 1945, had gotten tired of the FBI's failure to proceed with prosecutions against the communists she had named, so she went to the papers. Bentley told the *New York World-Telegram* that the Communists had penetrated the army, the navy, the OSS, the Treasury Department, even the White House. Within days, the "Blonde Spy Queen"—she was in fact a brunette, but the tabloids knew that the American public expected a femme fatale to be blonde—was called before a public session of HUAC, where she named eighty names and gave the United States a decisive lead in the Cold War. If Americans who found themselves on the left wing of the Democratic Party had been feeling the chill of the Cold War, taking more care with what they said and signed, the temperature had just gotten a few degrees colder.

Just days after this extraordinary coup on the part of HUAC, which was of course a setback for the FBI since it ruined a number of confidential ongoing investigations, even more spectacular news broke. Another former Soviet spy who found the FBI unwilling or as yet unable to use what he had to offer now appeared before the committee. Whittaker Chambers not only confirmed much of Bentley's testimony but added a few new names, among them Alger Hiss. Called before HUAC, Hiss denied the charges, but the damage had been done. Even if only some of Bentley's and Chambers's testimony was true, and even if less could be proven, the "spy mania" that their accusations inspired deeply divided the country, in effect shaking the confidence that many Americans had in their government, and with good reason.

This wasn't the first time that a Soviet agent had revealed, voluntarily or under the threat of prosecution, details of Moscow's operations in the

United States. But never before had defectors told such a damaging story; never before had they captured the attention of so many Americans, in part because of the new medium of television, which brought the masses into a kind of intimacy with their supposed enemies. Boris would have been even more worried had he known that back in Moscow, Beria was handing over responsibility for Soviet intelligence in America to his much-feared deputy Aleksandr Korotkov, who had started out as an elevator operator in Soviet intelligence headquarters in Ljubljana and went on to become Stalin's preferred assassin. One of Korotkov's first acts in his new job was to ask: Who is Boris Morros?

CHAPTER SIXTEEN
PONTIFEX MAXIMUS, 1948–49

Aleksandr Korotkov's idea was to bring Boris to Moscow. The FBI was delighted that one of their agents had worked his way so far inside the Soviet spy apparatus, though they did warn Boris that they wouldn't be able to protect him on Russian soil. Boris found a way out by suggesting that a visit to the Soviet Union at this time would raise eyebrows, so he asked Soble to set up a meeting with Korotkov on neutral ground, in Switzerland. But before that happened, Boris and Soble decided to indulge themselves, spending two weeks with their wives in Nice. Boris treated the Sobles to a taste of a life that, communist ideologues or no, they always longed for: exclusive restaurants and the front row at every show. Little did they know it was all on the FBI's tab. Catherine and Myra were free to enjoy themselves, but Boris and Jack were following the news closely, realizing that their jobs were getting more complicated every day. New accusations before HUAC against Alger Hiss shared the front pages with details about the expulsion of the Soviet consul general in New York, the Berlin Airlift, and the division of the Korean peninsula.

Eventually, Soble got a telephone call ordering him and Boris to Geneva on August 22, 1948. Korotkov would be disguised as a Soviet Ministry of Foreign Affairs courier at a meeting of the United Nations Economic and Social Council in Bonn, while Soble and Boris would pretend to be on vacation with their wives. The FBI tried to warn Boris how dangerous such a meeting was, but Boris laughed it off, joking that he could always let out his "distress yodel" if he got into trouble. But he knew precisely how high the stakes were.

Boris rented a car and the two couples headed from Nice to Geneva. It took most of the day to get there, though after they settled into their rooms at the luxurious Beau Rivage Hotel on Lake Geneva, a favorite of European aristocrats, there was still time for the ladies to go shopping. Soble took advantage of their time alone to prepare Boris to meet Korotkov. Boris put on a brave face, but he admitted to Soble how terrified he actually was. Switzerland was officially neutral territory in the Cold War, but that would only make it easier for Korotkov if he was planning on bringing Boris back to Moscow against his will.

Korotkov scheduled the rendezvous for the extravagant Eaux Vives Restaurant, on the east shore of Lake Geneva, a setting intended to communicate to Boris that he wasn't the only spy who could move easily between the worlds of capitalism and communism. As Boris drove across the Mont-Blanc Bridge, where the Rhône empties in the lake, Soble told him that he should mostly just listen to what Korotkov had to say. Boris stopped in front of the restaurant, handed the car keys to Soble, and went inside, where a giant, glowering figure waited for him. So this was the infamous Aleksandr Korotkov, Boris thought. He didn't know that Korotkov was just as curious to meet the short, bald, rotund fellow in whom Beria had placed so much trust.

It was a stifling summer evening, and as they were seated in the restaurant's sprawling garden, Boris couldn't help but think that Soviet spies seemed even more addicted to luxury than their capitalist counterparts, perhaps because those at the highest level enjoyed the kinds of food, wine, and accommodations that the typical Russian didn't dare even dream about. After ordering drinks and food, Korotkov conveyed Zarubin's greetings and then got down to business. It wasn't pretty. He was displeased at the way Boris had alienated the Sterns, who were highly valued back in Moscow, especially Martha. "What a little recruiter!" Korotkov enthused, as the drinks arrived. "A thousand more like her and the battle would be won." The fact was, Korotkov continued, the whole episode with Chord had damaged the cause. No matter how inept Alfred may have been, Boris should have put the revolution first. As their food arrived on enormous silver platters, Korotkov had one more comment before tucking his napkin under his chin: "The fight to save humanity from its own corrupt capitalism is much more important than such petty grievances." Korotkov appeared to have said everything he wanted to say and ate in silence. Boris was relieved to think that he had survived yet another rendezvous with a killer but then realized that he didn't yet have anything of value to bring back to the FBI. That's when Korotkov did something he rarely did: He made a mistake. Korotkov confronted Boris with the news that that not only were his brothers Isaak and Aleksander still up to their old tricks, but now one of his three sisters was also suspected of counterrevolutionary activity. Korotkov knew the truth: Isaak and Aleksander had died years before, and Boris knew as well, but Korotkov didn't know that Boris knew. Boris held his temper, realizing that he now had an advantage. They finished the meal, shook hands, and arranged to meet in the next day in Lausanne.

Soble picked up Boris in front of the restaurant and drove back to the hotel, where Catherine and Myra were dividing up the spoils of their shopping expedition. It hadn't gone well. Catherine's habit of histrionically, tearfully telling every Russian she met how the Reds had destroyed her family didn't sit well with Myra, who defended communism with an irrational passion. Myra had listened to Catherine with pretend sympathy for weeks. Now she went back to her hotel room and wrote a lengthy report to Korotkov detailing Catherine's hostility to the revolution.

At a meeting the next day, Korotkov exploded in anger at an astonished Boris. He accused Boris not only of insufficient devotion to the cause but an inability to control his wife: "Why don't you indoctrinate that vicious, lying bitch you're married to?" Boris realized that he would have to exercise a great deal of patience when dealing with Korotkov and came up with his usual retort, amazed that it still worked after all these years: "What better cover could I have than a wife who denounces all my Comrades and our Cause unceasingly?" Indeed, it was all an act, Boris claimed. The story of the Bolsheviks murdering her family was false, he told Korotkov. The last time Boris had been in the Soviet Union, he had actually visited her sisters. Catherine was a loyal Russian who longed to visit her homeland herself. Korotkov seemed convinced and scheduled another meeting for August 27, 1948, in Lausanne.

On the way to Lausanne, things got complicated. While making small talk with the driver who picked them up at their hotel in Geneva, Soble and Boris noticed that he had a Belarusian accent. Soble was suspicious. It turned out the man had fled the Bolsheviks back in 1917 and sat out the revolution in France, which was enough information to convince Soble that the man was not to be trusted. Perhaps he had been hired by the FBI? When they arrived in Lausanne, Soble refused to let the driver know the final destination. Instead, he insisted that they stop a few blocks away from where Korotkov was waiting. Boris went the rest of the way on foot. Boris thought Soble's precautions were silly. Why would someone looking to set up two Soviet spies, to test their loyalty, or to eavesdrop on their conversations use an admitted enemy of the revolution? Then again, what if the driver was a Soviet plant? Maybe Soble wasn't paranoid after all. Boris objected to being treated like an amateur, but at moments like this, it felt like he still had plenty to learn, and given Korotkov's reputation as a ruthless killer of so many of his own agents, Boris felt he didn't have much time.

The rendezvous with Korotkov was devoted to clearing up questions about Boris's background. Amazingly enough, no one in Soviet intelligence had ever bothered to hear Boris's full story direct from the source. Boris had been coached by the FBI to avoid talking about his time at the court of the tsar and to emphasize his service to the Bolsheviks during the Russian Civil War. Boris took things even further, confirming Beria's story that their friendship went all the way back to the early 1920s. It was the performance of a lifetime, giving Boris an authority in Korotkov's eyes that immediately changed the nature of the conversation. It effectively put Boris in charge, and he now complained that he had never been given clear assignments and that he had to deal with drunks like Zarubin and incompetents like Alfred Stern. If that was all the Soviets had in mind for him, he would rather "be discharged and sent to Russia together with his wife," Korotkov wrote to Moscow, adding that it seemed like Boris was bluffing, at least the part about returning to Russia. Nevertheless, Korotkov wrote back to Moscow: "His inborn energy, aptitude, cunning, and certain organizational and musical talents" made him worth holding on to.

Korotkov balked, however, when Boris asked him to invest not $150,000, which was the number Korotkov had heard from Soble, but $300,000 in the television production scheme. Boris was devastated, though he tried not to show it. As for Korotkov, he walked away from the meeting just as troubled. "J's desire to work with us again on an active basis is rooted primarily in his own business interests," Korotkov decided. There was no reason to think that Boris was working for the Americans, but Korotkov asked: Could he ever be more than just a business partner with the Russians? That was a question, he reported, that "we in Moscow have unanimously determined to be of utmost importance."

Korotkov summoned Boris to one more meeting before returning to Moscow, and this time there was good news. Moscow was willing to fund Boris's television project, offering as much as $350,000. "Money is nothing," Korotkov told Boris, if the project would bear fruit in terms of providing cover for Soviet agents. Of course, by now Boris had learned that Soviet spies never did any favors without expecting something in return. What would it be this time? Korotkov explained: In a few months, Americans would be electing a new president. The Soviets had found a useful adversary in Truman, a Democrat who was skeptical of Hoover and his anti-communist mania. In contrast, the Republican team of New York State governor Thomas Dewey and California governor Earl Warren, who were far more sympathetic to J. Edgar Hoover, was projected to win. Boris was in a most advantageous position as far as Korotkov was concerned, he explained, not only because of the debt that Dewey owed him but because of Boris's connection to Warren. Boris knew Warren when he was the attorney general of California, investigating the problem of adolescent sexual behavior, and Boris represented the Motion Picture Association of America's involvement in the efforts. Later, Warren had hired Boris to produce an English-language version of *Carmen*, with an on-stage bullfight, in connection with the centennial celebration of California's statehood. Korotkov wanted Boris to find a way to make sure Dewey and Warren lost, and Boris seemed like the man to do it.

It might have seemed like an act of desperation for the Soviets to depend on a Hollywood celebrity like Boris Morros to help keep the Democrats in power, but with his level of access, Boris could surely come up with something to use against the Republicans. After all, Korotkov insisted, wasn't it was in the nature of American politics to lie, cheat, and steal one's way into office? What about their finances? Who paid for their campaigns? Who was pulling the strings? Boris was mentally preparing a response when Korotkov pulled one of his oldest tricks: ending a meeting with an assignment, without giving the other party the chance to think it over. Suddenly Korotkov was saying goodbye, instructing Boris to start setting up his television production company and to make sure to offer Soble a position, a good one, maybe the best one.

Boris knew enough not to invest too much of his own money on the television production company until Moscow came through. In the meantime, he drove Catherine and Jack and Myra Soble back to Paris, where he debriefed his FBI minder and spent the next three weeks spending the FBI's money on hotels, restaurants, and shows, buying clothing for Catherine and presents for friends back in the States. Catherine never quite enjoyed nightlife as much as Boris did, and she had no acquaintances in Paris other than Myra. When Catherine told Boris she wanted to get out of town, Boris remembered the letter of introduction to Pope Pius XII that Cardinal Spellman had given him. Boris cabled Count Enrico Galeazzi, who was in charge of the pope's schedule, and asked if it would be possible to have a few minutes of the pontiff's time to discuss various film projects that might involve the Vatican. Galeazzi, who had been told by Spellman to expect Boris to get in contact, cabled back that they should come right away to Rome, where he would put them up in a hotel.

Soon after Boris and Catherine arrived in Rome, they got a telephone call from Galeazzi inviting them to the Vatican, where they could discuss the possibility of meeting with the pope himself. Galeazzi turned out to be a friendly, helpful, and intelligent conversationalist. They discussed Cardinal Spellman, Boris's European film projects, American and European politics, and mutual friends like James Farley, an intimate of Truman who had been the chairman of the Democratic National Committee, postmaster general, and then the chairman of Coca-Cola. Apparently, Boris passed the test and was invited for a formal audience with the pope on September 24, 1948, at 11:15 A.M. and was told that Catherine was welcome to come. The whole business was ruled by a sense of ritual and discretion that reminded Boris of the Soviet secret police. He wasn't even allowed to keep the invitation.

Boris and Catherine arrived at the Apostolic Palace on time and were led up to the third-floor papal apartments, where for thirty-five minutes they had the pope all to themselves. Pius XII was considered by many to be a saint in his own lifetime, but he was also accused of shocking indifference to Italy's Jews during the war. He is still known as "Hitler's Pope" because he saw the choice between Nazism and communism as a matter of the lesser of two evils. The pope knew from Cardinal Spellman that Boris and Catherine were Russian, and he began by mentioning that he had recently read Tolstoy's *War and Peace*. Sitting in the pontiff's opulent chambers, they discussed Dostoevsky and Russian literature in general before moving on to the current situation in the Soviet Union, about which the pope, otherwise a frail, soft-spoken figure, introverted and private to the point of secrecy, had very clear views: Among the signal dangers of modern life, including hedonism and existentialism, communism was the worst. Just two months before, the official newspaper of the Vatican, *L'Osservatore Romano*, announced that Catholic communists worldwide should consider themselves excommunicated. Meanwhile, Russia, the Pope insisted, must be fought "with all available means," as Boris reported back to Moscow. The whole subject was music to Catherine's ears, but Boris was working, for Moscow, for Washington, and for himself, so he was glad to chat about Cardinal Spellman and James Farley, but he perked up when the pope inquired about what things were like in Hollywood and about Boris's European film plans.

At 11:50, as Boris and Catherine got up to leave, the pope asked Boris to send his regards to Spellman and his brother, Martin. But it wasn't quite over. When Boris reached out to shake the pope's hand, he saw it held a gift: two papal medallions, with his image in profile and the words "Pontifex Maximus." The pope clasped their hands firmly, and then it was over. As Boris and Catherine made their way across St. Peter's Square to their car, they were too moved by the whole experience to look around and see that they could have bought the exact same medallions from any of the street vendors lining the square.

Stalin loved to dismiss the power of the Catholic Church by asking, How many divisions of soldiers does the Pope have? But Boris's tête-à-tête with the pope deeply impressed both Soviet intelligence and the FBI. If Moscow and Washington had their doubts about Boris, his visit to the pope, a contact of unique value when it came to penetrating anti-communist movements globally, eased them, at least temporarily. Boris might not have learned any Vatican secrets, but it was a turning point in his relationship with Moscow. For a while, the new generation of spymasters in Moscow would see Boris not merely as someone who could provide cover, dig up dirt on public figures, or carry cash across borders, but as an actual spy involved in bona fide intelligence gathering. Even Boris's minders at the FBI, usually less starstruck than their Soviet counterparts, saw him in a new light.

Before Boris and Catherine left Europe, Soble had disappointing news. The television production company would have to wait. Despite Korotkov's enthusiasm, he hadn't discussed the matter with Beria and didn't know when he would. The FBI counselled Boris to be patient and get to work on "the good stuff" that he had promised to dig up on Thomas Dewey and Earl Warren. In fact, the FBI did most of the work. The four-page report that Boris put together for Soble to send to Korotkov consisted of items dictated to him by the FBI and contained nothing that even a lazy reader of the *New York Times* wouldn't know.

At the same time, Boris was told by the FBI not to wait for Korotkov's money to come through before setting up the television production company. They agreed to pay $500 per month ($5,000 today) to rent and equip offices on the top floor of a midtown Manhattan office building next to the Plaza Hotel. Boris thought Soble would be delighted at a space that shouted legitimacy, but Soble as usual found problems with the security situation: The offices didn't have a separate entrance, which meant that their secret work would essentially be visible to anyone who wandered into the building. Boris gave his usual reply that hiding would only raise suspicions.

CHAPTER SEVENTEEN
INSIDE THE TEMPLE, 1949

After the revelations of Elizabeth Bentley and Whittaker Chambers before HUAC, there was a sense in Moscow that their American operations had weathered the worst. Then, on December 15, 1948, Alger Hiss was indicted for perjury, and five days later, Laurence Duggan, a State Department official whom the FBI had been interrogating on suspicion of being a Soviet agent, committed suicide. The following week, the FBI identified Judith Coplon, a twenty-eight-year-old analyst at the Justice Department's Foreign Agents Registration Section, as a spy. That fact wasn't made public and Coplon wasn't arrested, but Moscow found out soon enough. Coplon guessed correctly that she was being tailed and warned her Soviet handlers. Convinced that other agents would surely come under increased scrutiny in the months to come, Moscow ordered a full stop to its American operations. But Boris didn't fold just because the stakes had been raised. In early 1949, eager to find some way to change Korotkov's mind about investing in his television production company, he played a card that neither side knew he was holding.

Back in the summer of 1947, just weeks after he was turned by the FBI, Boris heard that President Truman's daughter, Margaret, who fancied herself a singer, would be debuting at the Hollywood Bowl. Boris had heard the gossip and knew that Margaret wasn't much of a singer. Something told him she would be worth getting to know, however, so he bought tickets. The concert was a musical disappointment, but it led to one of the most significant moments of his career as a spy. Boris invited himself to a party held for the singer several weeks later in the Palm Room of the Beverly Hills Hotel, and he worked his way into her confidence. Boris convinced her that she ought to be in the movies, all but promising her a starring role in one of his films. They stayed in touch, and when Margaret invited Boris and Catherine to have dinner with her folks in February 1949, he didn't have to think twice.

Compared to what it is today, security at the White House in the 1940s was minimal, so there was no complicated procedure to get inside. Margaret simply left Boris and Catherine's names with the ushers at the North Portico entrance, which led up to the State Floor, where Margaret and her mother were waiting. They took Boris and Catherine through the grand Entrance Hall and down the Cross Hall, but instead of entering the State Room, where dignitaries dined, they settled into the Family Dining Room, which was considerably more intimate. Even better, Boris thought, before he realized that they were going to start dinner without the president. Would he show up at all? Boris comforted himself by enjoying the food, the fine china, the heavy silverware, and the swanky surroundings. Boris had almost given up hope when just before dessert, the president of the United States himself walked through the door. Truman, who was a head taller than Boris and half his weight, bent over to shake hands.

Even for someone who had consorted with the tsar and the pope, with movie stars and millionaires, this was an unforgettable moment. The after-dinner talk, about Hollywood, the music business, and the future of television, wasn't anything worth reporting back to Moscow, but Boris still felt justified, thinking it might lead to something he could take back to Moscow, of course with the FBI's permission. All too soon though, the president stood up and apologized, saying he had to get back to work, and then the first lady did the same. Boris and Catherine were left alone with Margaret. He made the most of it, according to a report filed later by Soble.

While Truman was politically to the left of J. Edgar Hoover—who wasn't?—his daughter was a genuine progressive who hated Wall Street, HUAC, and racists, and she wasn't afraid to go public about it. Encouraged by Boris, Margaret divulged some very interesting information on tensions within Truman's cabinet and closest advisors over the direction the country was headed diplomatically. Margaret confided to Boris that the president had recently been involved with a heated discussion on foreign affairs with Vice President Alben Barkley, veteran diplomat and soon-to-be Soviet ambassador Charles Bohlen, Secretary of State Dean Acheson, financier and Truman advisor Bernard Baruch, and General Dwight Eisenhower, who was then president of Columbia University. Baruch and Eisenhower, neither of whom was considered an accommodationist when it came to communism, nonetheless "insisted that Truman shake off the influence of reactionary generals and Wall Street businessmen, and staff his cabinet with people who want to engage the Sov. Union 'in honest commercial language.'" Eisenhower became so passionate that he "pounded the table with his fist" while insulting hard-liners such as former under secretary of state Robert Lovett and secretary of defense James Forrestal. He went so far as to call Boris's friend General Lucius Clay "a protege of German Fascists."

At a time when the official message coming from Washington was that Americans needed to stick together in order to counter socialist expansionism across the globe, especially now that China had fallen to the communists, Boris had stumbled on an intelligence coup: a schism in the president's cabinet. But that wasn't all. Margaret also unwittingly leaked details of the group's discussion about the individuals Truman was considering appointing as ambassadors to Britain and France. Boris was so excited that he could barely muster up the facial expression appropriate to Margaret's lament that never in American history had a president had to battle such enemies. But he did manage to promise Margaret before leaving that he would do his best to cast her in his next film, or perhaps she might play a role in one of the television programs he was developing? As Boris walked Catherine out in the mild winter evening and looked out over the South Lawn, across the Ellipse to the Washington Monument, he felt a combination of pride and disappointment. He'd spent his life trying to get close to great men, but he'd never become one himself. Not yet.

Boris had been bragging to Soviet intelligence about his political connections, but now he was operating on an entirely new level. As Soble reported to Moscow, in the weeks to come, Boris met with Vice President Barkley and saw Supreme Court Justices Hugo Black and Felix Frankfurter, Secretary of the Treasury John Snyder, and Marshall Plan administrator Averell Harriman, who asked Boris to make a documentary film about the situation in postwar Europe. Aware that name-dropping never failed to impress Moscow's spymasters, Soble reported that Boris was close to Admiral Chester Nimitz, Secretary of Defense Louis Johnson, and General Omar Bradley, with whom Boris had worked in Hollywood on the Committee to Aid Victory. How close exactly, Soble didn't say, but it was close enough for Beria and Korotkov.

In early March 1949, Soble had returned to New York and settled into an apartment that Boris arranged for him—one that the FBI had selected and wired for eavesdropping. He called Boris to New York and announced that Beria had given his consent to spending $350,000 on Boris's television project, the first of many such dubious promises. A summer rendezvous with Korotkov was scheduled to take place in Vienna, whose divided status in the postwar years made it a place where spy agencies of every stripe could freely operate. There Korotkov would lay out all the details of how Boris would be paid and what he could expect in return. Boris didn't get his hopes up in terms of the money, but he looked forward to the trip to Vienna, especially now that both the FBI and the Russians would be footing the bill.

The rendezvous was postponed, however, when Judith Coplon, the Justice Department analyst whom the FBI was tailing, was arrested and charged with espionage. It didn't come as a surprise to the Russians, but Beria and Korotkov were troubled by the hysterical way the newspapers covered the story of the "red slut" of Barnard College who went on to become the "Spy Next Door." Despite orders from Moscow to lay low in the aftermath of the arrest of "Mata Hari in bobby socks," Boris pestered Soble to put the summer rendezvous with Korotkov in Vienna back on the agenda. Soble wasn't enthusiastic about the idea, which struck Boris as odd, since Soble had so much to gain from Boris's newly earned prestige with Korotkov. Soble wrote to Moscow that Boris had been "downright torturing" him for a meeting with someone, anyone in Vienna, but preferably a "heart-to-heart" with Korotkov. "It is an idee fixe for him," Soble complained, unaware that Boris was less interested in a meeting with Korotkov than an all-expense-paid trip to Europe to work on a film called *The Treasure*, a comedy about a poor French nobleman who returns to his family's castle in their ancestral village to find legendary riches hidden there, but he ends up sharing his newfound wealth with the whole village after they show him that true riches aren't a matter of gold and silver. It was yet another Boris Morros production celebrating socialist-style redistribution of wealth.

Eventually Korotkov agreed to a meeting, and Soble and Boris boarded the *Queen Elizabeth* on May 13, 1949, bound for France. Boris, booked into a first-class cabin, was looking forward to ten days of sea air and bridge, which didn't please his FBI minders, one of whom was travelling as Boris's lawyer and the other as his assistant; neither has ever been identified. They would rather have sat down with Boris to talk through the implications of events unfolding in Germany, including the Berlin Airlift and the founding of the Federal Republic of Germany, which they heard about as they approached France. Would the Soviets set up their own puppet state in the East? What did it mean for the Russian intelligence? Nor was Soble pleased to have to drag Boris away from the card table every day for strategy sessions at eleven A.M. and three P.M.

After they docked at Le Havre, they made their separate ways to Paris, where Boris was booked into the Hotel Raphael, a favorite of all of the big Hollywood stars, which was located on the Avenue Kléber, near the Arc de Triomphe. Soble stayed at the considerably more modest Hotel Racine, on the Left Bank. Now Boris got to work on *The Treasure*. The filming, which was taking place in Bois d'Arcy, near Versailles, didn't require Boris's presence—Boris had very little to do with the actual making of the film, which came out in 1950 as *The Treasure of Cantenac*—so he had plenty of time to enjoy Paris with the two FBI agents who gladly accompanied him as he ate his way through the city, from the rough-and-ready stalls of Les Halles to the chic brasseries on the Champs-Élysées.

In early June, Soble showed up at the Hotel Raphael, and after checking the room thoroughly for bugs, announced that he had someone he wanted Boris to meet, a "lovely American girl" who could be of much use to both of them. Down in the lobby, Soble introduced Boris to a diminutive woman named Jane Foster and a friend of hers who worked in the French Foreign Ministry, but whose sympathies were with Moscow. Anxious to impress, Soble made sure the ladies learned that Boris was an important Hollywood producer committed to progressive causes. After drinks at the hotel bar, they were joined by a nephew of Soble's, and they all stuffed themselves into a car and went out for the evening. On the way to Petrograd, the Russian restaurant that Boris favored, Soble and Foster couldn't keep their hands off each other. For Boris, it called to mind Zarubin and Martha Stern and made him wonder if everything would turn out the same way. Soble and Foster barely stopped kissing and groping long enough to have dinner. Then Soble took them all to the apartment of a couple he knew, where the lovers could have some privacy.

Later that evening, Boris was in his element, boasting of how he had recently conquered both the White House and the Vatican. Foster wasn't much impressed at first: "He was one of the ugliest men I have ever seen," she later recalled. "He looked like a fat toad, warts and all. He was about five feet two inches, fat and round, and his waist was under his armpits. He had pop eyes and blubbery lips." But those blubbery lips belonged to a masterful storyteller, and Foster had to admit that she was so charmed by his enthusiasm that within days she entrusted him with a file of confidential biographies of workers at her employer, the Economic Cooperation Administration, which was the umbrella organization that administered the Marshall Plan. The plan was for Boris to pass it on to Moscow. Soble hadn't made it clear at first, but Foster was a not merely a communist sympathizer but a full-fledged Soviet spy.

Foster had quite a story of her own to tell. Born in San Francisco in 1912, she grew up as a member of the West Coast aristocracy. After graduating from Mills College in 1935, she travelled to Germany, where like Martha Stern she fell in and then out of love with Nazism, or with a string of handsome young Nazi officers, to be more accurate. Back in California in 1936, she married a Dutch diplomat, Leo Kamper, whom she had met at a party thrown by the Institute of Pacific Relations, a communist front funded by Alfred Stern. Foster and Kamper moved to the Dutch East Indies, where Kamper was stationed—in fact, he was a Dutch counterintelligence officer charged with opposing the efforts of Chinese communists, and when he realized that his wife's politics made him a political liability, he ended the marriage. By the time World War II broke out, Foster had returned to the United States, settling in New York City. She formally joined the Communist Party and began attending meetings and benefits, where she struck up a friendship with Martha Stern. Foster sang along at concerts of the left-wing folk group the Almanac Singers—they were soon to be blacklisted—and knitted socks for Soviet troops. However, as a West Coast WASP, she felt out of place among all of the New York Jewish socialists, donning a mink coat on wintry days when she handed out *The Daily Worker* in Union Square. Foster told Martha that she longed to do more for the cause, and Martha soon gave her the chance.

It was around this time that Foster met and married George Zlatovski, a vain, handsome engineer with a passion for left-wing causes. Born in Russia in 1910 and raised in Duluth, Minnesota, Zlatovski studied engineering at the University of Minnesota but was swept up in the radical causes that attracted so many young people during the Depression. Impulsive and violent, especially when he'd been drinking, he joined the Young Communist League. After a two-year stint fighting fascists in the Spanish Civil War as part of the famed Abraham Lincoln Brigade, Zlatovski returned to the United States, drifting from job to job but hoping to be of some service to the revolution. That opportunity didn't appear until he met Foster, one of the few people he had ever met who could outdrink him. Galvanized by Pearl Harbor, Foster and Zlatovski threw themselves into the war effort, volunteering as airplane spotters and air-raid wardens.

There is much speculation about when exactly Foster formally became a Soviet agent, but it is indisputable that by 1942, having moved with Zlatovski to Washington, DC, she was stealing documents from her job at the Federal Board of Economic Warfare and passing them to local Soviet intelligence contacts she knew through Martha Stern. It wasn't until the summer of 1943, when Foster was preparing to join the OSS—outsiders joked it stood for "Oh So Secret"—specializing in morale operations and disinformation in the Southeast Asia section, that she was considered a real Soviet agent. Foster took to her new duties quite naturally. Foster was posted to Ceylon, where she became best friends with a tall Californian named Julia McWilliams, who later became the most famous chef in the world under her married name, Julia Child. As the war wound down, Foster was sent to Indonesia, then still a Dutch colony, to investigate whether the nationalist leader, Sukarno, could be counted on to resist the wave of communism that was rolling across Asia. The report that Foster wrote recommended that the US stand behind Sukarno, even if doing so alienated the Dutch, who were not yet ready to give up their colony. Truman doubted Sukarno's ability to resist the communists and made sure that the report was immediately classified and buried. Foster was a woman of contradictions, flighty and yet principled, so she quit and headed home with a copy of her report, more convinced than ever that her early passion for communism was not simply some youthful dalliance. The question was: What should she do with the report? How could she get it to Moscow? Who could be trusted to get it there? Martha Stern knew the one answer to all of those questions: Jack Soble.

Martha and Alfred Stern had a tradition of throwing a Christmas party for friends and fellow travellers at their apartment on Central Park West. During the war these were relatively subdued events, but the festivities in December 1945 were to be more lavish than usual. Boris was not on the guest list, of course, but Jack Soble was still close to the Sterns, and he always enjoyed meeting the celebrities that came to their parties. Soble had barely gotten through the front door when Martha pushed Foster into his arms, saying: "Here's a wonderful girl, Jack. She wants to do some work for you." For Martha to set up her old drinking buddy with her lover was hardly unusual in radical circles, which considered romance and monogamy to be capitalist myths, relics of bourgeois individualism.

Soble and Foster quickly became lovers and co-conspirators. A few weeks later, under the watchful eye of Alfred and Martha Stern, Foster passed her report on Indonesia to Soble across a formica table at an Upper West Side diner. Soble sent the report to Moscow, where it had quite an impact. In March 1945, seeking to portray its influence in the East Indies as a counter to the imperialist Allies, the Soviet Union entered the report that Truman tried to bury into evidence at a session of the United Nations Security Council meeting on Indonesian independence. It made Foster's reputation in the Kremlin. It didn't hurt Soble's standing either.

By 1949, when Boris first met Jane Foster in Paris, she was living in Austria and had been reunited with Zlatovski, who had fought in the Battle of the Bulge and helped to liberate the Bergen-Belsen concentration camp before joining military intelligence, interviewing displaced persons in Vienna. His real employer was Soble, who ordered him to use his connections with Allied intelligence and refugee relief agencies to track down Russians who had sought refugee status in Austria. Acting as what spies call a "raven," Zlatovski exercised his considerable romantic charms to get secretaries to open up locked file cabinets. Once these refugees found out how much he knew about them, including where their families lived, it was easy to convince them to "redefect" and start working for the Soviets. In the meantime, Foster made Zlatovski look like an amateur when it came to sheer depravity in the service of communism, an ideology that Boris often thought had more in common with the mores of Hollywood than most people realized. She got a cover job at a Salzburg radio station run by the US Information Service, where she managed a staff of ninety-five people, most of whom had until recently been committed Nazi propagandists. Her primary goal, however, was gathering information for Moscow on the sexual preferences, gambling debts, and drinking habits of American officials, information that might be used to blackmail them, particularly those from the Counter-Intelligence Corps, the CIA, or the US Army Information

Services. Salzburg was a small town where the expats all knew each other, so it was easy for Foster to play the part of a "honeypot," inviting them home or taking them on weekend trips to Vienna or Bad Gastein or Kitzbühel, where she dimmed the lights, got them drunk and naked, and took photos. Foster then passed the information and the pictures to Soble, who paid her a monthly salary of $150, plus bonuses of up to $1,000.

Boris soon started working with Foster. The FBI was increasingly interested in Soviet intelligence operations in Austria, and they had high hopes for the June meeting in Vienna, as did Moscow, which was hoping to hear from Boris about the progress he made with Dewey. They were also looking forward to a summary of Foster's activities in Salzburg. But once in Paris, Soble resisted settling the final details for the rendezvous in Vienna. Boris was at first mystified as to why Soble was dragging his feet, but eventually he came to suspect that one of Soviet intelligence's most distinguished and loyal agents was still looking for a way out. When the FBI heard that, they knew an extraordinary opportunity was staring them in the face, and that Boris might eventually be called upon to turn Jack Soble. But not yet.

Boris was simply planning to carry the intelligence that Foster and Zlatovski had gathered in his luggage by train across France and Germany to Austria, because it was too risky for Soble to carry. However, when Soble showed up with the files at Boris's ground-floor room at the Hotel Raphael, things turned out to be comically complicated, in part because the FBI wanted to get copies before he left, and in part because nothing was simple with Jack Soble. Boris had stacked up all ten of his suitcases and was ready to go. All he had to do was get the documents from Soble, slip them out the window to the FBI agents waiting across the street, wait for them to make photographs and return them through the window, and then put them in his luggage. After watching Soble go through his usual inspection of the room, Boris took the envelope with the reports that Soble handed over, put it into the suitcase on top of the pile, and waited for Soble to leave. But Soble thought putting the documents in the top suitcase was unwise. He made Boris unstack the suitcases, put the envelope into the bottom one, and then restack all ten suitcases. Only then was Soble satisfied. After he left, Boris had to unstack the suitcases, take the envelope out of the bottom one and hand it off to the FBI agent through the window, then restack them all over again in case Soble came back. It took the agent only a few minutes to return the documents, at which point Boris had to unstack the suitcases, put the envelope in the bottom one, and restack them again. It was like a scene out of *The Flying Deuces*.

Boris and Soble made their way separately to the Gare de l'Est station, boarded different cars on the Orient Express, and travelled through Strasbourg and Munich to Vienna, a luxurious trip that Boris found nonetheless nerve-racking, and not only because he didn't really know what awaited him in Vienna. Simply entering Austria in the early years of the Cold War was a complicated affair. The country had been subdivided, ruled by the Soviets, the Americans, the French, and the British, each of whom had to approve the entry of each traveller and his luggage, a time-consuming and tense process even if no top-secret intelligence was being smuggled into the country.

Boris, Soble, and the documents arrived safely in Vienna. Boris checked into the Ambassador, a massive, elegant hotel favored by diplomats, celebrities, and royalty, in part because it was located in the zone of the city that was ruled collectively by the four powers. After Soble's usual room check, Boris gave him the reports. Then Soble sat Boris down and explained that Boris needed to exercise great care while in Vienna, because Soble would be making a side trip to Moscow, leaving Boris alone in Vienna. Soble instructed Boris that he shouldn't trust anyone who tried to make conversation with him unless they used elaborate, multilingual, coded greetings. "Dritter, Romeo, Wagram," for example, meant Soble was back from Moscow and needed to meet. Soble's worries, however, seemed to be motivated more by his paranoid obsession with secrecy than legitimate security concerns.

Vienna in the postwar years was a gloomy backwater in ruins, far from the charming, glorious capital of the Habsburg Empire that Boris imagined. Most of its male citizens were dead, and the remaining population was plagued by food shortages and unemployment. More than seven hundred American bombs dropped in March 1945 left rubble-filled streets and bombed-out buildings still visible when Boris arrived. Residents joked that Vienna could survive a third world war but not a second liberation. There was a bitter core to the joke though: Vienna was a hive of espionage and political maneuvering, the place in Europe where the Cold War was the hottest.

While waiting for a signal from Korotkov, who apparently had no intention of funding Boris's television project—he wasn't even sincere about coming to meet Boris in Vienna—Boris tried to find Austrian exhibitors for *Carnegie Hall*. Mostly he played tourist, enjoying his luxurious hotel and dining out at the expensive restaurants that were just beginning to reappear amid the rubble, all of course paid for by the FBI. Finally, after ten days Soble knocked on Boris's door at the Ambassador. He was back from Moscow with good news, though he would only reveal it during a long "walk and talk" through the city. As Boris suspected, Soble had dreaded making the trip to Moscow because he feared being "put in cold storage." In actuality, Soble discovered that his stock in Moscow had gone up, in no small part because of Boris's recent trips to the Vatican and the White House. Soble had actually met with Korotkov and Fedotov, who were delighted with the work Boris had done, though not delighted enough to actually invest in Boris's latest venture, which Beria seems not to have learned. Simply renewing the promise that Boris could soon expect $350,000 from Moscow was the best they could do. That was fine with the FBI, which wanted to keep Boris in service to Moscow for as long as possible. But Boris no longer believed Korotkov's promises.

One reason Boris doubted that he would see the money anytime soon was the fact that Moscow was always playing catch-up with the latest news from America's ongoing spy mania. On July 1, 1949, Judith Coplon was convicted and sentenced to ten years in prison, a development that would have been enough to scare Moscow into pulling back or deactivating its American agents, and putting all of its plans on hold. Then later that month, Alger Hiss's perjury proceedings ended in a mistrial, which in a sense was even worse than if he had been convicted. A conviction would have blown over quickly, but now a prospect of a new trial promised to keep the entire subject on the front pages for months to come.

Soon after Coplon's conviction, Soble rang Boris at the Ambassador and told him he would be meeting a new contact, a Romanian named Vitaly Tcherniavsky, who would be running both of them from then on. Soble told Boris to meet him at Vienna's biggest and most famous attraction, the Prater, a former medieval royal hunting ground that had been turned into a park, with restaurants, promenades, and playgrounds. Most of the Prater was destroyed in the war, and though many of its attractions had been rebuilt, its dilapidated rides, crumbling streets, devastated bridges, and pathetic carnival gave it an air of menace. In other words, it was perfect for a secret meeting. Best of all, at least for Boris's Russian contacts, it was located in the Soviet zone.

When Boris arrived at the park's main entrance, Soble was waiting. They walked arm-in-arm over one of the Prater's many once-picturesque viaducts, then turned off the path and scrambled down to the road that ran underneath the viaduct, where a brown-haired, dapper young man whose suit made him look more like a Madison Avenue executive than a Soviet spy was waiting for them. Vitaly greeted Boris warmly. After all, Boris had become a legend as Moscow's celebrity spy. But then Vitaly and Soble strolled away, as if Boris wasn't even there, and he strained to hear their conversation in Russian and German. A few minutes later, Vitaly gave Soble an envelope stuffed with American money, turned to Boris, and told him that when they next met, it would be under that same viaduct, without Soble. Boris and Soble were to return to Paris. Someone would summon them back to Vienna in time. Once there, Boris was to telephone U-47306 to arrange a time to meet, calling himself "Riabov," the name of a well-known classical music conductor based in Kiev, as well as a character in one of Chekhov's best-loved short stories—these Russians were nothing if not cultured. If all went well, there would be good news about the money that Moscow still wanted to invest in Boris's cover operation.

On their way to Paris, Boris and Soble stopped in Zurich, where Soble deposited the money he received from Vitaly (Boris carried it across the border) into Credit Suisse Bank. Then they continued on to Paris, where Boris's FBI agents came up with a new idea: What if Boris could sell the Soviet rights to his films? They certainly weren't worth $350,000, but it would take care of Moscow's concerns about how to transfer the money to the United States, which Soble now said was the reason behind the delay. Boris wasn't enthusiastic about the idea, but he was willing to give it a try, and Soble was willing to set up an appointment with the Soviet ambassador to France.

Boris met with Ambassador Alexander Bogomolov and his cultural attaché, Nikolai Nagornov, on September 23, 1949, the very day that Truman announced to the world that the Soviets had tested the hydrogen bomb, an achievement that of course had only been made possible by the intelligence that Boris had helped Zarubin smuggle out of America. They agreed to showings of *Tales of Manhattan* and *Carnegie Hall* the next month. It was supposed to be a moment of glory for Boris, as the diplomatic corps and their invited guests admired his work. But by the end of the evening it had become clear to Boris that the Soviets hadn't enjoyed his films enough to make him an offer.

CHAPTER EIGHTEEN
BELIEVING IN TEARS, 1949–50

Moscow was where the money was. That's how Boris explained to Catherine why he was willing to risk his reputation in returning to the Soviet Union once again. The political atmosphere in Hollywood, where anyone with even the hint of a left-wing background was shut out of projects at the studios or even blacklisted, meant that his film career was on hold, perhaps permanently. *The Treasure of Cantenac*, which was a minor film even by European standards, and one that Boris had contributed little to other than his name, hardly counted. So even though he had little reason to think that the promises Soviet intelligence had been making for years about backing his television project were about to be fulfilled, it was the only prospect he had—at least the only prospect he could talk to her about. The other prospect, the one he couldn't tell her about, involved much less money and much more danger: The FBI was going to make him the first American spy to penetrate the Kremlin.

If Boris didn't know what to expect in Moscow—it might be money, or it might be a death sentence—Beria and Korotkov knew exactly what they wanted from him. Their classified "Plan of Action" from November 1949 confirms that Soviet intelligence was less interested in Boris's latest business schemes than his political connections. While some of his time in Moscow should be spent negotiating with the Ministry of Cinematography, the memo proposed, there would also be clandestine meetings to give him new assignments, like finding out more about an employee in the visa section of the American embassy whom Boris had recently identified as a possible recruit for the Russians. Moscow also wanted to assess his progress with Cardinal Spellman, Milton Eisenhower, and Earl Warren. There was one more thing: They still needed to "clarify the hazy parts of J's biography," especially from the period of the revolution and the civil war. After a decade and a half of active service, Boris's background was still a mystery to them.

Boris's FBI handlers normally prepared him carefully for his meetings with the Soviets, but there was nothing normal about this visit; it was unique in the history of American espionage. The Soviets had penetrated virtually every area of American life, every industry, every federal agency, every top-secret project, but an American intelligence operative had never been inside the Kremlin. In a meeting at the Restaurant Chez Vincent, near the Arc de Triomphe, Boris's FBI agents told him they simply couldn't offer him much guidance. They didn't know the players or the reception he would receive: "You used to be a musician," Boris recalled them telling him. "You'll have to play this one by ear." The only thing they could say for sure was that Boris was heading unprotected into a very dangerous situation, one that could easily end in a jail cell, on a chain gang in Siberia, or before a firing squad.

Soble was no more optimistic than the FBI, warning Boris that he would be followed, photographed, and bugged for his entire stay, and that the Russians would no doubt try to lure him into the arms of a honeypot. All Boris had to do was remember his paroles. Anyone who came up to him and asked, "How are you doing? Did you bring the Jascha Heifetz record with you?" was safe. Then again, why would his allies in Soviet intelligence need to use coded greetings in their own country? Was it Soble's paranoia talking again? Or was Boris not paranoid enough?

Boris used his contact at the Soviet embassy in Paris to arrange visas for himself and Catherine as guests of a new organization, Sovexportfilm, devoted to marketing Russian films abroad. Boris actually begged Catherine to stay home, not only because she had little family left to visit but because her vocal hatred of communism would surely get them both in trouble; but she insisted on coming along. So, in late December 1949, Boris took his show back to Russia, where he hadn't been since 1935, where he didn't want to go; everything he knew and felt told him he shouldn't go. Boris and Catherine boarded the Orient Express in Paris and headed for Zurich, where they spent two days, and then travelled on to Vienna. There they celebrated the New Year with Willi Forst, one of Austria's most beloved actors and directors, though his reputation was a bit off-color, owing to the way his career had flourished under the Nazis during the war. Was it another case of Boris protecting his secret identity by camouflaging himself with anti-communists? If so, it seemed to work, as Forst himself begged Boris and Catherine not to go to Moscow, warning them that it would be a miracle if they returned alive: "Innocents like you two usually don't," he told them.

After forty-eight hours in Vienna, Boris and Catherine boarded a train to Prague, where they booked themselves into the most luxurious hotel they could find, the Alcron, an art deco monument near Wenceslas Square. The hotel had attracted the likes of Charlie Chaplin and Winston Churchill before the war, but now it was being run by Czechoslovakia's Communist Party. As Boris suspected, all the rooms were bugged and the lobby was filled with bored young men who were no doubt secret police and women who were far too nicely dressed to be anything but Soviet operatives posing as prostitutes. Boris soon had a chance to find out who they really were. After they had checked in, Catherine went out shopping, leaving Boris alone in the room. He was daydreaming in a chair next to the window when he heard a knock at the door. It was a gorgeous young lady with a low-cut blouse and a burning desire to become a Hollywood actress. Could he do something about that? Boris remembered Soble's warning about honeypots and called downstairs to the front desk to have someone come and throw her out. Then he telephoned the Soviet ambassador and warned him: No more "whore spies" or other tricks. The message got back to Moscow, because Boris and Catherine were treated like returning heroes, both spoiled and undisturbed, for the rest of the journey, which took them to Warsaw and Brest-Litovsk on the way to Moscow.

The long train ride was a surreal experience. They enjoyed the luxurious but dilapidated fixtures of their first-class Pullman room, dining on caviar washed down with *yorsh*, an appalling Russian specialty of vodka mixed with beer. Meanwhile, they watched the grim landscape rushing by, the blasted bloodlands of Eastern Europe, which hadn't even begun recovering from the war. The war had left at least twenty-seven million dead in the Soviet Union, among them almost twenty million civilians, many of whose bodies had not yet been identified or even properly buried, and one-third of the nation's wealth had been destroyed. Five years after victory, the stunned survivors lived lives of privation and terror, though Stalin insisted that they were in the middle of a postwar economic boom. It didn't look that way to the visitors, who at one point were distracted by noises coming from the corridor. They poked their heads out to see a little boy playing not cowboys and Indians but Russians and Americans. It would have been amusing had it not been such a chilling reminder that they had passed through the Cold War mirror.

On the afternoon that Boris and Catherine arrived at Moscow's Belorussky Station, on January 15, 1950, it was already dark. They had forgotten how early the sun goes down in Russia in the winter. Korotkov made sure that a large greeting party, including the minister of cinematography Petrovich Ivanov, a delegation from Sovexportfilm, and E. V. Kovalenok of the Soviet Committee on Artistic Affairs (who was in fact an intelligence agent), was waiting for them. After an elaborate round of greetings, Boris and Catherine were bustled into one car with three of the officials, while another car was devoted to their luggage, as well as precious reels of *Tales of Manhattan* and *Carnegie Hall*, for the three-mile ride to the Metropol Hotel, an art nouveau building opposite the Bolshoi Theatre and a short walk from the Kremlin and Red Square. Along the way, Catherine and Boris marvelled at how gorgeous, clean, prosperous, and modern the capital seemed, "a city awakening from a thousand-year sleep," as Boris put it, compared with the ramshackle huts and impoverished peasants that they had seen from the window of their train.

When Boris saw that Kovalenok had arranged for the bags to be brought into the Metropol and that he had taken care of the bill, he realized that he ought to make the most of his status as an honored guest, so he asked for 1,000 rubles for spending money—the equivalent of about $150 today. Kovalenok opened his wallet and counted out the bills without comment and gave them to Boris, who later privately handed them over to Catherine, who was not merely an anti-communist in theory but a master shopper in practice.

To their surprise, Boris and Catherine were largely left alone to explore Moscow for several days, or so they had been told. But it was hard to enjoy their supposed freedom. No matter how good the shopping might be, Catherine was afraid to venture out alone, so the ever-curious Boris led the way. They didn't quite know what to make of so much that they saw. At the hotel, a band called the Moscow Boys was playing American jazz, albeit in a style that dated from the 1920s, and American-style technology was everywhere, from appliances to construction equipment. Muscovites were not the emaciated, shoeless wraiths they expected. Boris and Catherine ate at the city's finest restaurants several times, but they also sought out more modest establishments, where the menu consisted of smoked fish, black bread, and the inevitable *yorsh* that Muscovites seemed to drink from morning till night; but when Boris and Catherine tried to engage with the other diners, they seemed terrified to enter into conversation. Even getting them to accept an innocuous glass of tea was impossible: "I had never seen so many faces troubled by fear and worry," Boris later recalled. It didn't occur at first to him that what was so worrying to the average Muscovite might not just be life in general but also the loud American in the fancy suit throwing around rubles. Or perhaps it was the presence of the man who so conspicuously followed them wherever they went, even standing outside their hotel room all night? Boris and Catherine didn't let that get in the way of their trip. On the day of their arrival, they had taken in a screening of the film *Fire* at the Metropole Cinema, and over the next few weeks they went to the theater no fewer than nineteen times. They even saw an anti-American puppet show in which a character with a strong resemblance to the legendary Hollywood film producer Joseph Schenk, named "Mr. Pervertitis," ends up in bed with a starlet named "Miss Lay."

Finally, after Boris and Catherine had spent five days enjoying the city, the telephone in their hotel room rang. It was a contact from the Committee on Artistic Affairs with the news that he would be waiting at three P.M. at the Metropol with a car that would take Boris to his first meeting. Boris was already downstairs when the car pulled up. It took him on a short ride through the January dusk to an anonymous building in a leafy residential neighborhood. He was taken to a third-floor apartment filled with the latest appliances, including a television, radio, and record player, clearly installed to impress visitors, and told to wait. Boris had plenty to think about: If this wasn't the Committee on Artistic Affairs, what was it? Boris waited for a full two hours, becoming more and more anxious. Then Korotkov, the "King of the Illegals," a man who had virtually unchallenged authority to do what he wanted with his agents, walked through the front door.

After the usual round of ritual toasts, Korotkov got down to business. First came some good-natured criticism. Why had Boris come empty-handed? Had he nothing new to offer on the many assignments he'd been given? Then there was the matter of his past reports. Although Soble claimed that Moscow had been pleased with a report Boris had written on the state of the Republican Party, it turns out that Korotkov had read the same *New York Times* articles that Boris had used to put together the document. But Korotkov was genuinely pleased with another report that Boris had submitted about a secret meeting at the White House related to the American nuclear program. Boris had no idea what Korotkov was referring to. Apparently Soble had supplemented Boris's dossier with an item that was sure to please Korotkov.

With the question of Boris's performance out of the way, for now anyway, Korotkov turned again to the bottle, and the toasts resumed.

Boris had never been much of a drinker, and he was already tipsy from the last round, which is why he made a mistake that he would never have made while sober. He raised his glass and made a toast to the prospect of peace between the Soviet Union and the United States. He immediately regretted it, having forgotten that his drinking partner hated everything American. Korotkov launched into a tirade on everything from inferior American food and cars to the country's deplorable values, which he had seen undermine the ideological fortitude of Soviet agents who lived there too long. Korotkov hardly needed to mention Soble's name for Boris to get the message. Korotkov claimed that Moscow had spent $60,000 to help Soble buy and run the bristle factory in France—not the $30,000 that Boris had heard—and they were still paying him a quarterly salary. For what? Then Korotkov's face softened and he lowered his voice. Soble was still too important to ignore, Korotkov offered, and while Boris was going to be working his political contacts more intensively in the future, he would still be serving as Soble's bagman, taking cash across borders and making wire transfers. But that might change. If someone approached Boris on the street and whispered in his ear "the general died at dawn," that meant he wanted to talk about Soble. Strangely, the Soviets chose as Boris's new parole the name of the film for which he had been nominated for an Academy Award back in 1936. More precisely, it meant they wanted to hear what Boris had to say about Soble. It took some time before Boris finally understood: "You mean you want me to inform on Soble?" Korotkov answered: "The answer is maybe, soon." Then Korotkov raised a glass to toast Soble, but before he drank he warned Boris not to get too friendly with him or any agents he worked with in the United States.

Boris now felt confident enough to bring up the matter of the $350,000 that Moscow had promised to invest in his television project. He got an answer that was, predictably, both encouraging and off-putting: "Don't worry about money," Korotkov told him. "We'll give you more than you'll be able to use." He refused to say more and Boris dared not push him. The meeting was clearly coming to an end, but before making his farewells, Korotkov told Boris that he would be brought to the same apartment in three days. It wasn't exactly clear why, but Boris knew counterespionage leaks that might expose his real situation were always a possibility, and he feared that every meeting was a potential rendezvous with his executioner.

When he got home he had a hard time explaining to Catherine where he'd been. It was even more difficult to explain why he then locked himself into the hotel suite's bedroom for several hours. She would never have guessed he was putting together a lengthy report on Cardinal Spellman, which he managed to pass along through an intermediary to Korotkov the next day.

The car was waiting in front of the hotel on Monday, January 23, at three P.M. sharp. As expected, it brought Boris to the same place. This time, Korotkov was waiting for him with one of his deputies, Dimitrievich Petrov, a diminutive figure who seemed harmless except for the long scar that ran down his right cheek. This time there were no toasts, no compliments, no friendly inquiries. Instead, Korotkov began with a lecture about Marxism and ended with more criticism of Boris's report on Dewey and Warren. Then Petrov, who seemed to have been assigned to investigate Boris's finances, took over: How much money had he made over the years? How well had his movies done? How profitable had his other projects been? These were difficult questions for Boris to answer. First of all, he didn't really know the answers, because he never paid much attention to his own finances. He was used to lending and borrowing liberally and not paying much attention to the bottom line. Indeed, in the past, Moscow had seemed to know more about his bank balance than he did. And in recent years, the bulk of his income had come from the FBI, and he couldn't very well admit that. Moreover, while his popularity within Russian intelligence depended on his reputation as a millionaire celebrity, the more he had, the less likely he was able to convince Moscow to invest in his various schemes: "Why don't you give your millions to the Party?" Petrov asked. Had Boris's braggadocio been too successful?

When Petrov finished going over Boris's finances, he turned to his connections, and to Cardinal Spellman in particular. Might he be able to use his friendship to penetrate the archdiocese and develop sources, perhaps even place an agent in the cardinal's inner circle as a secretary or assistant? Boris went over his report item by item, admitting that he was "like one" with Spellman, whom he portrayed as a vain man that had his employees scour the newspapers for mentions of him, and whose "colossal influence on the domestic and international politics of the USA" would be easy to control. Petrov had clearly been thinking of Spellman's homosexuality, a secret closely guarded from the Vatican to Gracie Mansion. Boris was feeling genuine remorse at treating his old friend this way and said there were other ways that Moscow could influence the man everyone assumed would be the next pope. Boris explained that Spellman had a female chef and several female housekeepers, which looked quite suspicious for a man who was supposed to be celibate. Even better, for Moscow's purposes, Spellman seemed to have had a longstanding relationship with his literary agent, a young woman named Olga Algazi, who had unlimited access, day or night, to Spellman's private quarters, though it wasn't clear how intimate the two were. Other weak spots included Spellman's problematic brother and the fact that cardinal had close connection to the Orsatti organized crime family. It seemed that Boris would do anything to avoid outing Spellman, a position that neither Korotkov nor Petrov would have shared. With that, the meeting was over. This time there were no hugs or farewell toasts.

Boris was shaken as he made his way home. He'd given them almost everything that they could have wanted on Spellman, including details on his daily schedule, his family, and his friends, but they wanted to hear more details about his sex life. Several days later, Boris was summoned back to the apartment and was surprised to find Korotkov and Petrov waiting at a fully stocked dinner table. After a meal that lasted until well into the evening, they lectured Boris on the place of sex in the spy game. Teams of experts on sexuality had been sent all over the world to gather information on the amatory habits of men from different cultures, information that Soviet intelligence put to use in schools that trained agents whose primary weapon was their sexuality. There was even a commencement ceremony in which graduates were called upon to demonstrate what they'd learned about what Boris later modestly called "the boudoir science." Then the graduates were assigned abroad, targeting American military personnel in particular, whose supposedly puritanical backgrounds made them especially vulnerable to the kinds of exotic charms these women offered. Once in bed, Korotkov told Boris, the men were an open book: "Sex, comrade, works for better for us than dope." Boris remembered the encounter he'd had with their "honeypot" in Prague and wondered if they were having this conversation because he'd passed some sort of test. Or was it the vodka that was determining the agenda?

Korotkov began by asking Boris about the young woman who had served them dinner. Did he find her attractive? Would he like to get to know her better? Then it hit Boris: His rejection of the young would-be starlet in Prague, combined with his refusal to use Cardinal Spellman's homosexuality against him, suggested that he might also be gay. It didn't take much for Boris to dispel that notion.

Once they had exhausted the topic of sex spies, Korotkov had new assignments for Boris, all of which involved prominent American politicians and government officials that Boris had told Soble he was close to. First on the list was former president Herbert Hoover, whom Boris had known in Memphis back in the late 1920s, and who still helped steer the ideological direction of the Republican Party. Next on the list was California representative Helen Gahagan Douglas, a fearsome, elegant former actress who was said to be the inspiration for the Evil Queen in Walt Disney's *Snow White*, and who was an outspoken foe of fascism, sexism, and the bomb. Douglas leaned further left than most other Democrats, though Boris's take, that she was "one of ours" and might surreptitiously represent Soviet interests if she could take the Senate seat of Richard Nixon, was preposterous.

By the time Boris finished explaining how useful Douglas might be to the Soviets, it was late, and Korotkov and Petrov wanted to go home. But Boris had one more idea: It was something he'd only dreamed about in private. Boris had never been a particularly political person, but he recognized the theatrical element of American politics and long thought that if entertainers like Helen Gahagan Douglas and John Davis Lodge could enter politics, so could he. Congressman Boris Morros? That was something they could talk about next time, Korotkov suggested, not very convincingly. The fact that they would be meeting for a fourth time suggested that this was less a debriefing than a slow-motion interrogation. The next time Boris was brought to the apartment, on January 27, Korotkov wasn't even there. Instead Petrov and Kovalenok wanted to review yet again what Boris had on Cardinal Spellman, Earl Warren, and Thomas Dewey. Boris saw opportunities with Spellman and Warren, but Dewey, who had famously lost to Truman in the presidential election of 1948, was a dead end with no political future: "The USA does not like 'losers,'" Boris told them. They also had another assignment: Boris had indicated that while he was in Austria, he had become close to Michael Farrell, the head of the American Office of Displaced Persons. Boris was in the process of arranging for Farrell's mistress, the actress Inga Konrad, to get work in the United States. Since both Farrell and Konrad were politically far to the right and active in anti-communist circles, Boris had obviously stumbled upon a situation that was tailor-made for blackmail. That wasn't all. Before the rendezvous was over, Boris offered Moscow a chance to get inside the Marshall Plan. The chief administrator of the program, Averell Harriman, had been discussing with Boris the possibility of making a series of documentary films about the European postwar reconstruction. If the project went forward, Boris was considering putting his son in charge, and with Dick at the helm, it would be easy to put Soviet agents on the crew, giving them access to information about the Marshall Plan that ordinary Americans, much less Russian spies, did not have.

It was more of the same when Boris met with Petrov and Kovalenok the next day, January 28. At this fifth meeting, they wanted to go over all of Boris's political and business contacts again to see which one would be best suited for providing cover. They said nothing about investing in Boris's television company, and he didn't even get anything of interest to bring back to the FBI. Beyond frustrated, Boris was glad to have a few days off before being summoned back on February 1 for a sixth meeting, though his break had been taken up with meetings with Sovexportfilm functionaries that went nowhere. Nor did they express interest in one of Boris's new ideas: bringing Soviet films to the United States. But they were open to giving Boris permission to make his own films in the Soviet Union and show them, via Boris's company, on American television.

Given how little was getting accomplished in terms of his business deals and his assignments with Moscow—for Boris they were the same thing, while the Soviets seemed to want to keep them separate—Boris was even more gratified to see the giant Korotkov, the tiny Petrov, and the bespectacled Fedotov, who was Beria's much-feared number-two man, walk through the door a few days later for a seventh rendezvous. The meeting started off in a friendly enough way and then it got weird. Soble had described Fedotov as a "smoldering volcano of a man," so Boris expected that after the usual rounds of toasts would come the usual round of recriminations, criticisms, and threats. Instead, Fedotov leisurely chatted with Boris about the movies, economics, and politics. When Fedotov moved on to the topic of Jack Soble, whom he'd known since before World War I, he reminisced about the good old days. Korotkov and Petrov watched, their mouths hanging open in disbelief. This was a Fedotov they'd never seen. Boris waited and waited for Fedotov to get down to business, but the moment never arrived. Boris realized that Fedotov was really only there to say goodbye. Then Fedotov called in his driver and told him to make his own way home. Fedotov himself would drive Boris back to his hotel. It was unheard of, but then again, nothing about Boris's interactions with Soviet intelligence had ever had any precedent.

There were a few more days of shopping and sightseeing, then Boris and Catherine left Moscow for Vienna on February 6, 1950, with the same distinguished party of politicians and bureaucrats who had greeted them three weeks earlier showing up to wave goodbye until the station disappeared in the steam and smoke. They were treated like honored guests in Brest-Litovsk, Warsaw, and Prague. In between, Boris thought through the last month, and the months to come. The FBI would no doubt be delighted that the Russians had been so open about their interest in gathering information about so many of Boris's friends in politics, business, and the entertainment world. It showed that Moscow was at a loss as to the direction that American politics was heading.

And what about the $350,000? The Soviets hadn't thought much of Boris's idea to sell the rights to show his films to Soviet television and cinemas for that amount. Nor had they approved or even understood another of his ideas, in which they might buy those rights in exchange for returning to Germany valuable works of art that the Soviets had plundered from the Nazis in the last months of the war, art that the Nazis themselves had stolen from their victims. Where Boris fit into the scheme wasn't clear to the Soviets—and perhaps not to Boris himself. Given how harebrained some of his schemes were, Boris was perhaps unfairly disappointed that the money hadn't materialized. But he was rightly proud to have survived the nightmare world that existed on the other side of the Iron Curtain, where one was always just a few words or thoughts away from being denounced as an enemy of the people and whisked away to the gulag, or worse. Still, sometimes it seemed Boris survived and prevailed less because of his own talents and more because of the fact that Soviet intelligence was in disarray, following a strategy driven by personality, not policy. That had always been the case to some extent, but this level of disorder seemed unusual. The mystery was solved as soon as he crossed back into Western Europe, and for the first time in a month, saw the newspapers.

When Boris arrived in Moscow in mid-January 1950, Soviet intelligence was still jubilant over the recent founding of People's Republic of China and the German Democratic Republic the previous October, and if there was some concern about how obedient they would be as puppet states, Mao's humiliating visit to Moscow just a few weeks before Boris's arrival settled the question. It seemed that communist states around the world would continue to take their lead from Moscow for the foreseeable future. While Boris was in Moscow, Alger Hiss was convicted of perjury and sentenced to five years in prison, and a German scientist named Klaus Fuchs confessed that he'd operated as a Soviet spy at the Manhattan Project back in 1944 and 1945. Truman then announced plans to up the ante and accelerate production of the hydrogen bomb, which would make the destructive power of the weapons that won World War II seem mild. Then the Soviet Union temporarily lost its veto power on the United Nations Security Council when its representative walked out over the continued presence of Chiang Kai-shek on the council. Given the political turmoil in Moscow and its satellite interests, it was perhaps understandable that there was no consensus on what the Soviet intelligence strategy in the United States and Western Europe should be, no consistent or coherent plan on how to use Boris. Of course, the disarray was only good news for the FBI, and for Boris. In all the chaos, Fedotov had effectively promoted Boris into the top echelon of Soviet agents, while his penetration of the Vatican, the White House, and the Kremlin within a year meant that he had finally earned the nickname the FBI had given him: "Our special special agent." Of course, now the stakes were higher. Before saying goodbye one last time, Fedotov had said to Boris as the car idled in front of the Metropol: "If there is anyone you don't like, anyone who is annoying you and you don't want around any more, just let me know." Whether he said this because Beria demanded that they protect Boris or because Boris was Moscow's only way to get to Soble didn't much matter to Boris, who now knew for sure: "I was 'in.'"

CHAPTER NINETEEN
MY OWN FBI, 1950–51

Sometimes it was hard for Boris to remember who was working for whom. He left Moscow with the sense that Fedotov trusted him, though not when it came to money, which is what really mattered to Boris. If Moscow was stringing him along with promises of funding, Boris could still count on the FBI to pay the rent on his Manhattan production facility, not to mention the hotels, restaurants, and flights, as long as Moscow was convinced he was their man. It's why Boris joked about having "my own FBI."

When he got back to Vienna on February 12, 1950, things got even more complicated. Boris and Catherine had hardly settled into their rooms at the Ambassador Hotel when he was summoned by telephone to the Café Mozart, the oldest of Vienna's coffee houses. But when he arrived, there was someone suspicious loitering nearby. Boris couldn't tell if he was Soviet or American, or one pretending to be the other, but he went right up to the man, stuck out his hand, and said hello. The mysterious character fled, his cover blown. The man wasn't even out the door when Boris realized he'd made a mistake. Now he'd never know which side was watching him.

Boris sat down at one of the cafe's tables for two and was opening the menu when he heard a familiar voice behind him. It was Vitaly, his Vienna contact: "Quick! Follow me!" Vitaly dashed outside and led Boris on a roundabout path that after ten minutes brought them to a parked car. Vitaly got in and waited for Boris to close the door before instructing the driver to take them to one of the train stations in the Soviet Zone of the city. And then what, Boris asked himself. Was Vitaly being extra cautious, or were they planning on making a long, one-way journey?

Boris knew that Korotkov and Vitaly were troubled by a new development in America's ongoing obsession with the communists. While Boris was en route from Moscow to Vienna, Senator Joseph McCarthy had stood up before the Women's Republican Club of Wheeling, West Virginia, and declared: "I have in my hand a list of 205 members of the Communist Party in the State Department." At the time, McCarthy was a relatively obscure figure in Washington, DC, and the list failed to materialize, because McCarthy never had such a list—he was apparently holding in his hand a four-year-old letter from the then-secretary of state claiming that the State Department was riddled with traitors. But everyone in Soviet intelligence knew that their jobs had suddenly become much more difficult. The Judith Coplon and Elizabeth Bentley accusations were fresh in the public memory, and the Alger Hiss and Klaus Fuchs cases were still in play. Meanwhile, the Soviets were moving aggressively into Eastern Europe backed by a nuclear arsenal, and the communists had seized power in China. McCarthy's accusations understandably struck many Americans as worth taking seriously.

Where did events on the world stage leave Boris? Although Boris had returned from Moscow with the idea that Fedotov saw him as one of his most valuable agents, the rest of Soviet intelligence still had doubts. Classified reports composed in the days after Boris left Moscow cast doubt on Boris's accomplishments in the film world and questioned the story that he'd gotten his start as a spy under Beria in the early 1920s, a story that still accounted for his status in Moscow. Boris's business schemes didn't make sense financially and had no obvious intelligence payoff, the reports showed. He hadn't come through with the right kind of information on Cardinal Spellman and Earl Warren, and even worse, Moscow's Paris *rezidentura* had reported that Boris was in danger of being unmasked as a Soviet spy by French intelligence, based on a tip from Martha and Alfred Stern, who were still looking for ways to discredit Boris. There were also concerns in Moscow that Boris's trip had raised suspicions in the FBI that

he was a Soviet spy and that he was now being followed. At the same time, there was the still-unanswered accusation of Jane Foster that Boris was a double agent.

Once Vitaly's driver was headed toward the Soviet zone, Boris thought it would be safe to speak, but Vitaly shot him a look that said "not now." It wasn't until they had been dropped off at the South-West Railway Station and were strolling through the crowded concourse that Vitaly finally explained why he was being so cautious. "You better watch your step," Vitaly warned. Boris was not to contact Soble at all, but wait until Soble contacted him in person. Boris was to make his way to Paris and on February 20, stroll down the Avenue de l'Opéra, heading toward the Louvre on the left side of the street at four P.M. If Soble didn't show up, Boris was to return the next day, and every day after that until they connected. Boris was being used as bait.

Boris's FBI handlers ordered Boris to extend his stay in Vienna and miss the February 20 rendezvous with Soble in Paris altogether, reasoning that a real double agent would never be so careless. As it happens, Soble wasn't sticking to the plan either, but for very different reasons. Boris had a surprise waiting for him when he arrived in Paris on February 21. When he checked into the Raphael Hotel, the clerk at the front desk had a stack of messages waiting for him, all from Soble, who had not only refused to follow Vitaly's instructions about meeting on the Avenue de l'Opéra but indiscreetly left the messages for Boris in his own name, a serious breach of Soviet protocol. A few minutes after Boris unpacked there was a knock on the door. It was Soble. An odd combination of paranoia and careless-ness had increasingly characterized his actions, but this time there was a good reason. Soble explained: He had been tailing Boris since Vienna and believed that the FBI was following him as well, though en route to Paris he had apparently lost the men. It was exactly what the FBI wanted Soble to believe.

Now that the watchers were being watched, Boris's FBI minders had to think long and hard about how long they would be able to main-tain his secret status. Then, in late February 1950, Hal Eaton's nationally syndicated Going to Town column asked a very dangerous question: "It would be interesting to know what took producer Boris Morros to Moscow: What he had to do or give to crash the iron curtain; what he came out with." In an era in which even privately expressed innuendo could have very public consequences, this kind of publicity might have spelled the end of Boris's activities as a spy, or worse. Lucky for Boris, Soviet spies in the United States apparently still didn't bother to read the newspapers very carefully. At any rate, there was no sign from Moscow that things had changed. Indeed, a classified Soviet memo written several weeks after Eaton's column seemed unconcerned about the attention the FBI was apparently paying to Boris and instead focused on Boris's business sense in the matter of trying to fund his television project through various film schemes in the Soviet Union: "M's proposal stems from a desire to sell a million dollars [sic] worth of Amer. movies, and as for his promises to distribute Soviet films in the USA, they cannot be taken seriously." Boris had gotten that message long ago, so while Soble made a trip to the United States, Boris took meetings in Paris about buying the American rights to a World War II drama called *The Fall of Berlin* and a musical comedy produced in Vienna called *Child of the Danube*, and he also kept an eye on *A Tale of Five Women*. But mostly Boris dedicated himself to enjoying Paris.

When Soble came back to Paris, he had a report that Boris was to take to Vienna. It was a single sheet of paper that Soble had hidden in the lining of his jacket, which might have seemed prudent, except for the fact that he had also smuggled a box of American cigarettes in his luggage. If customs found the cigarettes, they would be sure to keep looking for more contraband, and they would undoubtedly find the document. It was simply not the behavior of a seasoned, dedicated spy, but such behavior was becoming increasingly common for Soble. More than once Boris wondered if Soble wanted to be caught. Boris certainly had little confidence in the way Soble was setting up the rendezvous with Vitaly in June. To begin with, there was a complicated new parole. Vitaly would meet Boris under the viaduct near the entrance to the Prater and say: "I am the representative of Almi Films," to which Boris would answer, "Fine. I want to see you." If all was well, Vitaly would then say: "Mr. Vitus from Rome has a message for you." Boris had been instructed by the FBI to try to get Soble to write out the parole, which could then be used as evidence in court, so he complained to Soble that the new one was too complicated to remember. But the Soviets were adamant, and wisely so, that a new parole must always be transmitted orally.

The timing of the rendezvous in Vienna was not auspicious. The blacklisting of Hollywood subversives, inspired by HUAC's relentless hunt for communists, was vying for space on the front pages of American newspapers with McCarthy's crusade. The Fuchs confession had led in late May 1950 to the arrest of Harry Gold, a mild-mannered chemical engineer whose enthusiasm for communism led him to help transmit America's atomic secrets from the Manhattan Project to the Soviet Union. Then in mid-June an investigation into Gold led to the arrest of machinist David Greenglass on charges of stealing documents from the Manhattan Project's facilities at Oak Ridge and Los Alamos. Finally, on June 22, the day before Boris was scheduled to meet with Vitaly in Vienna, a special report in the right-wing American newsletter *Counterattack* did the Hollywood blacklist one better and published a list of 151 actors, musicians, broadcasters, professors, and writers who were suspected of such communistic practices as agitating for civil rights, academic freedom, and nuclear disarmament. The list, contained in a pamphlet called *Red Channels*, read like a Who's Who of postwar American culture: Stella Adler, Leonard Bernstein, Aaron Copland, John Garfield, Dashiell Hammett, Lena Horne, Langston Hughes, Arthur Miller, and Orson Welles all made the cut. Boris wasn't on the list, but many of his friends and colleagues were. Moreover, he had an incessant need for publicity, which had recently resulted in newspaper stories about his acquisition of the American and European rights to the Soviet-financed Austrian film *Child of the Danube*, a deal that let everyone in the industry know he had violated an unofficial trade ban in effect against the Soviet Union. It had been years since Boris had done film work in Hollywood, and it looked more unlikely than ever that he would get that life back, given the suspicions that now clung to his name. It made him less valuable and more vulnerable to both of his spymasters.

Boris was in no mood to see how Vitaly was going to react to all the news when they met on June 23 in Vienna's Prater. Boris tried to set the tone for conversation by complaining that Moscow wasn't giving him any assignments, nor he was he allowed to act on his own initiative. Vitaly was hardly listening: "Stop worrying about little things," he scolded Boris, who didn't understand Vitaly's comment until two days later when he read in the newspaper that North Korea had invaded South Korea, opening up what was essentially a second Asian front in the Cold War. Vitaly had little more to say to Boris, except to set up another meeting a month later.

This time it wasn't Vitaly who showed up but an agitated woman who turned out to be his wife. She ordered Boris to come back again in two days. Boris thought that it was the usual story of Moscow reacting too late to damaging revelations in the West. To be sure, Soviet intelligence was alarmed by J. Edgar Hoover's request to President Truman in the wake of the Korean situation that he suspend habeas corpus and round up more than twelve thousand Americans who were suspected subversives. Then on July 17, 1950, the FBI arrested committed communist Julius Rosenberg, an engineer who, along with his wife, Ethel, was a commited communist who had conspired to steal atomic secrets from the Manhattan Project.

The news was totally unexpected in Moscow, and Boris assumed that it would throw Soviet intelligence into chaos, since such developments usually did. It would certainly explain why Vitaly had missed the June 23 meeting. But Boris was wrong. Vitaly failed to show up because he had been preparing for a daring operation: the kidnapping of Yugoslav premier Josip Tito, who had started out as a loyal servant of Stalin, but whose growing independence from Moscow's directives over the past decade had tested the Soviet supreme leader's patience too many times. Getting to Tito was Stalin's last great obsession, one that, Vitaly claimed, Boris might play a role in. Every possibility was being considered, including spraying Tito's clothing with plague, shooting him at a party in London, and putting poison gas in the box that contained his rings and cufflinks. The latest idea, Vitaly told Boris, was to seize Tito from a train as it went through a Soviet-controlled tunnel in Yugoslavia. This information turned out to be an extraordinary windfall for the FBI, but there was nothing else of substance that Vitaly had to tell Boris: nothing about his past performance, nothing about future assignments, and no plans for the next rendezvous. So Boris decided to take a vacation.

Between his trips to Vienna, Boris saw less of Jack Soble than usual, because in the spring of 1950 Soble had started a new business importing Chinese bristles through Switzerland to France. The business was so lucrative that Soble was able to bring Myra and their son, Larry, to Europe to spend a few weeks relaxing at a summer house he'd rented on the Normandy coast. Boris and Catherine were more than welcome to join them. It was of course a major breach of Moscow's ban on secret agents socializing with each other, but it wasn't the first time that Soble had been so indiscreet. Indeed, Soble had been distancing himself more and more from Moscow, emboldened by the success of his business, which he thought might make it possible for him to finally get out of espionage. When Boris arrived at the tiny town of Villerville, already concerned lest someone back in Moscow find out what they were doing, he was unpleasantly surprised to see Jane Foster enjoying the sun and the water, along with her husband, George Zlatovski, whom Boris had never met. Foster had a completely different response: "George and I nearly died of suppressed laughter when we first saw him in all his glory. He had on yachting slacks, coming up to his armpits as usual, he having no waist, bright red braces, very short naturally, a Breton sailor's shirt and a movie director's hat with visor."

The next few days were uncomfortable to say the least. Jane had no great love for Myra Soble, and she quickly grew tired of Catherine's constant harping on the evils of communism. Boris was relieved to learn that he would need to see Vitaly again in Vienna, and he was able to convince the whole group to take their moveable feast to Bad Gastein, a fashionable resort town in Austria where they could enjoy the thermal springs and classical music concerts while Soble and Boris waited for Vitaly's summons.

Still at heart a musician, Boris was in his element in Bad Gastein. When Foster and Zlatovski couldn't get tickets to a local performance of *Don Giovanni*, Boris, playing the big-shot Hollywood movie producer, reassured them: "I'll get seats for you through my good friend Yehudi Menuhin"—and did. When Zlatovski doubted whether Boris was really a musician, Boris approached a friend at the resort who was performing Tchaikovsky's violin concerto at the nearby music festival at Salzburg, borrowed his instrument, and performed part of the piece from memory. Every morning, every afternoon, and every evening, Boris regaled Jack, Myra, Jane, and George with a nonstop monologue detailing his fascinating adventures. Catherine—who genuinely seems to have been unaware that she was surrounded by Soviet spies—had of course heard it all before, and though Foster and Zlatovski liked to mock Boris for his looks, they were charmed by his tales, especially because Soble seemed to believe every word.

The Boris Morros show wasn't just about the past. One evening at dinner, he told his companions how earlier in the day he had gone for a walk in the mountains and noticed that an unseen source of magnetism or radiation was interfering with the functioning of his wristwatch. He surmised that it was an underground vein of uranium that would make him a millionaire all over again and boasted that he'd managed to buy the entire mountain and return in time for cocktails. Soble, Foster, and Zlatovski, like so many Soviet spies, couldn't resist such stories. Indeed, Boris might have looked silly in his mogul-on-holiday getup, but his driver and fancy car, his ability to get the best table in any restaurant and pick up the check with a thick wad of cash, and his connections in Hollywood spoke louder than his looks. Foster and Zlatovski might also have humored Boris because they now needed him. After leaving US Army Intelligence in 1948, Zlatovski had been unable to find a job in France that would guarantee him a residence permit. Foster waited for one of those rare moments when Boris stopped talking and asked him discreetly if he could help.

When did Boris ever say no? But first he needed to make a quick trip to meet Vitaly in Vienna. The rendezvous, on August 19, was shaping up to be one of their usual non-meetings, with Boris complaining about Moscow's lack of interest in his television and movie deals, and Vitaly complaining about Boris's failure to produce something really shocking about Cardinal Spellman and Earl Warren. But then Boris committed a strategic error. He mentioned that he had come for the day to Vienna from Bad Gastein, where he was enjoying the waters with his wife, the Sobles, Jane Foster, and George Zlatovski. Vitaly, already shaken by the widening nuclear spy scandal in the United States, was furious at this breach of protocol: In the first place, vacations were a bourgeois, capitalist luxury. Moreover, fraternizing with other operatives was strictly forbidden.

When he finished his diatribe, Vitaly outlined a new assignment for Soble and Zlatovski. The mission to neutralize Tito in Yugoslavia was still on, but they needed someone to assess Tito's popularity among the general population. Zlatovski would travel to Yugoslavia posing as one of Soble's brush salesmen and find out if Yugoslavs would be glad to see Tito gone and return to Stalin's embrace. Or would they favor replacing Tito with someone who would take even more distance from the Soviet line? If such an assignment seemed amateurish, it was because Vitaly needed to find a way to keep Zlatovski on the inside, without putting him in a position where he could do any damage.

Vitaly also had something in the works for Boris. The telegram that summoned him back to Vienna in early September said "contract prepared," which suggested good news. But when Boris arrived at the Prater, it wasn't Vitaly who met him but Petrov, whom he hadn't seen since Moscow, and a crew of bodyguards. Petrov walked Boris to the third-floor apartment of the nearby safe house where Boris had previously met Vitaly, closed the front door, and burst out in anger at everything from Boris's breach of protocol in vacationing with other agents to the ostentatious yellow tie Boris was wearing. Apparently, there was nothing else on the agenda except to order Boris to be ready again the next day at the usual place in the Prater. These non-meetings, Boris realized, were simply a way to keep him on a short leash. As he left the apartment building and walked back to his hotel, Boris noticed someone following him again. He led his tail on a long, pointless walk around Vienna before slowing down until the two were close enough to talk. "Hello, my faithful shadow," Boris called out to the man, who fled.

When Boris, wearing a more subdued necktie, showed up at the Prater the next day, Vitaly's wife was waiting along with Petrov, who held Boris tightly by the arm and walked him to another safe house, this time at Danhausergasse 10, where Vitaly was waiting. Then they all left Boris alone there for almost three hours without any explanation and returned only to complain again about the arrangements at Bad Gastein and Boris's clothing. Petrov grabbed Boris by his new necktie and pulled, hard. Boris had only one panicked thought: "So this is where it all ends." Petrov eventually let go, moving on to Boris's other shortcomings, most prominently his failure to use his connections in the entertainment world to advance the Soviet cause. Then Boris realized that Petrov was just working his way around to the next assignment: In October, it would be Boris and not George Zlatovski who would travel to Belgrade, under the cover story of trying to sell the rights to show *Carnegie Hall* in Yugoslavia. There he would talk to as many people as possible to try to gauge Tito's popularity. Boris was elated at the assignment, which indicated a new level of trust in his abilities. Just as important for Boris, and for the FBI, which was beginning to resent the way Boris was milking them for cash, Moscow would be picking up the tab.

There was one more meeting in Vienna, this time with both Petrov and Vitaly. After the usual sermons about wardrobe, punctuality, and general devotion to the cause, Petrov and Vitaly rehearsed Boris's new parole with him and sent him back to Paris to wait. Apparently not everyone in Soviet intelligence was feeling confident about the coming weeks, when they would be depending on Boris to carry out an assignment that was personally important to Stalin. Back in Moscow, a still-unidentified high-ranking intelligence official who never heard Boris talk about his assignments, but only his business ventures, was having serious doubts, writing to Vienna: "These profiteers are cheating us; they milk us for money and don't want to work. We have to put an end to this situation." But whereas the anonymous writer saw the problem as one of character, Vitaly saw it as a question of Soble's poor handling of his ring. Vitaly wrote back to Moscow: "J. requires constant guidance, which Czech cannot provide." There was no better proof than the fact that Boris, thinking he could parlay Moscow's new trust in him into cash, couldn't resist pitching, yet again, with a good deal of what Vitaly called "nervous insistence," his deal involving *Child of the Danube*. In a rare moment of weakness, Boris had pleaded that he needed it to save face in the film industry and was "especially agitated—and clearly upset," Vitaly wrote, to be turned down yet again.

All along, Boris had been wondering why Moscow didn't just send Soble to Yugoslavia. When he got back to Paris and met with Soble, he learned the reason. Soble was cultivating a new source that might allow Moscow to recover from the loss of the Rosenbergs. Soble had come into contact with a married couple, doctors originally from Austria who had been hired at various times in recent years to work in the vicinity of several of America's most important atomic weapons production facilities, including Los Alamos, and whose ideological proclivities meant they were willing to gather and share information about the locations and quantities of American nuclear devices. They even had photographs of the bunkers where the bombs were stored. Soble, who wanted the credit for himself, would not tell Boris any more details about "the atomic couple."

In mid-September, Soble had travelled to Vienna to hand over to Petrov the documents and photographs prepared by the "atomic couple," but Petrov never showed up. Waiting in a downpour at the designated drop-off site, Soble worried that Petrov had been arrested by the Americans or liquidated by the Soviets. And what to do now? Soble couldn't destroy the package and he couldn't bring it back to the hotel. Soble called Vitaly, who told him that Petrov was at that moment drinking himself into oblivion with a lady friend in Prague. Vitaly rushed over in the rain, accepted the package from Soble, and forwarded it in the next diplomatic pouch to Moscow.

Soble, who had long been looking for a way to end his spy career, now hoped for a promotion in return for this extraordinary scoop, which gave the Soviets an inside view of American nuclear weapons production. It was the kind of information that could help determine Moscow's bargaining position for years to come, which is why the FBI made it Boris's top priority to identify the "atomic couple"—after he returned from Yugoslavia.

Boris boarded the Simplon Express train in Paris bound for Belgrade on October 11, 1950, and arrived via Lausanne and Trieste two days later, heading straight for the Hotel Moskva, which during the war had served as Gestapo headquarters. As usual, there would be nothing but the best for Boris. He ate at Belgrade's finest restaurant, the Majestic, and soaked up all of the high and low culture that the city had to offer, including theater, classical concerts, popular music, nightclubs, and films. Because of Tito's independence from Moscow, it was simple for foreigners to enter Yugoslavia and move about. Boris talked to everyone he met: busboys, taxi drivers, and even Jack Soble's old Serbian running buddies from the University of Leipzig from two decades earlier. Boris being Boris, he even found someone he knew, a priest related to Tom Mix, Hollywood's "King of the Cowboys." No matter whom he talked to, Boris found that the love that Yugoslavians had for their benevolent dictator was matched by a hatred of Stalin and all things Russian.

Boris left Belgrade after a week, travelling via Zurich to Vienna, where he was scheduled to report to Vitaly one morning about what he had learned in Yugoslavia. At the safe house on the Danhausergasse, Vitaly told Boris: "All Moscow is waiting to read what you have found out for us in Belgrade." Vitaly put a stack of paper and a handful of sharpened pencils in front of Boris and told him to write down everything that happened to him on the trip, especially impressions of the residents, their attitudes toward the Soviet Union and the United States, and procedures regarding passports and customs. Vitaly left Boris alone with his story, returned four hours later with lunch, and then left again, returning only at seven P.M. to collect the results. He seemed impressed with the monograph Boris had produced and told him to come back the next day to fill in any details or explain anything that wasn't clear.

But Boris wasn't finished for the day. Feeling confident that he was now in the position to ask for something from Moscow, Boris once again brought up the subject of funding for his television project. The New York offices were very expensive, he explained, and he was paying the rent out of pocket. That of course was a lie: The FBI covered the rent every month. If the Soviets couldn't back that project, they could surely give him something else to do: "Let me move on from basic training; give me a good contact in the USA," he begged them. Let's talk more about it tomorrow, Vitaly answered.

By the time Boris returned the next day, Vitaly had read the report and was very pleased. He asked Boris to fill in a few details and then wanted to know how much Moscow should reimburse him for his week in Belgrade. Boris came up with a figure of $780, the equivalent of more than $8,000 today, but Vitaly wanted a precise accounting at their meeting the following day, at the Lindenkeller Restaurant on the Rotenturmstrasse. After Boris gave Vitaly a list of his itemized expenses, Vitaly reached into his pocket, took out a sheaf of American currency, and peeled off thirty-nine crisp twenty-dollar bills. Now that everyone was satisfied, Vitaly brought up the matter of Moscow coming up with $350,000 for Boris's television production company, telling him that it was almost a done deal. Fedotov would be making his final decision before the end of the month. Boris would have laughed out loud had his FBI contacts not explained to him that the longer it took to close the deal the better, because it meant more time "on the inside" for Boris. That theory was confirmed right away when Vitaly pulled out a list of new assignments for Boris, none of which Boris was to share with Jack Soble. The change was a first, and an ominous one.

Boris was to organize a trip to the USSR of a group of a dozen prominent Americans, not "comedian progressives," Vitaly warned, but influential and beloved figures. There they would observe the friendly and peace-loving nature of the Soviet people and bring home a message: "Another world war is the last thing the Kremlin wants!" Next, Boris was to get closer to another prominent American he had mentioned was a good friend and an even better source: T. Keith Glennan. Moscow hadn't been much interested in Glennan, a former engineer who had known Boris since they both worked at Paramount in the 1920s, and who had gone on to lead the Cleveland Technological Research Institute. But earlier in the month Glennan had taken a seat on the Atomic Energy Commission, with a special focus on the development of a hydrogen bomb. Perhaps there was something about Glennan's politics or his personal life that they could use against him? Boris promised to go digging, but he had to fake his enthusiasm. Boris had been the best man at Glennan's wedding, was an executor of Glennan's will, and was the legal guardian of two of Glennan's children. Boris warned Vitaly that trying to dig up any dirt on Glennan, a middle-of-the-road conservative with a solid family life, was futile. Vitaly wasn't discouraged. Perhaps Boris could convince Glennan, who would be known in coded messages as "Astrologer," to offer Dick a job on the commission? Then Dick, who was to be referred to by the code name "Reed," could be recruited, following his father's footsteps in serving the revolution.

Vitaly wanted to go slowly when it came to asking Boris recruit his own son, so he heard Boris out when he pitched a handful of ideas about doing movie business in Yugoslavia. Might Moscow be interested in helping Boris sell the rights to his films in Yugoslavia as a way of raising money for his television project in America? Perhaps they could get behind an idea for a television show based on Yugoslavian folk songs? How about a movie on the life of Tito? Would Stalin fund that? No wonder Fedotov wrote in a classified memo to Vitaly: "We have doubts about the seriousness of his intentions."

When Boris got back to Paris, all Soble could talk about was George Zlatovski, who had been assigned to hang around local airports and learn more about the military vehicles and equipment the Americans were shipping to France. The problem was that Zlatovski didn't have proper cover. Might Boris be able to help? Boris dreaded getting involved in Zlatovski's problems, but he needed to please both Moscow and Washington. Boris had his own troubles by now. The FBI gave him a monthly salary and paid for most of his basic living expenses, but they increasingly resisted funding the extravagant lifestyle Boris craved, and since none of his other projects were bringing in any money, Boris had started to borrow money. So in early December 1950, he told Zlatovski that $4,000 would buy him a job at a Paris movie theater that Boris supposedly owned and a 10 percent stake in the business. The story sounded far-fetched, and it was. One of Boris's friends, the son-in-law of the composer Sergei Rachmaninoff, Boris Conus, was the owner of the Studio Montmartre, a cinema at 43 Rue du Faubourg Montmartre, and was willing to play along in return for a piece of the $4,000, the rest of which would go right into Boris's pocket. Foster wired for the money from her father, who was relieved that it meant his no-good son-in-law would finally have a steady job and a piece of a good business. They did the deal, but Zlatovski didn't last long at the cinema. He had supposed he would be Conus's partner. He ended up being the assistant manager's assistant. Even worse, Zlatovski spent less time working than arguing politics with Conus, a man of the right who didn't appreciate hearing Zlatovski lecture him about the virtues of Stalin and the glorious Soviet future. Soble, who was following the whole business and sensed that Boris had pulled a quick one on Zlatovski, came up with a solution: He sent Zlatovski to Yugoslavia, using Soble's brush and bristle business as cover, to follow up on Boris's report, giving Boris just enough time to head back to the States with Catherine. They sailed from Cherbourg on December 28, 1950, bearing no fewer than twenty pieces of luggage, according to immigration records. After more than a year's absence from the United States, they arrived in New York five days later, heading directly from the piers to the train that would take them back to California.

CHAPTER TWENTY
ATOMIC BONDS, 1951—52

Boris was only home for a few weeks before he was gone again. What was there to keep him in California anyway? His film career was dormant to say the least, and his television project was based in New York. There was his family, but his father was safely ensconced in a Los Angeles nursing home, and he had little to do with Dick, now a grown man of twenty-seven, other than to bail him out of his debts from time to time. Things were different with Catherine, who still didn't know, or didn't want to know, that Boris was a spy, much less a double agent. She remained curiously loyal to Boris, and even pretended not to know about his infidelities, including the love affair that he carried on in the late 1940s or early 1950s, according to Jack Soble's later account, with a pianist named Elisabeth Schumann. Whether or not Boris had ever been in love with Catherine, the marriage had essentially ended years earlier, but they kept up appearances.

When Boris later remembered that "I did not mind leaving Hollywood behind me," he wasn't only talking about his personal life. It was also a matter of business. By 1950, Boris wouldn't have been able to make films in Hollywood even if he wanted to. Anti-communist hysteria was on the rise, and nowhere was it sharper than in Hollywood, where the studio chiefs, most of whom were bullies that were easily bullied themselves, essentially took their marching orders from Hoover and McCarthy. This made Boris a suspect character: A Russian immigrant with no visible means of support and plenty of blacklisted friends, who spent suspiciously long periods of time in Paris and Vienna, with mysterious jaunts behind the Iron Curtain. Widely considered "The Hollywood Eleventh," though not the only figure to claim that title, Boris heard people openly call him a socialist, and even old friends now snubbed or abandoned him altogether: "Those who did not suspect me of being a Russian agent thought me at least a fellow-traveler," Boris later wrote. Eventually, Boris revealed that the US Senate committee investigating communist subversion received numerous condemnations of him on political grounds, and the Justice Department had a thick file of letters denouncing him. The FBI made sure those efforts went nowhere.

In late January 1951, Boris travelled to Washington, DC, where he lunched with T. Keith Glennan, who seemed willing to join the board of directors of Boris's television production company. Getting Dick a job at the Atomic Energy Commission was a different story: Glennan wasn't allowed to have anything to do with hiring. While in the nation's capital, Boris also decided to do some sightseeing, starting naturally enough with the headquarters of the FBI, where he emptied the racks of every brochure that was publicly available. He even took a copy of the application to become an agent.

Summoned to meet with Vitaly in Vienna, Boris headed up to New York and steamed back to France alone, with the nominal goal of closing a deal on *Child of the Danube*. He found himself seated at supper next to Leonard Bernstein, who as a child had crossed paths with Boris in Jewish Boston back in the 1920s. In 1951 Bernstein was only thirty-three years old but already an international star who nonetheless had been publicly outed as a communist in *Red Channels* just months earlier. He expressed a desire to work with Boris on a project for the movies or perhaps television, but Boris, who naturally gravitated toward celebrities and rarely turned down the opportunity to work with one, had no choice but to put off Bernstein: "I could not hire a Red," he told Bernstein.

In Vienna, Vitaly was waiting for Boris at their usual meeting place, under the viaduct in the Prater. Moscow had been expressing doubts about Boris's reliability, but Vitaly forgot all about that when Boris showed him the materials he had picked up during his visit to FBI headquarters. Vitaly was one of Moscow's top spies, but he had almost no idea about how the FBI operated or how agents were selected and trained, so he was flabbergasted to see the actual application materials. He couldn't conceive of a national intelligence agency operating with that kind of openness and thought he knew for sure now that Boris was not the bumbling incompetent that Martha Stern or Jane Foster made him out to be, but a daring, bold, committed intelligence officer who, it seems, could find a way through any door. Boris decided to double down on this strategy and pulled out an honorary sheriff's badge that the Los Angeles police had given him. Anyone who had ever made a contribution to the Policemen's Benevolent Association got one, of course, but Vitaly was humbled, thinking that Moscow had seriously underestimated this agent because of his bad wardrobe and worse accent.

Boris capitalized on his advantage and took charge of the meeting, disingenuously complaining that the way Moscow was still stringing him along was costing him money—$10,000 a year in rent for office space. And then there was the matter of *Child of the Danube*, which was simply too expensive for Boris to acquire. Why couldn't Soviet intelligence exert its influence on Venfilm, the Austrian subsidiary of Sovexportfilm that made the movie, to have the price for foreign rights lowered? Boris's strategy failed on both accounts. He forgot that Vitaly considered him a rich man, which wasn't quite true.

When Boris left Paramount to go independent, he made good money, but there was no regular paycheck anymore, and there were more and more lean years as time went on. There was nothing Vitaly could do about the price of *Child of the Danube* anyway. As regards Moscow's investment in Boris's television project, the $350,000 had been approved, Vitaly insisted, but Moscow needed more from Boris, something to compromise Cardinal Spellman or J. Edgar Hoover. Boris seems to have somehow believed he would actually see the money someday, so he was willing to listen. What about Glennan? Boris countered that Glennan had agreed to sit on the project's board, but it wouldn't be possible to get Dick a job at the Atomic Energy Commission. Vitaly became frustrated, saying that they needed something to blackmail Glennan with: a girlfriend or boyfriend, a gambling debt, an addiction, anything. When Boris replied for the umpteenth time that Glennan couldn't be blackmailed because he was simply a hard-working, clean-living, faithful husband, Vitaly sighed loudly: "I'll never make a spy out of you, Boris." Boris took it as a compliment and headed back to Paris, where he met with Soble, who had fallen into a deep depression. He was hoping that the revelations of the "atomic couple" would change his status back in Moscow. Instead, all Soble got was a medal.

Vitaly had warned Boris to stay away not only from Jack but also from Myra Soble, who had started working for her husband as a courier and had moved up to writing reports and even substituting for him at rendezvous; the FBI ordered Boris to do the opposite. That wasn't difficult, since Boris always picked up the check. But it was still Soble and his mysterious "atomic couple" that Boris was focused on. So when Soble mentioned that he was headed to Vienna to meet with Vitaly about the reports on the "atomic couple," Boris tagged along, the FBI making it clear to him that getting the names of the couple was his highest priority. Soble invited Boris for dinner in Vienna on the evening of February 21, 1951, but when Boris showed up he saw that Soble was already seated with someone from the local film industry. Boris had only been invited to make Soble look good, and to pay the bill.

As the brandy flowed, Soble tried to impress his guests with a recitation, à la Boris, of the rich and famous that he knew, among them an old friend from his leftist university days in Leipzig. The man had inherited a fortune from his family in Austria and invested it all in coal mining schemes in Czechoslovakia, even as he remained active in the Austrian Communist Party. When the Czechoslovakian coal industry was nationalized in 1938, Soble continued, the friend lost all of his investment and fled to England, but somehow he'd managed to build his fortune back up and was richer than ever, despite remaining a committed communist and living in Austria. In fact, Soble continued, under the influence of the liquor, he'd dined with this millionaire, his wife, and her sister, a doctor who was married to another doctor, just a few weeks before. Boris's mind had been drifting, but when he heard about the married doctors, he could barely contain himself. This was the "atomic couple"! Boris hoped that Soble would let their names slip, but he was already on to something else.

Boris stayed in Vienna, mulling over ways to get Moscow moving on his television production plans. Boris also continued his negotiations to acquire foreign rights to *Child of the Danube*. It was a problematic deal in more ways than one. Venfilm wouldn't take less than $100,000, which Boris couldn't afford. In addition, the deal violated Hollywood's unofficial ban on doing business with the Soviet Union. Then again, Boris had already been essentially "gray-listed." Nor could Boris get another meeting with Vitaly, whose job had been made more complicated by the latest round of bad news from the States. The Rosenbergs had just been sentenced to death, and their handler, William Perl, an engineer who was old friends with Julius Rosenberg and who had passed on to Moscow intelligence he gathered working on supersonic flight at Cleveland's Jet Propulsion Laboratory, had been arrested.

Moscow reacted to the news that Glennan couldn't get Dick a job at the Atomic Energy Commission with deep disappointment. One memo to Vienna remarked: "As usual, he 'got our interest' and then didn't follow up." Now it seemed to Fedotov that Boris was only as productive as he wanted to be, and over the next two months, a series of cables from Moscow to Vienna once again cast doubt on their man in Hollywood, who wasn't even much in Hollywood anymore: "We have become increasingly convinced that the only motive for his cooperation with us is a desire to settle his own business at our expense." Vitaly was warned not to fall for Boris's "enticing proposals." Worst of all, Moscow couldn't use its traditional means of putting pressure on its agents when it came to Boris: "His relatives in the USSR cannot be used to influence him, b/c J. takes no interest in them whatsoever."

But those voices could not trump Beria's seemingly unshakeable trust in Boris, though that trust hadn't translated into cash so far. Boris needed to give Moscow something and Cardinal Spellman was his best bet. The way it happened was almost enough to make Boris a believer. In

April 1951, Boris was back in New York, staying at the Waldorf-Astoria and trying desperately to get in touch with Spellman by telephone. Frustrated and concerned about what he would tell Vitaly at their next meeting if he once again came up empty-handed, Boris took a walk to clear his mind. He was strolling absentmindedly along East Forty-Eighth Street, two blocks away from the chancery of the archdiocese where the cardinal lived, when he felt a finger on his shoulder. Turning around, he saw it was none other than Spellman, who said: "Boris, it seems that God wanted us to see each other, because I have been trying to get through to you."

Spellman invited Boris to dinner the next evening. When Boris arrived, he was disconcerted and also honored to see that he was the only person at the gathering who wasn't a church official. He was surrounded by priests jockeying for favor with Spellman—it was not the intimate evening Boris had hoped for. But after the waiters cleared away the dessert plates, Spellman invited Boris upstairs to his private chambers, where it became clear that Spellman wanted to talk politics. President Truman had just relieved General Douglas MacArthur of his command in Korea, a decision he justified by pointing to recent military setbacks. Spellman was livid, convinced that Truman had fired the most celebrated warrior in American history because he wasn't soft enough on the communists. Spellman, who believed it was impossible to be too hard on the communists, told Boris that he'd actually picked up his hotline to the White House and told Truman that if he didn't get tougher on communism, he would order Catholics, who comprised almost one-third of the American electorate, to vote Republican in the next election. "The country is in great danger," said Spellman, breathing heavily. He took off his sweat-drenched collar and, speaking with a halting wrath, predicted: "If power remains in the hands of Truman and his followers, the country will soon be in Uncle Joseph's hands in instead of Uncle Sam's."

This was precisely the sort of thing Boris believed Moscow wanted to hear, and he got more of the same the very next evening, when he dined with former president Herbert Hoover, who called Truman's actions not merely foolish but treasonous. And that wasn't the worst of it. According to Hoover: "The worst criminal of all is the brains behind that idiot—Acheson. Even now, that fashionable lawyer continues to flirt with Communists at fashionable salons. From top to bottom, the entire State Dept. is full of pederasts and pinkos." If that information wouldn't please Fedotov, what would?

A week later, Boris was on his way back to Europe. In Vienna, Vitaly seemed impressed by what Boris had to report on Spellman and Hoover, but the response from Moscow wasn't what Boris expected. Since both Spellman and Hoover were well-known anti-communists, Boris's report was "not very interesting." Boris walked back to his hotel deeply disappointed. As he passed through the front door of the Ambassador Hotel, he found himself face-to-face with an angry George Zlatovski, who had returned from Yugoslavia to find out that not only had he lost his job at the cinema in Paris but the manager claimed to know nothing about Boris's supposed 10 percent stake in the business.

With murder in his eyes, Zlatovski shouted that "one of us is not going to leave this room alive unless I get the $4,000." In full view of the crowd that had gathered in the lobby, he punched Boris in the mouth, breaking several of his teeth. It is a tribute to Boris's powers of persuasion, or to Zlatovski's gullibility, that while bleeding and terrified, Boris managed to convince Zlatovski to accept $2,000 of the rights to the English-language version of *Child of the Danube*, which Boris said he had finally acquired, as compensation. Once again, Boris had sold Zlatovski something he didn't even own. For the other half of the money, Boris called Catherine and begged her: "Darling, I will throw myself into the Danube if you don't cable me $2,000 immediately." It wasn't Boris's finest moment, but he came out even, except for the teeth. Of course, he knew a good dentist in Vienna.

Boris's troubles were nothing compared to what Jack Soble was going through. For a time, things had been going Soble's way, but when Boris met with him in May 1951 in Vienna, Soble was suffering from a mysterious skin ailment that resulted in boils all over his face. His mental condition was even worse. Soble looked like he was having a nervous breakdown as he bemoaned the state of Soviet intelligence, which was losing so many of its agents. He was referring in particular to the recent revelations that the veteran British foreign service officers Donald Maclean and Guy Burgess were in fact Soviet spies. The ones who remained in service, like George Zlatovski, often weren't worth the trouble they caused. What was also bothering Soble was that Moscow had decided to stop using his brush and bristle business as cover in France. Worst of all, Soble was convinced that the French police were suddenly taking an interest in him: They had paid a visit to the bristle factory and were looking into his mysterious trips to Vienna. "I'm spitting blood," Soble told Boris, using the old Soviet expression for being targeted by law enforcement.

The FBI saw the relationship between Boris and Soble changing: The apprentice seemed to be taking the master's place. Boris might speed up the process, they thought, by exploiting Soble's vulnerability. When Boris and Soble met in Paris on June 10, 1951, just a week after the Supreme Court upheld the convictions of the leaders of the Communist Party of the United States on Smith Act violations, Boris took charge, announcing that this might be the last time they ever met. Moscow had wanted to Boris to distance himself from Soble. Boris was inclined to agree unless Soble, who hadn't done any work for Moscow in months, made a gesture of good faith: revealing the name of the coal-mining tycoon whose sister was one-half of the "atomic couple." Soble realized that Boris was his only chance to escape the wrath of the Russians, so he told him: It was Paul Loew-Beer, whose wife's sister, Beatrice Spitz, and her husband, Henry, formed the notorious "atomic couple." After all the months of scheming to get Soble to reveal the name, Boris was at first disappointed: Soble had once introduced Boris to Loew-Beer at a train station in Zurich. Boris hadn't suspected that the tall, obese dandy, who was one of the most prominent communists in Europe and who funded a variety of communist initiatives via Swiss bank accounts, was the key to the mystery of the "atomic couple."

Boris had outwitted one of Moscow's most accomplished agents by getting him to reveal one of his most closely guarded secrets. Still, he felt a twinge of conscience at having taken advantage of Soble's misfortunes, but he had been doing it for years in order to survive. Boris headed straight for the café on the Champs-Élysées where his FBI contacts were waiting. Boris had hit what he called "the espionage jackpot." Could he finally walk away from it all and get back to his life? Did he even want to walk away from it all? And what kind of life was there to get back to? These were all pointless questions, because as far as the FBI was concerned, Boris's career as a double agent was far from over. Indeed, now that Soble seemed to be deactivating himself, Boris's work was more important than ever.

George Zlatovski also sensed that Soble and Boris were exchanging roles. He had never much liked Soble, and not simply because Soble had been his wife's lover. Rather, the way Zlatovski saw things, Soble had lured him and his wife to Paris with the promise of a proper job and an opportunity to serve the cause, but the job hadn't worked out, Soble had never given them valuable espionage work to do, and Soble had always taken credit for any results. Zlatovski might have patched things up with Soble, but Jane Foster and Myra Soble had gotten themselves into a vicious feud over the ownership of a refrigerator. No one seemed to notice the irony of two Soviet spies fighting over who owned a kitchen appliance, a prime symbol of American capitalism.

Now Zlatovski saw Soble withdrawing from active duty and thought that if Soble wouldn't promote him, perhaps Boris would. In June, Zlatovski travelled to Vienna to make his plea to Boris, who hadn't quite gotten over the humiliation of the scene in the Ambassador lobby. But when Boris learned that Zlatovski had brought with him a letter to Moscow detailing Soble's various misdeeds and shortcomings, Boris swallowed his pride. The FBI had long been urging Boris to find a way to lure Foster and Zlatovski back to the United States with the promise of a job stateside, but the couple simply didn't trust Boris that much. So the FBI asked Boris to try to get something incriminating in writing from Zlatovski and Foster, evidence that would hold up in court. When Boris saw Zlatovski's typed ten-page screed, signed with their code names, "Rector" and "Slang," he knew it wouldn't do. Truman had been doing his best to restrain Hoover's

FBI, pushing the Justice Department to end all of its "black bag" operations and adhere to legal standards of evidence gathering. For the letter to hold up in court, it would have to be handwritten and signed with their real names. Boris convinced Zlatovski to redo the letter, arguing that the new version would have a much bigger impact when he passed it on to Vitaly. Boris surprised himself by keeping both versions for the FBI. He wanted to protect Soble from Moscow, but not out of mere friendship. If the Russians sensed that conflicts in Soble's ring posed a security threat, they would break up the ring, lure them back to Moscow, and liquidate them all.

Boris couldn't protect Soble forever, and by the end of 1951, Moscow had lost patience. As far as Soviet intelligence was concerned, Soble was a rogue agent who had essentially deactivated himself and gone into hiding. Of course, Soble had accrued a library's worth of knowledge about Soviet intelligence over the past three decades, which was a grave danger to the Soviets if he should ever decide to switch sides—and a distinct possibility if the FBI got to Soble first. So when Boris was summoned from London to Vienna for a series of meetings in January 1952, there was only one item on the agenda: Find Jack Soble.

Boris knew exactly where Soble was, but he played along, with a twist: If the Russians wanted to find Soble, they would have to provide financial backing for a new branch of Venfilm, which had made *Child of the Danube*, to be located in Switzerland and run by Boris. In return, Boris was to lure Soble to Vienna on the pretext of a business meeting related to Venfilm, where Soviet agents would bring Soble back into the fold. Boris had a number of reasons to doubt that any of this would happen. To begin with, it was not Vitaly who was waiting under the viaduct in the Prater but a new agent by the name Yakov, and why should Boris trust him? Moreover, given Moscow's reluctance to fund Boris's past proposals, why would they suddenly become willing investors in a scheme that had considerably fewer dividends in terms of both money and intelligence? And who's to say that once Boris and Soble had been lured into the Russian Zone that Soviet spies wouldn't grab both of them and put them on a train back to

Moscow? Because of these concerns, Boris, with the help of the FBI, came with something to offer: In an effort to secure the Catholic vote in the elections later that year, Truman was planning on sending Cardinal Spellman on a tour of Asia as "Grand Vicar of the U.S. Army." In the context of the conflict in Korea, it was to be a full-on anti-communist offensive backed by the Vatican, and Boris could get the schedule in advance. It was a masterful ploy, designed to convince Moscow that they would still need Boris even after they'd gotten rid of Soble. Yakov seemed interested but said he would have to talk to Moscow. Of course, Boris knew that if Moscow didn't answer right away it wouldn't happen at all, so after waiting two more days without hearing anything, he headed back to Paris. The whole trip had come to nothing, but the FBI warned Boris to be patient.

Boris next saw Soble two months later in Paris, at a birthday party for Myra at the luxurious Dominique restaurant—hardly the conduct of someone who was poor and in hiding, as Soble apparently was. It was a happy occasion, and Boris managed to lure Soble to the men's room to talk business: Come back to the fold, Boris practically begged Soble. Come with me to Vienna, where you can lay your cards on the table. Soble refused, claiming that at this point he trusted no one but Korotkov, not even Boris, who just asked too many questions. Still, Boris was able to convince Soble to write a note to Moscow explaining that he had been out of touch because he and Myra, appearing under the code names "Peter" and "Ludmilla," had been ill.

After allowing the FBI to make a copy of the note, which they saw as a major piece of evidence linking Soble with Soviet intelligence, Boris returned to Vienna, where he passed on the document to yet another new contact, Afanasy Yefimov, who had been ordered to encourage Boris to find Soble and bring him in. Unfortunately, since Boris had spoken with Yakov in March, Soble's situation had changed. He needed to renew his passport, which required a trip back to the States. Yefimov was new to Vienna and to Boris, but he wasn't naive. If the goal was to bring in Soble, it would be much harder to do in America. Instead, Yefimov proposed that Soble meet with Korotkov in Switzerland and travel together to the Soviet Union for further instructions. Only afterwards would Soble be allowed to return to the States, and only in the company of Boris. Whether it would actually play out that way, or whether Soble was simply being taken back to the Soviet Union to be liquidated, wasn't hard for Boris to divine. Yefimov passed Soble's note on via diplomatic pouch to Korotkov, who wrote a long, personal letter back to Soble, exactly what the FBI was looking for. Boris returned to Paris and delivered the letter to Soble, who admitted that the way to make it right with Moscow was to do exactly what they said. But they were lying to each other, and to themselves, and they both knew it. Meanwhile, Soble was negotiating with a firm in New York that was planning to buy a large shipment of bristles from him, solving at once his cash and passport problems.

Boris's main job now for both the FBI and Soviet intelligence was to ensnare Jack Soble, but at the same time, he was being pressured by the FBI not to lose contact with Jane Foster and George Zlatovski. Foster generally avoided Boris's invitations, but she met him for lunch at Paris's Plaza Athénée Hotel. She had two requests. First, could Boris use his pull in Moscow to have her released from her duties for Soble and be assigned directly to Korotkov? She also pleaded with Boris to help find work for her husband, who had been translating a technical dictionary for UNESCO but still didn't have a proper job. Boris, who saw Zlatovski as "a one-man international unemployment problem," promised to do what he could on both accounts and asked her to put her requests in writing (as the FBI had instructed). Foster couldn't wait to get away, but Boris suggested a walk around the neighborhood. As they strolled along the Rue du Faubourg Saint-Honoré, Boris stopped in front of Lanvin, a famously luxurious boutique, to admire the neckties. Claiming that he was leaving for the States in a few hours and had to get back to the Hotel Raphael to pack, Boris asked Foster to pick out a few neckties and have them sent to the hotel. He would pay her back later. It was one of Boris's oldest tricks: owing money to someone as a way to stay connected. But Foster, who had loaned Boris money for the last time, refused.

Boris flew from Paris to New York on April 7, 1952. His first order of business was to shut down the television production offices he'd been renting since 1949 on West Fifty-Eighth Street. Later he claimed that he had only set foot in the offices twice in all that time, having thrown away $18,000 on rent. Neither claim was remotely true, since he had actually lived there from time to time, and it was the FBI who had paid the rent. Then Boris was off to California to make an appearance on North Beverly Drive, but there was really not much else for him to do there. Catherine had long ago stopped asking him to account for his comings and goings, and Boris was soon back in New York to meet his new Russian handler. The instructions were, as usual, obsessively detailed and maddeningly vague: Boris was to stroll the sidewalk in front of the television production offices building on the afternoon of Tuesday, May 6, holding albums of the latest Broadway soundtracks under his left arm. The person who came along and asked "Did you hear those records?" was to be his new contact. Boris would complete the transaction by saying, "No, I just bought them at the Liberty Record Shop on Madison Avenue," to which the new contact would reply: "Okay, let's listen to them together, John." If no one appeared, Boris was to try again at the same time and place, with the same props and parole, on the first Tuesday of June. If that didn't work, he was to try again in July.

Boris responded that he would prefer to meet in the afternoon, because he had to go to Broadway shows in the evenings for work, a request that Moscow found reasonable enough. In fact, the FBI asked Boris to make the change because they would be able to photograph the scene more easily in daylight. Boris otherwise followed instructions exactly, but no one showed up, and eventually he became so impatient and disgusted that he threw the records away and left. Nor did anyone show up in June. Both times, Boris learned later, an FBI tail had unnerved Boris's contact.

Boris's trip to New York wasn't in vain. Unsure whether Soble had in fact made his appointment with Korotkov in Switzerland, survived Moscow, and made it to New York, Boris tried to track him down via Soble's lawyer on Wall Street. He learned that Soble would be arriving on the SS *Liberté* on June 12. Soble was surprised to see Boris at the West Side piers to welcome him home with old country–style embraces and kisses. They stepped into a taxi and on the way to the decidedly down-market Governor Clinton Hotel where Soble was staying, Soble explained that his trip had been authorized by the agent he met in Switzerland and that he was only staying in New York long enough to arrange new passports for himself and his family. Clearly something had changed for Soble, but he wasn't talking.

When Boris and Soble met again the next day at Boris's rooms at the Meurice hotel, Soble's state of mind had taken a manic turn for the worse. He didn't even bother to check the room for bugs. As Soble feared, the State Department was holding up his passport request. He would have to remain in America for longer than planned, and he didn't have the money for that. There was an apartment at 210 Riverside Drive that he could rent: Would Boris be able to loan him $1,000 for the down payment? Boris was willing to reach out to one of his wife's friends, who worked in the passport office, to see what could be done, but when it came to the loan, Boris refused. He had his own money troubles. Still, he held out the possibility that if Moscow came through with financing for another one of his projects, he might be able to help. Soble frowned: "You will never get that money, Boris, because they are convinced you are such a wealthy man. You have played that part too long and too well."

Boris and Soble met regularly that summer in New York, and Boris watched Soble's mental health steadily deteriorate. Things got especially bad in late June, when Soble learned that one of his agents in Paris, who had been transferred to the Soviet embassy in London, had been identified by an employee of the British Foreign Office who was cooperating with the FBI. Now it seemed certain that both the Americans and the Soviets were after Soble. Boris reported back to Moscow on what he'd heard from Soble, and his report was accompanied by yet another scheme: a series of 104 television shows on the great men of history, to be backed by the Encyclopaedia Britannica company and to be made at new studios that Boris was prepared to rent at 160 Broadway. He wasn't surprised to find

Moscow uninterested in his business proposition, but he was shocked by their response to the situation involving Soble. It turned out Soble hadn't been to Switzerland at all, much less Moscow. Even worse, Soviet intelligence had learned that Soble was selling the bristle factory in France and planning to pocket the money. They had pages of questions for Boris: Where was Soble living and what was he living on? Was the FBI tailing him as he suspected? What was he planning for the future?

In August 1952, Yefimov called Boris back to Europe to answer these questions. He stopped first in Paris, where he met Myra Soble, who claimed she had finally made a deal on her husband's behalf to sell the bristle factory and that she had booked passage back to the United States, where Jack would support the family as a brush and bristle wholesaler. Boris then headed to Vienna, where Yefimov apologized for the botched rendezvous on West Fifty-Eighth Street and announced news that was both disturbing and encouraging: Korotkov had given up on Soble. From now on, Boris would take over Soble's contacts and run Soble himself. It was the best news Boris could have hoped for, at least from the perspective of the FBI. But this raised the stakes considerably. Boris, who had already been physically threatened by these men more than once, wasn't sure if he should celebrate the promotion or take out another life insurance policy.

When Boris showed up several days later for his next appointment with Yefimov at an abandoned Viennese ice-skating rink, he saw the teenage girl who had kept their glasses full at the safe house. She took him back there, where Boris was surprised to see not Yefimov but a friendly stranger with an American accent who introduced himself as Christopher Georgevich Petrossian and explained that he'd be temporarily taking over the Vienna operations. Where was Yefimov? The answer, that he was away on business, wasn't convincing or encouraging.

Boris was worried that he'd have to start from scratch in earning Petrossian's trust. As it turned out, Petrossian seemed to be the one looking to earn Boris's trust by sharing with him insights into Moscow's long-range plans on the international stage. The Kremlin was in the midst of an effort to divide England and France via a propaganda war. After that,

Moscow intended to court Egypt and Turkey by reaching out to politicians and religious figures sympathetic to communism, or simply hostile to the United States. It was exactly the sort of intelligence that the FBI had hoped Boris would bring home. Petrossian brought up the possibility once again of Moscow investing in the television project, but it depended on Boris's ability to get Soble back on Soviet soil, where Soble would finally account, one way or another, for the money he had "borrowed" from the Soviets to start the bristle factory. Boris had long ago grown tired of such promises, knowing that they were merely being used to keep him on the inside. He admitted as much to Petrossian, warning him that getting Soble back across the ocean, with the money he owed Moscow, would be almost impossible. But a significant investment would improve the odds. Petrossian heard this with a straight face. Moscow did not. One of the operatives handling Boris's affairs back in Moscow wrote of Boris and Soble in an internal memo just days later: "We need to make a concerted effort to drag out both of them, take their money, and arrest them." But Beria and Korotkov were still convinced of Boris's value.

Boris spent the next several months crisscrossing Europe, developing his own projects. There were the usual nascent film, music, and television deals, and even a beryllium mine in Austria. None of them worked out, but he always managed to get potential investors to cover the costs of his travel. What he did not do was make any effort to rein in Soble, which led to increasing frustration back in Moscow, where there was a feeling that Boris and Soble were in league together somehow. "We have begun to have certain suspicions," an internal report admitted, referring to Boris in code: "We do not trust J."

CHAPTER TWENTY-ONE
IN CHAINS, 1952–54

Returning to New York on November 30, 1952, Boris found himself in a country that had Dwight Eisenhower to the presidency. Eisenhower was a Republican who promised to act far more decisively against the communist threat that the Democrats under Roosevelt and Truman had so grievously underestimated, even if it meant using the hydrogen bomb—but rumors coming out of Moscow that Stalin's health was declining, and that his inner circle was jockeying for power, meant that Eisenhower would certainly not act on those promises until it became clearer which way the Soviet Union was heading.

The adamantly apolitical Boris hadn't even voted, and never did. At any rate, Boris was having his own problems finding Soble and urging him to repay the money he owed Moscow. Soble, however, was on an "up" cycle, believing he'd found a way back into Soviet intelligence's good graces: a new source. "Slava" was a former US Army officer stationed in Germany who recruited potential Soviet spies for the military before moving to the State Department and then the War Department. Slava would prove so useful to Moscow that all would be forgiven, Soble hoped. Boris returned to Vienna in late December 1952 bearing Soble's report on Slava, but Yefimov was not impressed. Maybe Moscow was right, he speculated. Maybe Soble was causing more trouble than he was worth. Maybe he should just be shot. And Boris too.

Far from being shot, Boris was now running Soble's ring, and Moscow needed to arrange a time and place where Boris could meet with a new handler. It was decided that on the first Tuesday of January, Boris would wait by the statue of Simón Bolívar at Central Park South and Sixth Avenue. It was a bizarre choice of location, just a brief walk from Boris's television production studios, conspicuously close to both the Soviet consulate and a police station, where he would be in full view of thousands of passersby every day, not to mention the full-time doormen just across the street.

If no one appeared, Boris was instructed to return the next month, and then again the next month, until they were able to rendezvous or Boris got new instructions. An agent named Vasily Molev, whose official job was custodian and chauffeur at the Soviet consulate, was waiting at the appointed time and place on January 6, 1953, observed by both the FBI and another Soviet agent named Mikhail Svirin. Boris never showed up, however, because he was back in France, cultivating sources among the delegates from the Congress of Nations in Defense of Peace. It didn't take long for Yefimov to check the story and catch Boris in a lie: The Congress had taken place in December. Boris expected the worst when he met with Yefimov later that month in Vienna, but Yefimov didn't make much of it. After all, Boris was the only agent who might be able to bring in Soble, and motivating him to do it meant pulling off a tricky balancing act. Even if Boris was a mercenary in the eyes of Moscow, he could hardly be expected to lead his friend and mentor to the scaffold.

Moscow's new instructions to Yefimov were clear as far as Boris was concerned: "On no account should you let him find out our true intentions." It was yet another sign that Boris's status in Moscow was not as certain as it had once been. That is why Moscow left Boris alone in early 1953, giving him the chance to return to New York to supervise the American premiere of *Child of the Danube*, now retitled *Marika*, at New York's modest Beekman Theatre. Gone were the days when the premiere of one of Boris's movies could command the biggest theater in town. Nor did tepid reviews help to fill seats in the weeks to come. Boris's attempt to re-conquer the film world hadn't succeeded, and his spy career seemed on hold as well. Moscow instructed its New York *rezidentura* that

Boris needed to "avoid flaunting his connection with Sov. people," but he was still expected to keep showing up on the first Tuesday of the month underneath the statue of Simón Bolívar. No one appeared in February, but on March 3, Molev was ready and waiting with the new parole, after which they had coffee at a nearby diner. There Boris handed over Soble's latest intelligence from Slava, the entire transaction photographed and filmed by the FBI.

Moscow didn't react right away to the new report from Soble, because things were about to change again, and not only because of the new Red Scare led by McCarthy and the new generation of Republicans occupying the White House and the Capitol for the first time since 1932. Even as Boris handed over the report, Stalin was on his deathbed, muttering his last words: "I don't even trust myself." The seventy-seven-year-old ruler, who had led the Soviet Union for three decades, who murdered ten million of his own citizens, and then murdered the executioners, and then murdered those who counted the number of dead and the technicians who retouched the dead out of old photos, had failed to name a successor. After his death on March 5, 1953, which despite widespread knowledge of his declining health came as a surprise, a triumvirate of consisting of Georgi Malenkov, Vyacheslav Molotov, and Boris's old friend Lavrenti Beria began writing a new chapter in the Cold War, one that would be marked by a thaw that was no less significant because its pace was so glacial.

Beria's newfound power was indeed good for Boris, who for a time commanded more authority in Moscow than ever. Boris had assumed Soble's duties, but Soble himself was still out there somewhere, and that was a problem Moscow still needed to solve. Two weeks after Stalin's death, Boris was back in Vienna, where he learned he would have a new contact, a Lithuanian forger named Jacob Albam, code-named "Belov," with whom Soble had been working since the late 1940s. As for Jane Foster and George Zlatovski, Moscow's sense was that they posed too many security risks and should be sidelined. In essence, Soble himself was to be considered as having resigned from active duty as a Soviet intelligence officer. That wasn't Soble's decision to make, of course, because in the world of international espionage, the only thing more dangerous than a spy was an ex-spy. That point was made all the more obvious the next month, when a former high-ranking Soviet secret agent published a tell-all in *Life* magazine. The agent had escaped the purges of the late 1930s and settled with his family in the United States under the name Alexander Orlov. As it turns out, Orlov's insights into the Soviet intelligence apparatus were past their expiration date. Nor did he have much new to say to the FBI or the Senate committee that grilled him. Orlov's revelations, coming on top of news that President Eisenhower had issued an executive order allowing the Justice Department to target federal employees based not just on political convictions but on personal character, should have worried Moscow, but the Kremlin was focused on troubles closer to home.

Beria's commitment to sharing power with Malenkov and Molotov was questionable. In what many observers saw as a coup, he merged the Soviet military and civilian intelligence services into a new agency called the Ministry of Internal Affairs, or MVD, effectively raising his own political status above that of the other two ruling members of the triumvirate. In that position he made a number of decisions that his colleagues considered counterrevolutionary, including cancelling plans to assassinate Tito and indicating that he would be willing to accept a unified, capitalist Germany. Beria was even willing to talk to the United States about winding down the conflict in Korea. He promoted moderates, banned torture by police and security services, and emptied jails of more than one million suspected enemies of the revolution. It wasn't long before Malenkov and Molotov determined that Beria, the man who had purged more of the revolution's enemies than any other figure in Soviet history, but who had now apparently gone soft, must himself be judged and found guilty.

If Boris had breathed a sigh of relief when he heard that Beria was part of a new ruling triumvirate, he felt he was suffocating when he learned in July 1953 that his protector had been arrested, fired as first deputy premier and head of Soviet intelligence, kicked out of the Communist Party, and charged with treason, terrorism, and counterrevolutionary activity. A new purge would surely target anyone who had been close to Beria, but

Nikita Khrushchev, who was consolidating power in order to take over from Malenkov as the first secretary of the Central Committee of the Communist Party of the Soviet Union, was determined not to repeat the kind of purges that had done so much damage back in the 1930s. Nonetheless, he ordered a secret trial charging Beria with putting state security above the party at the behest of foreign capitalists, impeding the progress of Soviet agricultural policy, engaging in moral depravity, and promoting bourgeois nationalism in the Soviet republics. While this was all good news for the United States, since it indicated that there was political dissent at the very highest levels of Soviet politics, it was the worst kind of bad news for Boris. Beria was the most feared and hated man in the Soviet Union, which is why his memory of having worked with Boris back in the 1920s in Baku seemed to have been the only thing that kept Boris alive.

Horrified about what was happening in Moscow, Soble told Boris that he was considering defecting, which wasn't what the FBI wanted—at least not yet. Boris tried to keep Soble from doing anything rash, convincing Soble to accompany him to Vienna to set things straight in the fall. Then Soble saw a newspaper column by Leonard Lyons that made everything more complicated. Joseph McCarthy had announced plans to question the daughter of a former United States ambassador. The article didn't mention Martha Stern by name, but it wasn't hard for Soble to guess her identity, and he feared that he would be next. Under such conditions, he felt that a trip to Vienna would attract far too much attention: "We'll all end up in Leavenworth," Soble muttered. Boris reported to Vienna that Soble had gone from being one of the Soviet Union's most valued agents to being "something of a coward."

Cowardice seemed to be contagious that summer. The fighting in Korea was over by late July, but the armistice that divided the country in two was far from ideal, ending only active military engagement. Two weeks later Soviet scientists tested their first workable hydrogen bomb, but with the fate of Beria and his allies still uncertain, Yefimov, who was being questioned in connection with Beria's trial, realized that Soble might start to consider the FBI a safer haven than Soviet intelligence and so he started to protect himself. Until things settled down, Yefimov maintained, any more meetings with Boris were inadvisable. When Boris asked what he should do, Yefimov had a one-word answer: "Disappear!" But two weeks later, Yefimov set up a rendezvous with Boris and claimed that operations at KGB headquarters in Moscow were returning to normal, and that the interrogations and purges surrounding Beria's fall were not only normal but necessary "to preserve the system requiring continuous examination and re-examination of each of us." The ideas, the very language told Boris that someone had gotten to Yefimov, and that Boris would have to be even more careful in the future.

Back in New York, Boris met again with Jack Soble, who was happy to report that the knock on the door from the Senate subcommittee hadn't come, but the State Department had refused to renew his passport. He feared the attentions of the FBI or the CIA and asked Boris to deliver a letter to Vienna in which Soble offered to come back to work in Europe. In the meantime, Soble confided in Boris: He was going to take his family and disappear, perhaps to Canada.

Boris, who worried that Moscow's interest in him had narrowed almost exclusively to his relationship with Soble, a man who surely didn't have much of a future either in the Soviet Union or America, was covering his own broad backside, which meant planning for a life that wasn't funded by the FBI or Soviet intelligence. Falling revenues had led the Hollywood studios to experiment with a variety of gimmicks intended to lure audiences back into theaters. One of these was a process by which the simultaneous projection of two superimposed strips of film resulted in images that appeared three-dimensional when viewed through special glasses. The idea hadn't really caught on. Viewers didn't take to the glasses, and most cinemas couldn't afford the system. Desperate to find some way back into the movie business, Boris had been in contact with the developers of a new method of showing 3-D movies that involved only one strip of film and did away with the glasses. Boris actually invented the process, according to the medium's one and only historian, receiving two patents in England for an "improved apparatus for stereoscopic optical projection." One of the reasons Boris returned to the United States in the summer of 1953 and remained through October was to find a way to sell this system to theaters, and he staged a demonstration in New York of what he called the Moropticon. It was a gimmick with potential. The system started to catch on under the name Depix/Pola-Lite/Moropticon. The 1954 film *Creature from the Black Lagoon*, for example, was filmed and screened this way. However, theater owners eventually realized that they made so much more money from the selling of 3-D glasses that Boris's invention ended up being a failed novelty, not a way back to Hollywood.

On Christmas Eve 1953, two days after Beria was convicted of being "an agent of imperialism" and shot, Boris found himself waiting in the Prater, with a letter from Soble, offering to come back into the fold, carefully tucked into his breast pocket. A car pulled up on time, with the usual driver, Alexei, at the wheel, but in Yefimov's place in the back seat was a young agent who stuck out his hand and introduced himself in Latvian-accented Russian as Sokolov. Boris knew better than to ask about Yefimov.

Instead of heading to the usual safe house, Alexei drove the car out to one of Vienna's thickly wooded suburbs, to a modest house with a basement garage. Boris followed Sokolov up from the cellar to the living room, where he handed over Soble's letter. Sokolov proceeded to read the letter carefully, twice. Then, with no discussion at all, the meeting was over. Boris felt no need to mention that Soble had gone missing. Alexei took Boris back to the Prater and Boris walked all the way back to his hotel, where, for the first time in years, Boris wasn't alone on Christmas Eve. He had fallen in love with a much younger cabaret singer right there in Vienna. Marion Sklarz came from a Berlin family that was rich in history if not money: Her father helped arrange for Lenin's return to Russia in 1917. She also had a natural sense of discretion, never asking questions when Boris disappeared. Over the years Boris been unfaithful to Catherine many times, including the long affair with Elizabeth Schumann, but this time things were different. Time flew when Boris was with Marion, and the several days he had to wait for the next message from Yefimov were spent with her, going out and sleeping in. Eventually Boris was summoned again to the Prater, where once again Alexei picked him up and drove them to the house in the forest. Boris noticed that this time there was already a car parked in the garage, and when he came upstairs, two priests were waiting. Yefimov was there as well, apologizing to Boris, saying they would have to keep things brief, because he had some business with one of the priests, who was also a Soviet agent organizing French factory workers. Yefimov acknowledged that Boris had long deserved to take over Soble's position, though of course Soble had essentially turned over all of his assignments to Boris anyway.

Yefimov told Boris that they needed to talk about Soble, but he seemed distracted, his eyes continually darting in the direction of the basement. Finally it came: a muffled gunshot. "Well, that's over with," Yefimov calmly told Boris. "And it was done on schedule." The meeting over, a bewildered Boris saw on the way out just one priest, bent over in prayer. The execution of the one priest had apparently been arranged to teach the other a lesson. Boris learned something else that day as well, something about himself: "I knew that day, if I had ever doubted it before, that helping to smash these killers, these ruthless destroyers of human life, was the most important thing I ever had to do in my life. God willing, I would continue doing that just so long as the FBI felt they could use me."

As moving as this lesson was, it's important to remember that whatever his ideals, Boris was using both of his spymasters as much as they were using them, and Boris had become far more entangled in the lives of Moscow's murderers than he was later willing to admit. But it did mark a turning point in his career as a spy. It came at just the right time, because Korotkov had decided he had finally had enough of his two American agents, who were rarely worth the trouble they caused. After learning from Yefimov that Soble was missing, Korotkov wrote in a classified internal memorandum: "How are we going to get our hands on these bastards?"

Boris headed back to the United States with Marion, settled into a room at the Essex House Hotel, just down the street from the statue of Simón Bolívar, and set out to bring in Soble. Exercising his newfound authority as Soble's handler, Boris summoned Soble from Montreal by telegram and set up a meeting at the Essex House. After Soble went through his usual inspection of the room, he explained that he hoped to get a Canadian passport based on yet another hare-brained business idea. Unlike the United States, Canada had no trade restrictions in effect against China, so Soble planned to import inferior Chinese bristles, relabel them as American, and sell them, making a profit of almost two dollars per brush. Maybe Boris would be willing to invest $10,000 in the business? Maybe he could convince Korotkov to put Soviet money into the business? Soble had obviously learned something from Boris about how to try to make espionage pay.

Taking Yefimov's advice not to get involved in Soble's personal problems, Boris cut him off. "You are a highly ranked Soviet spy," he reminded a dismayed Soble. "Start acting like one! I have instructions for you. *Instructions* this time, not requests." From now on, Boris was officially in charge of all of Soble's contacts, starting with Slava—though Boris still didn't know his true identity—and starting immediately, Soble would report only to Boris. Shocked, Soble began to weep uncontrollably. Boris was heartbroken to see him reduced to such a state, but he steeled himself like a good Soviet spy and ordered Soble to stop blubbering and repeat the instructions word for word. Then Boris sent him away and ordered him to return in a week.

When he came back a week later, Soble was so depressed that he didn't even bother to check the room for microphones. He did, however, work up the courage to ask Boris again if he wanted to invest in the Canadian bristle business. It would make Boris a fortune by year's end, Soble promised. Boris ignored the offer and instead sat Soble down and ordered him to write a letter to Moscow explaining his situation, a letter that, needless to say, went directly to the FBI. At their next meeting, a few days later, an increasingly manic Soble wouldn't venture past the lobby. This time it wasn't bugs he was worried about but Boris, who seemed to be setting up Soble to be kidnapped or worse: "You want to put me in chains," Soble moaned. Instead they headed to a nondescript bar on Sixth Avenue, where a pathetic Soble tried to buy some time and goodwill by offering

Moscow a list of all of his contacts over the years. Boris slid a pen and paper across the table but was disappointed when he saw that Soble was not using his contacts' real names but their code names. Boris knew that "Roman" was Soble's brother, Robert Soblen, and that "Belov" was the Lithuanian forger. But in addition to having no idea who "Slava" really was, Boris had no clue as to the real identities of the rest of Soble's ring, or even if there had been contacts that he'd left off the list. Clearly, Soble had a few cards left, but he didn't know that the game was changing.

CHAPTER TWENTY-TWO
THE AGENT IN BLACK, 1954–55

It is one of the ironies of Boris's spy career that he took over Soble's stable of contacts and became one of the Soviet Union's most important secret agents just as the golden age of espionage seemed to be ending. In fact, the platinum age of spycraft was just beginning. After Beria was gone, Khrushchev, having replaced Beria's entry in the *Great Soviet Encyclopedia* with an entry for the Bering Sea, transformed the security services again. The MVD was renamed the KGB, or the Committee for State Security. The KGB was potentially much more powerful than its predecessors, in part because it had been elevated to the status of the army and the Communist Party. There was also a determined effort to take resources out of promoting a global socialist revolution, instead focusing on internal threats. At the same time, Khrushchev had entered on a program of reconciliation with the West: A relaxing of politics, economics, and culture at home would supposedly promote peaceful coexistence with Europe and the United States. Khrushchev's timing was perfect. The anti-communist hysteria that was such a central feature of American life was fading. In public hearings held starting in April 1954, Joseph McCarthy tried to revive it by focusing on subversives in the United States Army, but the public thought he had gone too far. So did J. Edgar Hoover, and so did McCarthy's colleagues in Congress, who stripped him of his committee chairmanship and formally condemned him on the Senate floor. But fighting Soviet influence in American society remained central to the FBI's mission, so making sure the Bureau's seven-year investment in Boris paid off was more important than ever.

For a time, it looked as if the Cold War was thawing out, which was both good news and bad news for Boris. Falling in love with Marion had inspired him to think about their future together. Boris went over possible scenarios in his mind. The only one with a happy ending was one in which both Moscow and Washington needed him more than he needed them. He was one of the KGB's top agents. It was time to start acting like one. At the next rendezvous in May in Vienna, Alexei drove Boris and Yefimov to a lavish restaurant, where Boris sat up straight in his chair, looked Yefimov across the table, lit a cigarette, and took control. He had worked faithfully for years, providing cover, transporting cash and documents, developing contacts, and extracting intelligence. He had put his own life, and his family's lives, at risk. Why? He had been strung along with the television production project and other ideas, wasting a fortune and years of his life for them, and for what? Did they really think he would keep coming when they called? "Korotkov can come to Vienna," Boris warned a shocked Yefimov, "or the KGB can forget about finding their rogue secret agent."

It worked. Boris put out his cigarette and stood up to go, but Yefimov pleaded for him to stay, promising that he could convince Korotkov to come to Vienna. But when Boris showed up several days later in the Prater, Yefimov was there again; he had been ordered to do what it took to prevent the KGB from losing its only link to Soble. Yefimov took Boris to an expensive seafood restaurant overlooking the Danube and started asking questions, writing down everything Boris said. What was the status of Soble's bristle business in Canada? What were his plans for the future? How well did Slava and Soble seem to know each other? Had Boris met Slava? Boris revealed as little as possible, which was apparently enough, because Yefimov ended the meeting by suggesting that Boris be patient. Korotkov might very well be in Vienna soon.

Boris waited and waited, looking for reasons to leave Vienna until he finally found one—actually two. When he had the chance to demonstrate the Moropticon in England and Switzerland again he took it, and then came a brief trip to Florida for Dick's second marriage. It wasn't the happiest of occasions for Boris, whose involvement in Dick's life for years was mostly limited to creating companies that could hire him without requiring him to work—providing cover for his own son, in essence. But Boris, who claimed to have such a strong family feeling, had never been much of a husband or father in practice—and he rarely visited his own father, whose nursing home was "a real hole," Marion later remembered.

When Boris returned to Vienna in July, Korotkov was waiting for him. Boris made his way to the designated rendezvous point, at the back entrance of the new Burgtheater, where he was expecting to be picked up by the usual chauffeured sedan. He was shocked but also secretly pleased to see that Korotkov himself, one of the top-ranked security officials in the Soviet Union, had arrived early and was waiting for him. Korotkov greeted Boris warmly and together they strolled to a run-down house in the Russian Zone. Inside was a different story.

Korotkov began by bemoaning Soble's situation. "My heart aches for Abram," offered Korotkov, using one of Soble's code names. How could such a heroic figure of Soviet history have fallen so low, Korotkov wondered. Boris knew the right answer to that question even before Korotkov provided it: "It must be his surroundings that overwhelmed my old Comrade," he insisted. "Easy living! Idealists have something soft in them—always, and that soft side, exposed to sufficient temptation, will corrupt them." Then Korotkov made a prediction about the coming conflict between capitalism and communism that was no less bizarre for being so familiar to Boris: "When the time is right we will strike, Comrade. In one day we will wipe out all the American air bases from Spain to Alaska. And on that very same day the one hundred most important Americans will die. Some of them will be poisoned, some crushed under falling rocks, some in unavoidable accidents. The sooner these capitalist exploiters, these bloodsuckers of the poor are liquidated, the better!" This would be hastened, Korotkov told Boris, by a reorganization of the

KGB's American presence. Soviet agents in Europe and Asia had been quite successful, Korotkov boasted. In contrast, he continued, "In America my men have failed me, utterly failed me."

Much of that failure was being blamed on Beria, and the KGB had clearly not finished purging its ranks of his allies, which should have meant trouble for Boris. Korotkov slid a piece of paper across the table. "You may be shot for signing this paper," Korotkov half joked. Boris didn't have much of a choice. He might be shot for not signing it. In a gesture that he hoped would reassure Korotkov, he boldly scrawled his name across the bottom of the page without reading it. It was only later that Boris discovered it was a statement swearing he had never known Beria.

Now that he had protected himself against having had one of Beria's allies in his service, Korotkov turned to Soble's situation. No matter how loyally Soble had served the party in the past, Korotkov explained, no matter how good a friend he was, he had to submit to the discipline that the cause demanded, or else. It was up to Boris to bring him in: "Stop at nothing in getting Abram to Europe," Korotkov instructed Boris. "I leave his fate now completely in your hands."

Boris flew back to the United States via London with Marion in September 1954. He stopped off in New York, setting up Marion in a hotel before connecting with Soble, who pressed Boris for $5,000 and pleaded with him to deliver yet another note to Moscow promising that if he could resolve his passport and money problems, he could still be of use to the KGB. Boris was in no mood to hear either request and it showed. The reaction wasn't strategic on Boris's part, but it had the effect of accomplishing something that all of his skills as a spy hadn't until now: Soble suddenly revealed Slava's identity. He was Soble's nephew, Ilya Wolston, who had been in army intelligence before running the midtown lunch counter with Soble back in the 1940s. Slava had been in plain sight all along. This was a real windfall in the eyes of the FBI, but they wanted more.

Boris continued on to the West Coast alone, but there was little for him to do in California and he was anxious to get back to Marion in New York. Catherine had seen a photo of her husband and Marion, identified as his secretary, in the papers. Catherine didn't have to think twice before realizing what was going on. She wasn't sorry to see him leave. Back in Vienna, Boris telephoned the prearranged number, U-47306, at the prearranged time. No one picked up, which had never happened before. He tried again, without success, and then tried one more time. Now a man with an unfamiliar voice answered and instructed Boris to meet him the next day at six P.M. in front of the Tabor Theatre. Apparently, this was Semyen, a new contact that Korotkov had said would be taking over in Vienna, because it was this same voice Boris heard greeting him when he arrived at the rendezvous point. Without so much as mentioning his name or relation to Yefimov or Korotkov, this stranger, who carried himself less like a spy than a military officer, brusquely expressed surprise that Boris hadn't brought Soble or Slava. Perhaps Boris needed to pay a visit to Moscow to explain? Reminding Semyen that he had already effectively replaced Soble, Boris had his usual excuses about his other assignments, including Spellman, Glennan, Harriman, and Lodge, as well as new targets like the journalist Edward R. Murrow, who had been so damaging to Senator Joseph McCarthy's crusade against communists. Semyen was not impressed. Boris also introduced Semyen to a plan he had just come up with to stage Prokofiev's *War and Peace*, which had never been seen outside the Soviet Union, in the United States with the original score and libretto. Might Semyen help find them? No answer. Then there was an optics firm that Boris was setting up in Liechtenstein, which could provide cover for up to four KGB agents. Again, Semyen said nothing.

Boris again asked himself: Was this even Semyen? If not, who was in charge? "I suspected that Soviet intelligence had been taken over lock, stock, and barrel by the military," he later wrote. If the Soviet intelligence had decided to take such a step, which would explain Semyen's seeming lack of familiarity with Boris's old assignments and his failure to commit to the new ones, it would have been justified. In recent months, America's spy mania may have diminished, but J. Edgar Hoover had been emboldened by McCarthy's exit from the scene and was stepping up his efforts, legal and illegal, against subversives. Hoover announced that a "no rules" rule would now guide his pursuit of Soviet subversives, a change supported by Attorney General Herbert Brownell's decision that the FBI's infamous "black bag" jobs were protected by law.

Boris spent the next several weeks showing Marion his Europe, until he got word that Korotkov wanted to meet again in Vienna. Boris showed up behind the Burgtheater at six P.M. on November 5 and once again the mysterious Semyen was there, with a different attitude, having heard, inexplicably, from Moscow that "J. has our complete trust in politics and business."

Boris and Semyen walked arm in arm all the way to a safe house on the Faulmanngasse, where Korotkov was waiting. Like last time, Korotkov wasted no time with polite greetings and inquiries into Boris's health and family but launched into his usual complaint about Soble's failure to submit to party discipline, and all of the lies, prevarications, and broken promises. Boris suggested that Soble was still a loyal servant of the revolution and that he would soon remember where his loyalties must lie. Korotkov anticipated Boris's next question: "And if he does not? I suppose then there will be nothing for me to do but order him liquidated." Boris had gotten used to such talk, but this time his blood froze: If Korotkov could speak so casually about murdering a figure like Soble, what would they do to Boris if he didn't produce?

Boris anticipated his final meeting with Korotkov that fall with a combined sense of boredom and dread. The rendezvous at the safe house left Boris in an even greater state of dismay about what the KGB was planning, if there was a plan at all. Korotkov told Boris that he was going to be travelling to the United States to reorganize operations there, but it was essential they secure Soble before that happened. Boris wasn't going to learn anything more about where he stood that day. Korotkov had barely started to explain when he was called away, and Boris was hustled by Korotkov's driver toward the front door. Would there be a chance to say goodbye to Korotkov? The driver answered: "Don't bother." Boris did speak to Korotkov once more, to set up another rendezvous on November 8, 1954, to discuss Korotkov's trip to America. But when Korotkov's car pulled up behind the Burgtheater and a new driver named Vladimir opened the back door, Boris was met by a grim, beetle-browed man. He was large, powerfully built, and dressed all in black and he bore an uncanny resemblance to the American character actor Charles Bickford. Had Boris just met his executioner?

There was no greeting, no introduction, just a gesture for Boris to get in and a few words ordering the driver to proceed to a safe house in an apartment building on the Operngasse, a residential neighborhood in the Soviet Zone. The Agent in Black, whose name Boris never learned, hurried Boris out of the car, into the building, up the stairs, and through the front door, not even waiting for Boris to take off his coat and take a seat: "Alexander Mikhailovich is no more!" the Agent in Black shouted, using Korotkov's patronymic. "He is gone. We will forget him." Boris was speechless, unsure whether to believe the news, which was not in fact true (Korotkov didn't die until 1961 when he ruptured his aorta playing tennis). Boris's shock, the Agent in Black remarked, was proof that Boris was a sentimentalist, not a true revolutionary. Then came an inevitable question: "Do you wish to continue working for the Cause?" Answering no meant almost certain liquidation, but Boris couldn't know what yes would mean. When Boris answered "of course," he wasn't encouraged by the agent's response: "Perhaps you will be given the chance, that all depends on what happens tonight."

The Agent in Black handed Boris several pencils and a stack of blank paper and ordered him to produce a full accounting of his career as a spy, with special attention to Soble and Korotkov, and a full biography, complete with family history. He was even to detail his private financial condition, including the name and size of his investments. "Leave nothing out," the Agent in Black demanded.

Boris had long prided himself for being cool-headed. It had allowed him to survive revolution and war, bankruptcy and wealth, to play his role before an audience of thousands, to lie to the pope in the Vatican and to the president in the White House, to play both the FBI and the KGB. But now he found himself unable to talk, unable to write, unable to pick up the pencil. The Agent in Black stepped out for a few minutes, and when he returned and saw Boris hadn't even started, he burst out in anger: "There are many kinds of persuasion, Comrade!" Boris stifled an irrational urge to laugh as the Agent in Black now sat down beside him and wrote out twenty questions. "I am not going to leave this room until you have answered all of the questions—to my satisfaction," he warned. "Neither are you." Boris was still frozen in fear, so the Agent in Black decided to walk him through the list, question by question, allowing Boris to rehearse his answers before actually putting pencil to paper. They began at eight P.M. with the basics: What tasks had Moscow asked him to perform over the past two decades? How long had he known Soble and Korotkov? Who came to his rendezvous in Vienna and what were the paroles? How did he communicate with Center?

Now Boris was confused. Was the Agent in Black referring to Moscow? Boris had referred to Moscow as "Center" until 1952, when Soble instructed him that the new code word was "Home." Was it some sort of trick? Had the code names been changed again without Boris's knowledge? Or was it the Agent in Black who wasn't up to date? Finally, Boris's mind began to thaw, and he realized: "I, the little roly-poly man from Hollywood, would have to defeat him with my mind alone. I couldn't outwrestle this man, outfight him, outjump, or outrun him. I had to outthink him." Doing so was, he knew, a matter of withholding just enough information to remain alive to talk another day.

The Agent in Black continued: What could Boris tell him about Jane Foster and George Zlatovski? What did he think should be done about Jack Soble? This last question was complicated, and when Boris asked for some guidance, the Agent in Black flew into a rage and made a mistake, revealing why after all these years Moscow was still trying to bring Soble in: They believed he had a list of Trotskyites operating both inside and outside the USSR. It may seem bizarre for the KGB to have gone to so much effort to secure such a list. After all, hadn't Stalin gotten rid of the Trotskyites in the Soviet Union in the purges of the late 1930s? How many "Trotskyites" were even left after the assassination of Trotsky himself fourteen years earlier? Apparently enough to cause Moscow to take whatever steps necessary to find the list. What about Slava? And Boris's Vienna contacts, Vitaly Tcherniavsky, and Afanasy Yefimov? Finally, they came to the last question: "Why are you working for the Russian communist cause?" Boris answered that he was trying to protect his family back in Russia, but it was an answer that neither of them believed, and not only because most of Boris's family was either dead or in the United States. Perhaps it was the exhaustion talking. After all, it was almost four in the morning. Boris couldn't resist adding: "Not that it did me any good. Two brothers of mine were killed by you Soviets." If Boris was hoping for sympathy, he had the wrong man. The Agent in Black remarked casually: "It must have been for a good reason." This was too much for Boris, who pounded the table as he defended the memory of his brothers, and raising his voice, reminded the Agent in Black how things actually stood: "Every time that I work for the Soviets I risk my life," he shouted. "For the Revolution! Every time I enter the Soviet Zone I risk my life for the Cause!" The FBI had coached Boris very carefully in how to deal with KGB enforcers, but Boris had learned by himself that standing up to KGB bullying inevitably transformed even the most cold-blooded hitman into a reasonable, even sympathetic figure. That was certainly the case with the Agent in Black, whose face went from rage and disdain to surprised sympathy. The rendezvous was over anyway, though he did have some parting words for Boris: "As long as your main purpose is a revolutionary purpose, then you can help us. But I tell you with the utmost seriousness that you better keep your promises. From now on you must prove yourself by your deeds." Boris rose, put on his overcoat, and walked out of the apartment, down the stairs and out into the streets of Vienna's Soviet Zone. He had survived. He scanned the rooftops for a hint of light. Daybreak wasn't even close.

When Boris told his FBI minders about the all-night interrogation by the Agent in Black, they suggested that he might want to get out while he still could: "This is getting dangerous, Boris." Nonetheless, he decided to stay: "I was sick to the point of revulsion of their tricks," he later recalled, "their despicable lies and traps and acts of cruelty. I was disgusted with their rigid, Simple Simon philosophizing, their whole 'You're for us or against us' attitude, their conception of good and evil. Most of all I was disgusted with their maniacal pride, the pleasure they took in their acts of terrorism." Of course, that insight had the benefit of hindsight, and a strategic rewriting of history. The fact is that Boris remained a double agent at least in part because the FBI had become his only reliable source of income.

A few days later, Boris once again found himself in the same building, but in a different apartment. He was uncertain about the agenda and was surprised to be treated to an extended round of drinking and eating and more drinking before the Agent in Black got serious. From now on, he explained, you are officially the head of Soble's ring. Soble may have been less productive in recent years, but it still took seven hours for the Agent in Black to detail the full scope of the job Boris was taking on. It wasn't just a matter of the number of agents that Soble had supervised, which now appeared to be more than Boris had anticipated, but the mess that Soble had made of things. This was in addition, the Agent in Black explained to Boris, to previous assignments involving Jane Foster and George Zlatovski, Cardinal Spellman, T. Keith Glennan, and a dozen other prominent figures Boris was working.

The Agent in Black also laid out the methods by which he would communicate with Boris, making all of his previous handlers look like amateurs. Instead of waiting for a rendezvous to hand over materials in person, which was inefficient and indiscreet, Boris would mail reports to a Viennese lens and camera company that he had patronized in the past. The packages would be intercepted by a Soviet operative in the post office long before they reached their destination. There was an elaborate code that any correspondence was to use, drawn from the lens company's catalog: "Compensator" meant Boris, "Spanningspruefer" meant Foster, "Optische" meant Zlatovski, "Minilux" meant Soble, and "Prizm" meant rendezvous. That way the letters, which were not to be written in Russian, would seem to be innocent orders of photography equipment. The Agent in Black also laid down new rules for meetings. At an agreed-upon time,

Boris would appear in front of the Burgtheater, with his gloves in his left hand and a newspaper tucked under his left arm. If someone approached and said, "Have you seen Paul Scott lately?," Boris was to respond: "Yes, I saw him three or four days ago in Rome." If the contact answered, "Fine, John," it was safe to proceed to a safe house.

The reason for the new procedures was a new assignment, perhaps the most important that the Soviets had ever given Boris. They needed his help with two separate, but related problems. The Agent in Black explained that the Soviet Air Forces, locked into a technological war with the Americans over the domination of the skies, had been having trouble with their fleet of supersonic jets. They hadn't been able to come up with a suitably frictionless coating for the transparent canopies covering the pilot, and as a result, tiny bubbles formed during flight, clouding up the acrylic glass and preventing the pilots from being able to see through it. Apparently the Americans had solved this problem by coating the canopies with a combination of the newest generation of plastics, including Orlon and Perlon. Moscow was hoping that Boris's military and aviation industry contacts in California could deliver the formula for the coating. In addition to the problem of canopy friction, there were problems with the landing gear of these supersonic jets. The high-velocity landings were shredding conventional tires, and the Americans had apparently solved this problem as well. It was up to Boris to find out how.

This assignment was the latest manifestation of the shift in KGB strategy to emphasize technology, a shift that had started during World War II, when it became clear that America was outpacing the Soviets in weapons technology. After the Americans tested their hydrogen bomb in late 1952, the power of the explosion, seven hundred times greater than the bombs that ended World War II, surprised even the scientists who had designed the device. Clearly, the Soviets still had some catching up to do. The Soviets were also at a disadvantage in the field of high-altitude surveillance, with the US Air Force boasting that it could see President Eisenhower's golf ball on a putting green from an altitude of fifty-five thousand feet, and American U-2 planes almost ready to make their first forays into

Soviet airspace. But catching up didn't always require spies. Around this time, the Soviets went on a buying spree at the US Department of Commerce and the US Geological Survey, acquiring publicly available topographical maps and pilot handbooks with detailed technical information about major American airports. They bought aerial photographs of areas including military air bases, ports, nuclear plants, research and training stations, and industrial areas; or they hired photographers to make them. They subscribed to dozens of military, technical, scientific, transportation, and industrial journals; newspapers and magazines published in American military bases; and freely attended academic conventions and meetings devoted to scientific matters. Once again, the closed nature of the USSR was undermining its progress, while it was the openness of American society that made it vulnerable.

All of these activities were perfectly legal until mid-1954, when the federal government began restricting public access to these materials, which is why the KGB turned to Boris, who in turn went to the FBI to help him with the KGB's latest requests. As it turned out, the KGB had mixed them up. Orlon and Perlon weren't used for the jet canopies, but for the tires, which put Boris in a difficult situation. Should Boris give the KGB what they wanted and risk exposure when his intelligence got back to the Soviet scientists who would see that it was useless, or should he embarrass them by pointing out their error? In the end, the FBI decided that Boris should wait on the matter of the canopies but submit a report, with imaginary data, on the use of Orlon and Perlon in the tires and transmit it to Vienna via the optical-firm procedure. How would Boris account for having found this report? He would claim to have treated an air force general who happened to be a long-time buddy to dinner and a Broadway show, after which, on a stroll around Times Square, the conversation somehow ended up involving the chemistry of aviation technology. Would the KGB accept such an improbable story?

CHAPTER TWENTY-THREE
A COOKED GOOSE, 1955–57

The Soviet Union and the United States wanted very different things from Boris. While the KGB had Boris focus on science and technology, the FBI was interested in people; and in early 1955 they wanted Boris to bring in Jane Foster, who had reluctantly returned to California for an extended visit to care for her sick mother. The problem for Foster now was that the State Department had seized her passport, though not without a struggle: During an interrogation at San Francisco International Airport, Foster became so frustrated that she slapped the immigration officer in the face with the passport. Needless to say, when it expired shortly afterwards, a renewal was not forthcoming, and not only because of her behavior at the airport. At a private hearing before the State Department, Foster denied having been a communist, except for a brief period of youthful enthusiasm for America's most important ally early in World War II. Boris tracked down Foster in Los Angeles and made an appointment to meet her in the bar of the Beverly Wilshire Hotel. It was a sign of Foster's desperation that she not only agreed to meet with someone she wanted nothing to do with but went upstairs to a room with him for a private conversation, or at least one that seemed private to Foster.

Boris and Foster cracked open bottles of Seagram's and 7 Up and talked about her passport troubles, and how difficult the American government was making it for her. She claimed that the FBI was harassing her. At one point the Justice Department had even accused her of illegally entering Cutter Laboratories, where her father was on the board of directors, and tampering with their vaccines. When Boris asked her if she in fact had ever been a formal member of the Communist Party, she denied it out loud, but at the same time she nodded in the affirmative, an old spy trick that the communists taught their members, in case they were being recorded. At one point she got up to use the bathroom and Boris leapt out of his chair, his face gone white. "Don't go in there!" he pleaded. "It's too messy." It didn't take long for Foster, who hadn't checked the room the way Soble had taught her to do, to suspect FBI agents were listening there. The truth would have been hardly less welcome—that's where the recording devices had been set up.

Foster asked point-blank: "Could you be working for the FBI, Boris?" His answer was perfectly calibrated: He threw back his head and laughed, as if the question itself was preposterous. But Foster had decided once again that she'd had enough of Boris Morros and headed for the door. He followed her out into the hallway, imploring her to stay, if for no other reason than to write and sign a letter to Moscow asking for their assistance. Foster had been less active in her espionage work in recent years, but she knew an old KGB trick when she saw it. Waiting for the elevator, she suspected more strongly than ever that her own ring leader was helping the FBI build a case against her. "Go to hell, Boris," she told him as the elevator doors closed.

They saw each other again sooner than either would have predicted. On a trip east to consult with her lawyers in early March 1955, Foster ran into Boris in the lobby of New York City's Barbizon-Plaza Hotel, where he had just met with one of Soble's old agents. Foster cut the conversation short, worried that she was still being followed. It was the last time they ever saw each other. That summer, the Board of Passport Appeals recommended denying Foster a new passport, and the next day the secretary of state confirmed the decision; but eventually Foster won in court, because in order to argue its case, the Justice Department would have needed to reveal that Boris Morros was a double agent, which would have jeopardized its case against Jack Soble, who was then living in Canada.

With the chances of turning Jane Foster worse than ever, the FBI put Boris back on Soble's trail. Perhaps the news of the supposed liquidation of Korotkov, the closest thing to an ally that Soble had in Moscow, would convince him to defect. Boris boarded a train bound for Toronto, hoping that his old friend would be desperate enough to see that his chances of survival would be better with the FBI than with the KGB. Boris hadn't made a hotel reservation, and he walked Toronto's frigid streets for an hour looking for a room before ending up at the seedy Edgewater Hotel, across from the lakeside Sunnyside Amusement Park. As he scanned the depressing, run-down room, he thought to himself that he was getting too old to play this game. Would it ever end? Boris hurried over the more elegant Park Plaza, where Soble was staying. They had switched roles in more ways than one. Boris was shocked to see how much weight Soble had lost. They decided to talk things over at a nearby restaurant, and over coffee Soble admitted that he had never quite understood Boris, someone who would throw away a career as a Hollywood filmmaker, alienate friends and family, and live a life of constant danger, and without any real ideological commitment. "What *are* you?" Soble asked. "A noble fool? Do you imagine for one moment that the American authorities are not following you?" But that wasn't Boris's biggest problem, according to Soble: "Either the Soviets will double-cross you, or they'll use you to double-cross me." They finished their coffee, but there was still much business to take care of. Boris suggested going back to one of their hotels, but the ever-vigilant Soble preferred to talk outside, where Boris told Soble the news: "Korotkov is no more." Under the glare of a street lamp, Boris saw tears come to Soble's eyes, slowly freezing as they ran down his cheeks.

"This is the end," Soble muttered. "At least of the regime that we have always known and respected." He paused, distracted, and then the blood rose in him and he stared hotly into Boris's eyes and gave his one-time protégé his very last instructions: "You can tell them all for me that they can go to hell. They are butchers! They are sadists, tyrants."

Boris had to play things carefully now. "I am now your superior," he said, "and my first task is to bring you back."

"I'm not a fool," Soble responded. "If they ever got me to go to Europe, I'd never come back alive. I have only one message for Moscow. Tell them for me to go to hell. Tell them that I am no longer in sympathy with the Soviet Union."

Boris thought the moment had come; Soble was ready to be turned. But as they started walking again through the snow-packed streets, something in Soble seemed to melt, as four decades of devotion to an ideal reasserted themselves. The Agent in Black was apparently right about Soble when he talked about the sentimentalism of true ideologues. Soble turned to Boris and admitted that he would never, ever desert the cause: "No matter what the Communists do, I'll always be loyal to them, ideologically." Boris knew then that he'd failed the KGB, the FBI, and himself.

Boris's next rendezvous was scheduled for March 26, 1955, in Vienna, where he was expected to report on Soble. He was right on time in front of the Tabor Theatre. Almost immediately, Vladimir pulled up, alone in the car. Apparently, Vladimir had been promoted from driver to full-fledged agent, because instead of taking Boris to a safe house in the Soviet Zone, he held their meeting as they cruised around the city.

Boris had little good news for Vladimir. He'd gotten nowhere with Soble, who considered himself retired and wanted Moscow to know that he could only pay back half of what he owed them, having spent the rest. Slava, mentally unstable and unable to hold a job, was of no use to Moscow. Jane Foster was wrapped up in her own problems, and anyway, she was under surveillance. Nor could Boris describe as active Soble's other agents, including Jacob Albam and Mark Zborowski, who had been a legendary assassin of Trotskyites, including Trotsky's own son, before he came to the United States in 1941, serving as an army consultant during the war and then working as an anthropologist at Columbia University. In other words, Soble had all but destroyed his ring of spies before handing it over to Boris. With every piece of bad news, Vladimir would suddenly brake and then accelerate, sending Boris flying forward into the dashboard and then lurching backward into his seat. Then there was the matter of the supersonic jets. Vladimir said that Moscow was pleased that Boris had been able to help with the matter of the tires, but what about the canopies? Boris, who had been well-rehearsed by the FBI, promised that he would have answers to that question soon.

It was close to midnight when Vladimir finally brought Boris back to his hotel, his farewell a lecture on the glories of the Soviet revolution and the dangers of the capitalist menace. Then he gave him a warning: There had been good progress on the supersonic jet issues, Vladimir admitted, but Boris must not forget that Soble's former ring was his top priority, and so far Boris had let them down. When Boris was called back to the Tabor Theatre in early April 1955, it was the Agent in Black at the wheel, and he wasn't happy. They were silent all the way to the safe house and Boris once again feared for his life. He was not comforted by the fact that once inside, the Agent in Black explained that the KGB was in the process of reviewing its American operations. He had clearly washed his hands of Soble: "Our Abram is a cooked goose," he warned Boris. It was only a matter of time before Center solved their Soble problem their own way. And what of Boris? "The vital question," Boris later wrote, was whether they would label me 'To be liquidated' or 'To be forgotten.'" As it happened, Boris was safe for now, but he needed to demonstrate his loyalty in a way that even the socialist true believers of the KGB understood: money. The Agent in Black, like everyone in Soviet intelligence, believed that Boris was a very rich man and ordered him to produce his checkbook. It was an object of much interest to the Agent in Black, who had never seen such a thing.

"Now, if you please," he asked Boris, "Sign four checks and give them to me. I will fill out the amounts later." Boris, who rarely had much money in the bank, hesitated. There was no way for him to cover even small amounts, but if he refused he would be accused of insufficient loyalty to the cause, and his reputation as a millionaire would be shattered. Boris protested that his money was spread out among his various investments. The Agent in Black was as unimpressed by that excuse as he was by Boris's suggestion that it was unwise to create a paper trail that the FBI could easily trace. In the end Boris had to comply, though he beseeched the Agent in Black to keep the amounts of each check below $300. But even that amount was too high. When the rendezvous was over, Boris took the next train to Zurich in order to arrive before the checks cleared. He asked the bank manager not to honor any checks made out for more than $300, which struck the banker as bizarre, given that Boris had endorsed the checks himself.

Boris was summoned back to Vienna for a May 10, 1955, rendezvous with Vladimir. He lingered in front of the Tabor Theatre, but no one showed up. He tried again the next day, as he had been instructed, and this time he was met by a young, blonde agent with very crude dental work but the right parole. She warned Boris that he had only a few months to wrap up all of his current assignments. If he didn't, he shouldn't even bother trying to reach them again, the implication being that the KGB would make sure he wouldn't be able to. Two days later, Boris got a telephone call from Credit Suisse in Zurich with the distressing news that a man with an English accent had tried to cash one of Boris's checks for $2,000. Of course, there wasn't enough money in the account to cover it.

Bouncing a check to the KGB wasn't only a problem because it inconvenienced them; it also meant that Boris, whose supposed wealth had always been part of what made him attractive to the KGB, had been unmasked as an impostor. Was this how it would end? Boris fled Vienna and took a plane to the United States, where he felt marginally safer, but the FBI insisted that he finish what he started, so in July 1955 he was back in Vienna, a city in the midst of a major transformation.

The postwar division of the city into zones controlled by the Allies was ending. Indeed, the balance of power in Central Europe as a whole was shifting, and Vienna's Soviet Zone would no longer offer a safe haven for Soviet secret agents. That is part of the reason why the Soviet Union had forced a Treaty of Friendship, Cooperation, and Mutual Assistance, better known as the Warsaw Pact, on its neighbors. At the same time, Khrushchev was preparing to denounce Stalin and announce his vision of "peaceful coexistence" with the new Europe in a secret speech to the Twentieth Party Congress. His vision included accepting Austrian neutrality, reaching out to the United States as well as to nonaligned countries like Egypt and India, and a more independent Poland and Yugoslavia. "Socialism with a human face" went only so far: Khrushchev would soon draw the line in Hungary.

Boris tried for days to reach his Viennese contact at the U-47306 telephone number, but no one answered. Finally Vladimir picked up the phone. He told Boris coldly that there was no use in a rendezvous until he had solved the problem of the jet canopies, but Boris insisted on a meeting. The next evening in front of the Tabor Theatre, Vladimir pulled up in the usual car but, without getting out, signalled to Boris that they couldn't talk. Boris pointed a finger at Vladimir and then two fingers, a sign he had learned long ago from Zarubin that meant they should try again the next day. This time, Vladimir showed up on foot, but instead of exchanging the usual parole, he hurried away toward the Russian Zone. After checking surreptitiously to make sure no one was following, he indicated for Boris to follow. After a few minutes, when they had reached the Russian Zone, Vladimir whirled around and confronted Boris: He had been spotted chatting on a street corner with Austria's socialist minister of reconstruction, Karl Waldbrunner. It wasn't the indiscretion that bothered Moscow, but his failure to let the KGB know that the two were on such good terms. What else was he holding back, and why? Boris apologized, but Vladimir had already made up his mind: "Ah, Comrade," he sighed. "You know too many people but do too little for the Cause." Boris hung his head and admitted that he had nothing else to offer in the way of the jet canopies. "Forget about it," Vladimir interrupted. "We got the information somewhere else."

When Boris was called back to Vienna in October 1955, Vladimir was again unreachable by telephone, but there was another voice on the line, one that Boris had never heard before, one that seemed to know a great deal about Boris's comings and goings and the fact that he wasn't staying in his usual hotel. Clearly, the KGB had been following Boris, which was not good news. Nor was Boris relieved to hear the voice tell him that perhaps it was time for a visit to Moscow, perhaps for Christmas? "You will be welcomed by all your friends there." Boris politely declined but noted that he would remain in Vienna in case they needed each other, at which point the voice ordered Boris not to contact the KGB in writing. When Boris countered that telephone contact was so uncertain, the voice calmly answered: "We will be able to find you, either here in Vienna or at your house in the United States."

Boris, who had the sense that there was no one in charge in Vienna, kept calling, but no one answered until Christmas Day. The voice was interested in only one thing: "When can you go to Moscow?"

"I cannot say right now," Boris answered.

"You must say!"

But when Boris tried to explain, the line went dead. He kept calling back in the days that followed, to no avail. Then early one morning in January 1956, Boris was sleeping the troubled sleep of a double agent when he was awakened by a ringing telephone. It was someone named Riabov—a bizarre development, considering that Boris had long ago been instructed to identify himself by that name when calling the Vienna *rezidentura*. This Riabov demanded that Boris come to Moscow. In his drowsy confusion, Boris thought they were calling him Riabov, which was the name he'd been told to use for all of his telephone communications. It was a distressing development, even given Moscow's bizarre way with code names. When Riabov again demanded that Boris come to Moscow, Boris gave up and said he'd think about it and get back to them. Riabov answered: "Do not call. You will get calls. Wait for them. Wait." Then there was only a dial tone.

Boris was used to mixed signals and even no signals coming from Moscow, but this was something new. He spent the next two months travelling with Marion, his business with Moropticon and the optics firm in Liechtenstein taking him to Germany, Switzerland, France, and South Africa. He didn't see the sense in continuing to reach out, but the FBI insisted, so he returned to Vienna in early March 1956 and was soon back on the telephone with the unknown voice.

"Shall we meet—someplace—in?"

"When? Where?" Boris asked, bewildered.

"In the near future," the voice said.

Boris would have read this conversation as permission to give up espionage for good, but the FBI wasn't about to throw away a decade's investment, so they demanded that Boris keep trying to reactivate himself, or at least get someone on the telephone. Later in March 1956, another unfamiliar voice was on the line: "Why not go to Moscow, John? Would you not like to see your friends there?" Boris admitted that he'd be willing to talk about it face-to-face, but when? "Very soon," the voice offered and then hung up. Very soon was sooner than Boris thought. On April 1, 1956, he picked up the telephone in his hotel room and heard yet another unfamiliar voice tell him that the KGB had a new assignment for him: "You will have your orders soon." Boris stayed several more weeks in Vienna, hoping for another call, but it never came. In the meantime, he had heard from Soble, who was going to be moving back to New York and wanted to meet. "There are things to talk over," Soble told Boris. "Many things."

Back in New York with Marion in late May, Boris checked into the Savoy Plaza and invited Soble to his room while Marion went shopping. Soble didn't trust hotels at all anymore, so they went for a walk in Central Park. Soble looked like he had suffered a nervous breakdown. Indeed, Soble's slow transformation from one of the Soviet Union's most fearless spies into a helpless paranoiac roused the pity in Boris's heart. Soble was still wrapped up in his old problems with passports and money, and he was still spending much of his time composing desperate letters for Boris to forward to the KGB, letters in which he begged for forgiveness and an invitation to settle in Moscow with Myra and Larry.

Soble wasn't naive. He'd once sat down with one of his fellow agents and tallied up all of the operatives they'd ever known. Out of 150 names, only three had survived. Now Soble imagined he had found a way to get back in the KGB's good graces. It had to do with one of his old agents, Mark Zborowski. Although Boris had alerted the FBI in the late 1940s that Zborowski was a spy, it wasn't until five years later, when Zborowski had been identified by Alexander Orlov as a Soviet agent, that he was called to testify privately before the Senate Committee on Internal Security and apparently started naming names. Now Moscow wanted to get to Zborowski before he told the Americans more, and Soble could help them. Of course, Soble also knew that if Zborowski talked, his own name would surely come up. The letter about Zborowski that Soble gave to Boris to forward to Vienna and then Moscow was less a blow for socialism than a desperate attempt at self-preservation. "Don't you see that Moscow is my last hope?" Soble asked Boris.

In June 1956 Boris was back with Marion in Vienna, bearing a bulging file of desperate letters from Soble. He tried calling the Vienna station but there was no answer. There was, however, a call to his hotel room on June 10, a voice cryptically asking: "When will you be ready?" After a quick trip to London, he was back in Vienna on June 22, when another voice on the telephone asked, "Are you ready to go?" Boris was certainly not ready to go to Moscow and never would be again, and he remained for the time being in Vienna, both hoping for and dreading the telephone call that never came. By early August 1956, he was back in New York, where he met with Soble, who was drinking heavily and sleeping badly. "They will take me back, Boris, they must, they will," Soble maintained. "I am after all, a true revolutionary." The truth was that Boris hadn't handed off Soble's letters to Moscow. Instead, they all went into a safe deposit box in Zurich, waiting for the moment when the FBI could use them against Soble, either to turn him or try him.

Boris spent much of the summer and fall 1956 touring Europe with Marion, hard at work trying to raise money for yet another project, a multi-part documentary about the most prominent scientists of the era. He managed to make it back to Vienna in early October. Desperate to make some kind of contact with the KGB before the FBI stopped seeing his usefulness, he walked in the front door of the Soviet consulate, refusing to leave until someone was willing to accept his latest reports. A KGB agent stationed in the embassy, startled at Boris's indiscretion, took the reports, if only to make Boris go away. Then it was back to England, France, and Germany to interview more scientists. Boris returned to Vienna in mid-November, calling the Vienna residency over and over again. He even went back to the Soviet embassy, where the KGB agent who had accepted the reports a month earlier realized that someone had to put a stop to this. Come back in January, the agent said, and we can give you a new assignment.

Boris celebrated New Year's Eve according to the old Gregorian calendar, on January 13, 1957, at a Berlin restaurant with Marion and a group of friends, among them an old acquaintance from Hollywood's Russian community, Vladimir Pozner, a cameraman whom Boris also knew as an executive at Sovexportfilm. They agreed to meet the next day for dinner, but at the last minute, Pozner's wife called Boris to cancel without explanation. Boris correctly surmised that something unusual was going on. Pozner, who was obviously more than a film executive, must have learned that the KGB's long-standing doubts about Boris had been confirmed. Had he seen the memo from Moscow calling Boris "very suspect"? Had rumors about Boris's suspect allegiances travelled that fast? "This was a warning if I ever had one," remembered Boris. But whether it was the loss of his patron in Soviet intelligence, or the cumulative effect of years of suspicions on Moscow's part, or some new information, Boris now wondered whether or not it was a good idea to travel to Vienna, where he had a rendezvous scheduled with the Soviet ambassador at the Vienna Opera House. Instead, he left Marion in Berlin and took a train to Munich, where in the early hours of January 20, 1957, in the Bayerischer Hof Hotel, a telegram was slipped under his door, its contents consisting of a single word: CINERAMA.

CHAPTER TWENTY-FOUR
ABOVE THE FOLD, 1957–63

Boris's decision to fly to Vienna instead of taking the train saved his life, because a team of KGB kidnappers was waiting to snatch him at the Vienna train station. Now he was on his way back to America. The seven A.M. flight from Munich stopped at Frankfurt and Paris before landing in New York at Idlewild Airport—later renamed after President John F. Kennedy—at six A.M. the next day. Boris took a taxi to Pennsylvania Station, put in a call to the FBI, and boarded the Constellation express train to Washington, DC, where the agents who had been following—and leading—him for over a decade were waiting at Union Station with a greeting he'd fantasized about for years: They would thank him and let him know that he could now go back to his old life in the movies.

But not yet. First, Boris needed to testify before a grand jury looking into what the FBI called "Mocase," named after the investigation's chief witness. They started with Jack Soble. Telling the truth, from his first meeting with Soble in 1944 at the Far East Restaurant near Columbus Circle to their most recent rendezvous in New York, wasn't the hardest part of the job. What was much more difficult for Boris was being sequestered, which the FBI insisted upon out of concerns for his safety, concerns that lasted for the rest of his life. Within a few days, Boris had provided the testimony that gave the FBI what it needed to issue arrest warrants for Jack and Myra Soble.

Although the FBI showed up at the Soble home at 321 West Seventy-Eighth Street at 6:30 A.M. on January 25, 1957, Jack and Myra were already awake and preparing to flee. Once the KGB assassins saw that Boris had fled Munich, word spread that his entire ring should expect the worst. Boris never found out how he'd been unmasked or how word about his defection spread so quickly, but the fact that Soble was preparing to flee when seven FBI agents showed up at his door to arrest him suggests that he had still had some old friends in Moscow protecting him and that the KGB's claim that they needed Boris to find him was false. It didn't much matter now, not to Boris.

The Sobles were arrested, along with Jacob Albam, and brought to the US Attorney's office, where they were confronted separately by Boris. He implored them to tell the government everything they knew, which is what he had done, though it was unclear to the Sobles at that point whether or not Boris had also been charged. Either way, it was clear which side Boris was now on. The Sobles stoically refused to cooperate and were indicted on charges of a decade of giving classified American defense secrets to a foreign government. Among those secrets were details on the number of nuclear weapons stockpiled by the United States, the current rate of production of atomic bombs, and photographs of the bunkers where such weapons were stored. Such crimes had been made capital offenses in the wake of the Rosenberg case, but the Sobles seemed untroubled by the possibility of facing the electric chair. Soble, held on $100,000 bail, at first shook off the charges. "I will get your man and prove him to be a liar," he promised, in part because he still wasn't aware that Boris was the government's main witness. Yet at his plea hearing, the secret agent who'd once had nerves of steel seemed chastened in his wrinkled gray suit, an overweight, prematurely aged brush-and-bristle importer who held Myra's hand as if it were the only thing holding him up.

The Sobles underwent a grueling series of prison interrogations, which were particularly difficult for Jack Soble. Over the next year and a half, Soble was questioned more than 120 times, under circumstances that were uncomfortable to say the least, in federal facilities in New York City; Lewisburg, Pennsylvania; Springfield, Missouri; and Danbury, Connecticut, just a few minutes from Alfred and Martha Stern's old country house. The man described somewhat dramatically by the Justice Department as the "head of Soviet espionage in the United States"—it had been years since Soble had done significant intelligence work—complained of exhaustion, chest pains, anxiety, memory loss, and depression, which was treated with electroshock therapy, before collapsing in prison. Eventually, he and Myra agreed to cooperate in return for reduced charges, but that hardly solved all of his problems. Once word spread that he had turned state's witness, the other inmates began harassing him. Soble, never particularly psychologically stable, had a nervous breakdown and was transferred to Bellevue Hospital for observation. He tried to commit suicide by slashing his left wrist with a razor blade, but he was eventually judged fit to stand trial and began expressing remorse for his deeds, a development that made the front page of newspapers across the country.

The Sobles gave up "Slava," now publicly unmasked as Ilya Wolston, who pleaded guilty, not to using his job as the foreman of a New York herb and spice business as cover for delivering top-secret government files to the Soviets, but to criminal contempt related to failing to comply with a subpoena in the case. It was all they had against him. Jacob Albam pleaded guilty to one count of conspiring to obtain national defense secrets for the Soviets and received a reduced sentence of five years in return for his cooperation. Mark Zborowski was convicted of perjury in relation to charges that he'd delivered classified documents to Jack Soble, although that verdict was reversed on appeal. After testifying at Zborowski's trial, Soble, whose health had been precarious for years, had a heart attack. Myra pleaded guilty to obtaining and receiving defense materials and was sentenced to four years in jail.

With all the blood seemingly drained from his sunken cheeks, Jack sobbed quietly and moaned "I can't forgive myself" as he pleaded guilty to conspiring to obtain vital information from the United States to give to the Soviets. He received a reduced sentence of seven years, dependent on his continued cooperation. He did get a chance to tell his story his way in a series of articles, "How I Spied on the U.S. for the Reds," written with the anti-communist journalist Jack Lotto and published in the *New*

York Journal American and nationally syndicated via Hearst's International News Service. Advertised by previews that shouted CONVICTED RED, MASTER SPY, TELLS ALL! it was a purely self-serving gesture. Still, Soble's claim to have been a refugee in America, a victim of the Soviets, forced to become a spy in order to preserve the lives of his wife and child, didn't help his case much, though it did bring in some income to help support his seventeen-year-old son, Larry.

As the Sobles began to open up to FBI interrogators, the FBI began focusing more closely on Jane Foster and George Zlatovski, who had been contacted by the Justice Department a day after the Sobles' arrest and given the opportunity to come to the American embassy in Paris and tell all. They indignantly declined, knowing that even if Soble were to provide evidence that they had spied for the Soviet Union, France traditionally refused to extradite legal residents accused of political crimes.

"You refuse?" an official at the embassy asked. "So much the worse for you." But Foster and Zlatovski, who were convinced that the United States was trying to turn them into the next Rosenbergs, played a shrewd game. Starting the next day, they volunteered to speak to the French secret service and admitted to having once been members of the Communist Party. It was, Foster later explained, a short-lived, youthful passion: "a strong, uncompromising stand against the economic crisis, Fascism, Nazism, and Colonialism." The explanation was of course irrelevant: Whatever they said was not admissible in an American court, even as they publicly proclaimed their innocence. Foster, whose mental condition had been fragile for years, collapsed and was sent to a Paris mental hospital, where she tried to kill herself by slitting her wrists. A visit from two American Justice Department officials, Thomas Gilchrist and William Tompkins, who intended to secure her cooperation, bring her back to the United States, and make her testify against Soble, certainly didn't lift her spirits. When Gilchrist and Tompkins failed to convince her, they tried baser tactics on George Zlatovski, threatening to blackmail him with information Boris had provided about his sexual proclivities. But the couple's ideological connection to the Soviet Union was firm, and their legal standing was even firmer. When Foster heard that the Sobles had cooperated in return for reduced sentences, she remarked that Soble should have taken the insanity defense. As for Myra, Foster joked, she might easily have used the stupidity defense. When the indictment in absentia on conspiracy to commit espionage eventually came, Foster and Zlatovski not only denied the accusations to the newspapermen who tried to get through the door of their run-down Latin Quarter walk-up, but they called the charges absurd and unjust and refused to take them seriously. Zlatovski claimed that Justice Department officials had been "reading too many comic books on junior G-men."

Boris wasn't publicly connected with any of these developments at first and had initially been described by the Justice Department as an "unnamed government informant" who was in protective custody. Boris read the newspaper stories describing the case as the biggest since the Rosenbergs, with Soble being described as the spymaster of a "mammoth" ring, and thought: "All those missed opportunities for publicity!" But eventually the FBI realized that they would have to publicly identify the figure at the center of what was indeed looking like a second Rosenberg case.

On the morning of August 12, 1957, Boris testified before a closed-door session of the Senate Subcommittee on Internal Security. Afterward it was difficult to keep his identity secret, so later that day at a packed press conference at the office of the US district attorney, Boris answered the questions that the rest of America was asking: How deeply had Soviet agents penetrated the United States government, and whose fault was it? What kind of danger to the American way of life did that represent? How did such a figure as Boris Morros—unassuming but nonetheless charismatic—manage to fool the most sophisticated spy apparatus in the world for a decade? Were other revelations to be expected? Gilchrist didn't quite trust Boris once he started improvising, so he passed out a prepared statement that detailed his history and motivations. Even so, Gilchrist had to rein Boris in more than once before the crowd of reporters and photographers: "Don't talk so much, Mr. Morros," Gilchrist offered, to much laughter on the part of the press corps. But Boris had waited a long time for his moment in the sun and was determined to enjoy it. He bounced around the room, grabbing a reporter's hand as he rehearsed all of the old lies with the practiced skill of an advertising man or a Hollywood agent, explaining that it was hatred of the "vicious ideology" of the communists that had inspired him and a lifetime in the entertainment world that showed him how to pull it off: "I really had to do a more realistic acting job than any of the players I had ever directed in Hollywood." No one in the room let the fact that he had never directed a Hollywood movie get in the way of the story.

The next day, Boris achieved the kind of fame that music or the movies had never brought him. The newspapers covered Khrushchev's speech to the East German Parliament in which he claimed to want an end to the Cold War but was willing to use nuclear weapons in a conflict with the United States. But it was Boris's day at last, from coast to coast. The *New York Times* ran a front-page story, three columns above the fold, alongside a photograph of Boris, appearing slim but disheveled in a tuxedo and crooked bow tie, while he held a Chesterfield cigarette in one hand and jabbed a finger at the reader with the other. The article led with a made-for-Hollywood introduction of Boris as a "shadowy figure," an "ebullient, rotund person with a Russian accent," a "bald, moon-faced" polymath who "speaks nine languages and has a penchant for travel." Inside the paper, one sidebar, titled SPY ON A WORLD STAGE, detailed not only how this "short, pudgy character . . . danced with equal sure-footedness over pitfalls of the most perilous of commercial enterprises—show business" but how this "genius at walking on eggshells . . . has nimbly tiptoed and hop-scotched internationally through the tightest places and around the craftiest people." The image of Boris as a star witness in the free world's battle against the evil Soviet empire, as a daring, multilingual patriot who risked his own life—and spent $2 million of his own money—for the country that had taken him in, was on display in all of the newspaper and wire-service stories that day and for months and even years to come, though they couldn't agree on the basics. Was he a "master counterspy" (*Los Angeles Times*) and America's "secret agent number one" (*Paris Match*)?

Or was he an amateur forced to rise to the occasion? Was he smooth and unflappable or irrepressibly exuberant? Humble or self-confident? Did he have a "heavy accent" or was his speech only lightly marked by a Russian lilt? Was he motivated by patriotism or by self-interest? The only party that seems to have made up its mind about Boris was the KGB, which carefully followed the news regarding what secret cables called "the traitor Boris Morros."

Boris used these moments with the press as opportunities to rewrite his story—or stories. As always, if the press got most of it wrong, this lovable liar had only himself to blame, because he refused to get his own story straight. He gave himself not only a new date and place of birth but claimed that he came from a long line of court musicians in St. Petersburg. He exaggerated his record at the conservatory and his early career in the Russian music world. He made himself out to be a war hero during the revolution and civil war, and he conveniently left out his time in Baku and Constantinople, except to claim sole authorship of the biggest hit to be featured in *The Bat*. He buried his years in Boston's Jewish ghetto, making it seem as if Adolph Zukor had plucked him off the boat at Ellis Island and made him a Paramount executive. Some of this rewriting of history was innocuous, but Boris was also thinking about his reputation in Hollywood after Jack and Myra Soble, Martha and Alfred Stern, Jane Foster and George Zlatovski,

and the rest of his contacts in America were safely behind bars. Now he claimed that he was only approached by the Soviets in the mid-1940s and immediately went to the FBI, meaning that he had never actually worked for the Soviets.

A backlash against Boris was building. The syndicated columnist Dorothy Kilgallen was the first to pounce, calling the other reporters naive for reflexively believing everything Boris had to say. He never directed a Hollywood film and he did not write the song "March of the Wooden Soldiers," he did not come to the United States with the cast of *The Bat*, and he was not happily married to Catherine. Following Kilgallen's lead, Bob Thomas of the Associated Press published a three-part series in which he tracked down Boris's old friends and enemies—none of whom were willing to speak on the record—in an attempt to get to the bottom of it all. Not one of them believed he had been a prodigy at the tsar's court or that Rasputin had given him those beads. Not only did Boris not write "March of the Wooden Soldiers," but he was not even a proficient composer or conductor, they claimed. His real talent was his ability to sell himself to people: "Put him in a room full of talented and famous people and before long they will all be clustered around him," Thomas wrote. In fact, many of the sources Thomas spoke to were not surprised that Boris had turned a talent for telling people what they wanted to hear into a career as an international counterspy. But there were also doubts that Boris could have fooled the KGB: "Boris as a cloak-and-dagger man? It's very bad casting," one source offered. The fiercest criticism came, ironically enough, from anti-communists like Walter Winchell, who seemed to believe Boris's work for the FBI was undertaken to save his own skin, not to oppose the Soviet menace.

Four days after Boris went public, representatives of the notorious House Committee on Un-American Activities met with the man they called one of the KGB's "top agents in the United States" and "the man who fooled the Kremlin" in his room at the Hotel Warwick, where he was then living with Marion. The session lasted from two thirty in the afternoon until eleven thirty that evening, and was only interrupted to allow Boris to have dinner with Cardinal Spellman, who hadn't yet learned how Boris had traded on their friendship. But Boris seemed in no hurry to cut things short. On the contrary, for all of the usual half-truths and untruths that Boris told during this session—he maintained again that he went straight to the FBI in the mid-1940s on learning that the Soviets were recruiting him to spy against the United States—he demanded that they get the facts straight. The transcript of this secret session has Boris at one point scolding HUAC investigators for not paying attention. But HUAC rarely had a friendlier witness. Boris told HUAC that he considered what he did a patriotic duty in a time when democracy itself was under assault from within, that there was a war being waged that very day on American soil by an undercover Soviet army: "We should fight—all of us—with all our might against it. There is a great danger that looks us straight in the eye. It is much more dangerous, and much more serious, than any of us can ever imagine." That was something, coming from a man with no small imagination. "Let's stop being naive," he told them. Even as he spoke, Boris claimed, the Soviets were running dozens of businesses that provided cover for their spies, though he conveniently wouldn't or couldn't name even one.

Nonetheless, it is no wonder this "suave Slav charmer," as *Time* magazine put it, was spoken of in the highest terms by HUAC Chairman Francis Walter. Indeed, his testimony seemed to temporarily revive the committee at its most desperate and irrelevant stage. Since Boris was "regarded by the Soviets as a key instrument of espionage in the West," Mocase was "the biggest espionage haul in history," according to Walter. Still, Boris was surprised to be honored with a Congressional Citation that noted his "great personal sacrifice" and praised his bravery and loyalty: "With direct danger to your life and safety, you have made a magnificent contribution to the cause of freedom."

The real legacy of Boris's testimony before HUAC is mixed, given that it helped inspire a number of important but dubious new laws related to national security, including preventing attorneys who were acknowledged communists from representing clients before congressional committees, limiting access to public information that Congress considered confidential, broadening the powers of the State Department to revoke citizenship in the case of those suspected of misrepresenting the facts on their naturalization applications, and reinterpreting what "organized" means in the context of groups suspected of subversion.

After being "front-paged," Boris was "prime-timed," appearing on some of the country's most popular television talk shows. It was a medium Boris had been trying to break into for years, and if it didn't happen in the way he imagined, it was still a thrill. Boris was a guest on the *Ed Sullivan Show*, which aired from eight to nine P.M. on the CBS network, at the peak of its popularity, appearing alongside the jazz musician Cab

Calloway, tennis star Vic Seixas, and "nature girl" Dorothy Brown. If Boris had long played the fool in his public appearances, since January he had learned to be the "serious" guest. Rebranding himself as the world's most trustworthy Kremlinologist, he told Sullivan that his audience shouldn't trust Khrushchev's talk about peaceful coexistence but should instead see him as a pan-Slavic dictator who made Hitler's ambitions look modest. The warnings he sounded soon afterwards on *Face the Nation*, broadcast just before dinnertime on NBC and rebroadcast across the country later that evening on the radio, were even more dire. Introduced as "a genius of world music" and "a man of prominence in Hollywood," Boris told viewers and listeners that he had started spying for the Soviets in 1945 after they held his father hostage and that he began working for the FBI shortly thereafter, falsehoods that no one challenged. It was only with the assistance of "my very own FBI," as he put it, that he survived, which was exactly what America's dwindling community of anti-communists wanted to hear, and though he could soon no longer count on the FBI's protection, he felt perfectly safe in the United States and was planning to split his time between New York and Los Angeles, where he was going to get back into the entertainment world.

He wouldn't be going back to North Beverly Drive. On October 9, 1957, Catherine announced that she had officially separated from Boris, and a week later she sued for divorce in Los Angeles Superior Court, alleging cruelty and seeking maintenance for herself, as well as reimbursement for money she had spent on her father-in-law during Boris's years on the run. According to Catherine, Boris had "extensive holdings" and extramarital affairs that he had never told her about. She requested an injunction to prevent him from further hiding or spending his assets, which to Boris's distress made all of the papers. He refused to contest any of Catherine's claims, gave her everything she asked for, and got on with his life with Marion, which seemed to be a good one.

Boris was named one of *Family Weekly*'s "Americans of Achievement" for 1957, along with actress Kim Novak and evangelist Billy Graham, and he was now making almost daily public appearances, many of them intended to drum up support for his new projects, most prominently a television program about Europe's Nobel Prize winners, to be narrated by Burgess Meredith and then turned into a series of books. That project led to a rather unlikely invitation in January 1958 to address the Nobel Anniversary Committee's fourteenth annual gathering at the Waldorf-Astoria. Otherwise, Boris and Marion travelled constantly, as they had for years, though of course now instead of hiding and lying, Boris was celebrated wherever they went. When Boris and Marion were in New York, they stayed at some of the city's fanciest hotels, including the Warwick, the Sherry-Netherland, and the Essex House, still paid for by the FBI, which at this point was also keeping Boris's many creditors at bay. "He was always spending and spending," Marion remembers. "He would spend $1,000 to fill the hotel room with flowers. But once on the street I asked him to buy me a little ring for five or ten dollars and he said: 'You know I can't do that—you know I'm broke.' So the flowers were there because someone was coming. It was for show, the flowers—and me." Eventually, once he had told the FBI everything he knew, they stopped paying, and the creditors appeared. "They all came for their money," Marion recalls. Eventually, the couple settled into a spacious two-bedroom apartment at 50 Riverside Drive, where they loved to entertain friends. "It was a party a minute," remembers Marion, who was finally married to Boris in Germany. When they got back to New York, however, City Hall wouldn't accept the documentation. That didn't matter to Marion, who never minded that Boris didn't talk about his early years and never told her that he was a spy until it was all over. "I was madly in love with him and he was good to me," she said.

Boris told HUAC that his realization that he was being asked to become a Soviet spy was like something out of a book. Even as he spoke, he was planning on writing a memoir or having someone write one for him. A week after telling the world the truth about his career as a spy, he boasted about his life story being bought by the *Saturday Evening Post*, *Reader's Digest*, and Simon and Schuster. Instead, his byline appeared in the *Chicago Tribune* for a ten-part series that covered his entire story in all of its flamboyant falsehood. Those articles, reworked by Charles Samuels, who had ghostwritten the autobiographies of Ethel Waters and Buster Keaton, formed the basis of Boris's memoir, which the *New York Times* called "more fantastic than any scenarist could invent with or without Benzedrine." Published as *My Ten Years As a Counterspy* in late 1959, the story of what Boris called "my weird adventures" became a bestseller and remained one for months, despite dismissive reviews. *Time*'s reviewer thought the book read "like a bad novel" but reserved his worst vitriol for Boris himself, focusing on his "late-Picasso haberdashery, borscht-and-bagel accent, and a personality as outgoing as a trombone." As for the book itself, it demonstrated that "while it may not be true that anyone can be a spy, it is painfully certain that a spy can be anyone," according to the *New York Times*. The most positive review came, not coincidentally, from *Studies in Intelligence*, a CIA-sponsored journal that found Boris had produced "intimate and damaging data" on the "objectives, personnel, modus operandi, and vulnerability" of the Soviet intelligence operations.

When Boris's photograph appeared on the front page of the *New York Times* on August 13, 1957, the caption had noted: "It couldn't even happen in the movies." Of course, Boris had told his story in a way that was as Hollywood-friendly as possible, but despite early interest from all of the major studios—at one point, Dorothy Kilgallen called it "Hollywood's hottest property"—the movie was slow in becoming a reality. Eventually, Columbia Pictures bought the rights for *Spy and Counterspy*, which later would be given the title *Man on a String*. Boris got $125,000 up front, 22 percent of the big screen earnings, and 11 percent of television income. The movie was directed for Columbia by André de Toth, a one-eyed Hungarian director of B movies who had made the transition to television, and was written by a team of Hollywood second-stringers, but it had a fine cast, including the young Ernest Borgnine and Colleen Dewhurst. The film took liberties with Boris's story, conflating the Sterns and the Foster-Zlatovskis, substituting the "Central Bureau of Intelligence" for the FBI, and showing the Boris character murdering an East German police officer and beating up a former Gestapo informer. Nonetheless, the advertisements promised TRUTH, NOT FICTION! and in a tribute to Boris's interesting way with reality, Columbia's publicity department recorded a double-sided LP with Boris answering questions that disc jockeys would pretend to ask him, a promotional stunt that eventually became quite common in the music and film worlds.

Man on a String premiered in May 1960 in New York, with news of the shooting down of an American U-2 plane over the Soviet Union three weeks earlier still dominating the headlines. It held its own against Graham Greene's *Our Man in Havana*, Jimmy Stewart in *The FBI Story*, and *Who Was That Lady?*, a story about Soviet spies starring Tony Curtis, Dean Martin, and Janet Leigh. Although the film hasn't aged well, coming across as an alarmist and unconvincing piece of anti-communist propaganda, reviews were strong. Howard Thompson of the *New York Times* called it "a small miracle of Hollywood alchemy" and "a crackling good thriller." *Man on a String* had Boris back in his beloved limelight, and he did another publicity tour with Marion in 1960, hitting many of the same places he'd been a year earlier on his book tour.

The ring of traitors that Boris betrayed, "supporting actors in a major world drama," as the *Nation* put it, didn't have it so easy. The most sensational news to come out of Boris's testimony before HUAC was Boris's identification of Martha and Alfred Stern, the ambassador's daughter and her millionaire husband, as longtime Soviet secret agents. It was a shocking development, and the newspapers portrayed it sensationally. The failure of the Boris Morros Music Company back in the mid-1940s hadn't meant the Soviets were willing to let the couple go in the years that followed. Alfred wasn't much of a businessman, but the Soviets needed his deep pockets, and Martha had been one of the NKVD's most productive recruiters, though after the couple adopted a son in 1945 she temporarily lost interest in politics and went back to writing, publishing a novel, *Sowing the Wind*, about the horrors of Nazi Germany. But the Sterns' commitment to communism was long-term, and by the time of Henry Wallace's Progressive third-party presidential campaign in 1948, they were back in the limelight as celebrity subversives and communist operatives. Moscow set up Alfred in a scheme importing penicillin to Mexico. In fact, it was a front used to provide cover for agents in Latin America, but the business foundered, in part because Alfred was secretly skimming off the profits. Apparently he'd learned a thing or two from Boris after all. After the Sterns were targeted by McCarthy in 1953—Jane Foster was convinced that the American government never really wanted to bring the Sterns to trial because it would have ruined too many careers—the Kremlin realized they had no more value as spies, and the Sterns had to agree. They sold their New York apartment and their country home and fled to Mexico City, where they fell in with a large group of Americans, among them three of the "Hollywood Ten"—John Howard Lawson, Albert Maltz, and Dalton Trumbo—whose embrace of communism made going back home impossible. Alfred built a weekend getaway home for them in Cuernavaca and collected Mexican art. He also loaned out money to the other exiles at usurious interest rates, while Martha kept writing. In 1955 she published *The Searching Light*, a novel about a small-town college professor who is undone by his refusal to sign a loyalty oath. The book had some success, in part because of an endorsement by no less a figure than Albert Einstein. The Sterns enjoyed their lives in Mexico, but after Boris identified them as Soviet agents in 1957, which led to a subpoena before a grand jury and then an indictment on espionage charges, they didn't feel confident that they were beyond the long reach of the Justice Department. One of the accused spies in the Rosenberg case had been seized in Mexico and brought to justice in America, and the Sterns feared the same might happen to them. At the same time, it had been years since they had done work for the Soviets, who weren't willing to cause an international incident by taking in two of its accused spies—especially not these two.

When they were indicted in absentia on espionage charges as a result of the testimony of Boris and the Sobles, the Sterns claimed the charges were preposterous. How could Boris Morros's failed little record company come back to haunt them more than a decade later? But they feared extradition from Mexico on capital offenses, so they illegally acquired Paraguayan passports and fled to Europe in search of refuge behind the

Iron Curtain. The press followed the Sterns' flight with their son, Bobby, every step of the way, from Mexico to Montreal, Dublin, Amsterdam, and Prague, and the coverage was anything but objective. *Top Secret* magazine published a breathless tell-all, "The Spy Queen Was a Nympho!" that was filled with the most preposterous and misogynistic details about the Sterns. The "love-thirsty Miss Dodd" was sensationally and at least in part falsely portrayed as a decadent flapper from the Roaring Twenties who developed a crush on Nazism and then on communism. Meanwhile, the story celebrated Boris as the hero of "the most extraordinary spy drama ever staged."

The Sterns made a trip to Moscow to try to settle there but weren't welcome, so they moved to Prague, where Alfred claimed to work as an importer and exporter and Martha helped edit a local English-language newspaper. Eventually they spoke up and spoke out: "The accusations by Boris Morros that we are or were Soviet agents are the fantastic invention of a Hollywood imposter, a part and parcel of his lurid career." The Sterns claimed to be enjoying the freedom from "fear and persecution" that they faced in the United States, but they were unhappy in Prague. Their son suffered from schizophrenia and was sent back to Mexico, and in 1963 they moved to Cuba, where until 1970 Alfred claimed to be one of Fidel Castro's top advisors. They eventually resettled in Prague, where they lived in an expansive villa near the Moldau River and were chauffeured around in a Mercedes, while Alfred worked as a consultant to the state construction ministry and tried to find a way to return home. Espionage charges against them were finally dropped in 1979 because of a lack of evidence, and they got new American passports, but they remained in Prague, where Alfred, the "Pink Millionaire," died in 1986. Martha stayed on, living in Miss Havisham–like conditions—or was it more like Norma Desmond from *Sunset Boulevard*? She slept late, spent the afternoons buying closets full of fancy clothing that she never had a chance to wear, and devoted her evenings to poring over imported copies of *People* magazine. In the chaos that followed the fall of the Berlin Wall, their house was ransacked, and the looters tied up the woman known as the "American Mata Hari" and left her on the floor. It was days before neighbors found her. She died shortly thereafter and was buried next to her husband in Prague's New Jewish Cemetery.

As for Jane Foster and George Zlatovski, they had served the Soviet Union more effectively than the Sterns, and were for that reason hotly pursued by the American government, but there was no danger of extradition from France. Even if they had come home to trial, Foster was confident of acquittal if all the government could muster in the way of witnesses was "the testimony of a madman, Soble, and of a psychopathic liar, Morros." But Jane still told anyone who would listen that she had never been a spy and that she only learned in the late 1940s that Martha Stern was a Soviet agent. They made an unsuccessful attempt to become French citizens, then Foster tried to kill herself again, and then again. As late as 1970, the FBI still considered Foster and Zlatovski "a grave danger to internal security" and warned that they would be arrested if they tried to enter the United States. But the couple never tried to have the indictment overturned, the way the Sterns did, and they lived out the rest of their lives as exiles. She never stopped blaming Boris, "the most contemptible creature I have ever known." Foster died in 1979 and was buried among the *vrais Parisiens* in Père Lachaise cemetery, followed six years later by Zlatovski.

By 1960, between Boris and the Sobles, the FBI had enough evidence to charge Jack Soble's brother, Robert Soblen, the supervising psychiatrist at Rockland State Hospital, in Orangeburg, New York, for having given to the Soviets classified OSS documents during the war and photos of Los Alamos taken by the "atomic couple," Henry and Beatrice Spitz, in the 1950s. Anguished at the prospect of serving as a witness against his own brother, who was suffering from leukemia, Soble swallowed one-and-a-half pounds of nuts, bolts, rivets, and screws—some as long as three-and-a-quarter inches—that he stole from the workshop of the federal penitentiary in Lewisburg, Pennsylvania, in a desperate, unsuccessful attempt to kill himself. Once on the witness stand, Soble disrupted the trial in a fugue of anger, shouting that he would never implicate his own family, but the plea agreement proved stronger than his family loyalty. Soblen was convicted and sentenced to life in prison but escaped while awaiting imprisonment and fled to Israel, which refused to offer him asylum and instead put him on a plane to the United States via London. Desperate to avoid extradition, Soblen used the knife from the airline's dinner service to cut his wrist and stab himself in the stomach, which bought him a few extra days in England. Faced with certain extradition to the United States, he took a fatal overdose of painkillers.

Soble was released early from prison in 1962, having shown himself to be a model prisoner, working in the prison library. He lived a quiet life with Myra, who had been released in 1961, and found work as an accountant, continuing to cooperate with the government until his death in 1967. Myra received a full pardon by President George H. W. Bush in 1991 and died the next year.

As for the Soviets who had made Boris's life a nightmare for more than two decades, very few died in bed. Lavrenti Beria, Vitaly Tcherniavsky, and Afanasy Yefimov were all purged. Someone who did manage to survive was the man who made Boris a spy, the man who stole the American atomic bomb, Vasily Zarubin. He left the intelligence service in 1948 and became the chair in charge of tennis at the KGB-affiliated Dynamo Sports Club before coming out of retirement in 1953 to help train intelligence officers. Incapacitated by a stroke in 1968, he was awarded his second Order of Lenin medal the next year, and he died, much decorated, of a heart attack in Moscow in 1972, though his name lives on, not only through his two children but through a town called Zarubino, in the far east of Russia. His wife, Elizabeth, the "Red Joan of Arc," survived him for fifteen years. She was hit by a bus in Moscow and died of subsequent injuries.

Boris claimed that he became a spy to protect his family back in Russia, but he seems to have failed when it came to his American family. Boris's father, Mendel, died in 1960 in the Los Angeles nursing home Boris had put him in, the two having become estranged. The next to go was his son, Dick, who had little to do with Boris when he finally came of age, except when he needed a handout. He eventually had some success as a film and television producer. Dick's second marriage, to Jo Ann, who is still alive as of this writing but who refuses to speak publicly about her father-in-law, lasted longer than his first. They had two sons, Bruce and Michael, before Dick committed suicide in 1967 in Los Angeles. After divorcing Boris, Catherine lived on at 916 North Beverly Drive in as much anonymity as she could muster. She died in 1968.

As time went on, Boris began to doubt whether he'd really been able to change history, especially when in 1961, he sat down to breakfast and read about the Bay of Pigs incident and the building of the Berlin Wall. But soon the success or failure of American-Soviet relations seemed somehow less important. In late summer of that year, Boris found out he had cancer. Advised by his doctor to slow down and enjoy his time with Marion, Boris charged ahead with the usual full schedule of publicity for his book and film, meetings to promote Moropticon, his television series about Nobel Prize winners, and a dozen new projects, though as always, current events were inseparable for Boris from his own career. The Cuban Missile Crisis had barely died down when Boris found out he was being made an honorary member of the Criminal Investigation Division of the Armed Forces, but he collapsed on December 14, 1962, and spent his holidays in Beth Israel Hospital in New York City, where he died on January 8, 1963. Even as he drew his last breath, the United States and the Soviet Union were engaged in disarmament talks that led to the Partial Test Ban Treaty later that year.

In death, Boris was celebrated as a Hollywood eccentric who fooled them all, starting with the press, which still couldn't agree on the origins, age, or even the real name of the "master counterspy who duped the Kremlin itself." The newspapers all agreed that Boris would have been a significant figure even if he had never become a spy. And then they moved on.

To say that Boris was the longest-serving and most successful double agent in the history of espionage, who not only lied his way into the Kremlin and the White House, but who brought the Cold War to Hollywood, Wall Street, and the Vatican, doesn't explain how this immigrant outsider with his embarrassing accent, clownish manners, and preposterous clothing, became one of communism's undertakers. His crass, insatiable hunger for fame may have conflicted with the Kremlin's need for secrecy, and his impossibly amateurish bearing may have surprised more experienced agents—what spy agency would send Maxwell Smart to do the job of James Bond?—but in the end it was exactly his status as an outsider on the inside that made him so effective for so long.

Of course, as a central player in the Cold War strategy of both the FBI and the KGB, Boris didn't operate in a vacuum. As distressing as it may be to admit, J. Edgar Hoover may not have been good, but he was right, at least in his conviction that for most of the Cold War the Soviets successfully infiltrated American politics and culture at the highest levels. Boris revealed another side of the Soviet intelligence apparatus: It was an organization marked by not merely by inefficiency and a lack of focus but by chaos and self-destructiveness, an organization whose strictly controlled rituals of secrecy were undermined by stunning carelessness, whose priorities were determined not by ideology but by personalities, and shockingly unstable and unpredictable ones at that. Boris learned and told the world that for the Soviet Union, enemies were dangerous but friends were fatal, which is why KGB headquarters never displayed the traditional wall of portraits of past leaders that most large organizations do: Every single one of them was purged, victimizers who themselves fell victim to the culture of deadly fear that Stalin maintained. Like Hoover, who sometimes seemed to rival Stalin in the extent of his paranoia, if not the means to express it, Boris knew that until communism destroyed itself, staying ahead in the Cold War was not just a matter of political strategy, though the Russians apparently didn't learn how to successfully manipulate presidential elections for more than half a century. The biggest decisions, including military strategy and economic programs, turned on the most human of qualities: anger, loyalty, pride, ambition, jealousy, fear, greed, and lust. Boris knew all about every one of those.

If Boris didn't master all of the instruments of the orchestra before he was a teenager, as he so often claimed, and if his taste in music wasn't terribly sophisticated, his ability to compose, arrange, and conduct consistently impressed the most talented musicians in the world for decades. But his real instrument was his own story, and he was willing to take whatever liberties with the facts were necessary in order to inspire applause, even if that meant betraying both the country of his birth and the country that adopted him. Dissembling had been second nature to Boris ever since his childhood in tsarist Russia, when concealing his Jewishness was a matter of survival, and for the rest of his life he struggled unsuccessfully to avoid being a player in someone else's game. In that sense, lying was less a matter of representing reality than performing it. It was a matter of entertainment, telling others what they wanted to hear. "Boris was a pathological liar," remembers Marion, who insists that *My Ten Years As a Counterspy* is pure fiction. "But people believed him, and I like to think that he believed himself."

In the end, the question is not whether Boris was Falstaff or Prospero. He was both. He was an insider and an outsider, a winner and an almost-ran, a millionaire and a desperate debtor, a patriot and an opportunist. He was a brilliantly indiscreet social climber who knew the difference between the truth and the facts. His life had often depended on that distinction. Perhaps it is best to give the last word to Marion Morros, who still lives in the apartment overlooking the Hudson River that she shared with Boris in his last years. Still officially in charge of the moribund Moropticon business, Marion has mostly cleansed her home of anything that reminds her of Boris, including his diaries, which she claims to have just thrown away every time she's asked to show them. As for snapshots of Boris, she says she has nothing to show. Then she digs out the photo books from her bookcase, with photo after photo of Boris, not as a Hollywood producer or a Soviet secret agent, but as a husband, a neighbor, a friend. Ask her about Boris and she'll say she has nothing to say about him and no desire to say it, and then she spends the afternoon reminiscing about the love of her life. What Marion learned from Boris is that in the end what counts is not family or friends or colleagues but the applause of audiences. Like the wounded child that Marion says he always was, Boris dealt not in good or evil but in situations. He trafficked not in truth or lies but in stories.

Acknowledgments

Notes on Sources

Index